The Craft of Political Research

Eighth Edition

W. Phillips Shively
University of Minnesota

Longman
Boston   Columbus   Indianapolis   New York   San Francisco
Upper Saddle River   Amsterdam   Cape Town   Dubai   London
Madrid   Milan   Munich   Paris   Montreal   Toronto   Delhi   Mexico City
Sao Paulo   Sydney   Hong Kong   Seoul   Singapore   Taipei   Tokyo

To Barbara

Acquisitions Editor: Vikram Mukhija
Editorial Assistant: Toni Magyar
Marketing Manager: Lindsey Prudhomme
Production Manager: Wanda Rockwell
Project Coordination, Text Design,
   and Electronic Page Makeup: Shiny Rajesh/Integra Software Services, Ltd.
Creative Director: Jayne Conte
Cover Designer: Bruce Kenselaar/Mary Steinert
Cover Illustration/Photo: Corbis Corporation
Printer and Binder: Courier Companies, Inc.

Library of Congress Cataloging-in-Publication Data

Cataloging-in-Publication Data for this title can be obtained from the Library of Congress.

1 2 3 4 5 6 7 8 9 10—CRS—13 12 11 10

Longman
is an imprint of

www.pearsonhighered.com

ISBN-13: 978-0-205-79120-0
ISBN-10:   0-205-79120-4

Brief Contents

DETAILED CONTENTS   v

FOREWORD   ix

PREFACE   xi

CHAPTER 1   Doing Research   1

CHAPTER 2   Political Theories and Research Topics   13

CHAPTER 3   Importance of Dimensional Thinking   32

CHAPTER 4   Problems of Measurement: Accuracy   41

CHAPTER 5   Problems of Measurement: Precision   57

CHAPTER 6   Causal Thinking and Design of Research   74

CHAPTER 7   Selection of Observations for Study   97

CHAPTER 8   Introduction to Statistics: Measuring
            Relationships for Interval Data   112

CHAPTER 9   Introduction to Statistics: Further Topics on
            Measurement of Relationships   133

CHAPTER 10 Introduction to Statistics: Inference, or How to
            Gamble on Your Research   150

CHAPTER 11 Where Do Theories Come From?   167

            SELECTED BIBLIOGRAPHY   170

            INDEX   174

Detailed Contents

FOREWORD   ix

PREFACE   xi

CHAPTER 1   Doing Research   1

SOCIAL RESEARCH   2
Types of Political Research   4
Research Mix   8
Evaluating Different Types of Research   10
ETHICS OF POLITICAL RESEARCH   11

CHAPTER 2   Political Theories and Research Topics   13

CAUSALITY AND POLITICAL THEORY   14
WHAT DOES GOOD THEORY LOOK LIKE?   15
Example of Elegant Research: Phillip Converse   17
To Quantify or Not   20
CHOICE OF A TOPIC   21
Engineering Research   22
Theory-Oriented Research   22
DEVELOPMENT OF A RESEARCH DESIGN   23
Observations, Puzzles, and the Construction
of Theories   24
MACHIAVELLIAN GUIDE TO DEVELOPING
RESEARCH TOPICS   27
Further Discussion   31

CHAPTER 3   Importance of Dimensional Thinking   32

ENGLISH AS A LANGUAGE FOR RESEARCH   33
Ordinary Language   34
PROPER USE OF MULTIDIMENSIONAL WORDS   37
Example of Dimensional Analysis   38
Further Discussion   40

CHAPTER 4   Problems of Measurement: Accuracy   41

RELIABILITY   45
   Reliability as a Characteristic of Concepts   46
   Testing the Reliability of a Measure   47
VALIDITY   48
   Some Examples   49
   Checks for Validity   51
IMPACT OF RANDOM AND NONRANDOM ERRORS   53
IMPORTANCE OF ACCURACY   54
Further Discussion   56

CHAPTER 5   Problems of Measurement: Precision   57

PRECISION IN MEASURES   58
PRECISION IN MEASUREMENT   61
   Innate Nature of Levels of Measurement   63
   The Sin of Wasting Information   64
   Enrichment of the Level of Precision
      in Measurement   66
   Examples of Enrichment   67
   Quantifiers and Nonquantifiers Again   71
Further Discussion   72

CHAPTER 6   Causal Thinking and Design
             of Research   74

CAUSALITY: AN INTERPRETATION   75
ELIMINATION OF ALTERNATIVE CAUSAL
   INTERPRETATIONS   76
   Summary   77
A FEW BASICS OF RESEARCH DESIGN   78
   Designs without a Control Group   79
   Use of a Control Group   81
   True Experiment   83
DESIGNS FOR POLITICAL RESEARCH   85
   Special Design Problem for Policy Analysis:
      Regression to the Mean   88
USE OF VARIED DESIGNS AND MEASURES   90
   Example of Varied Designs and Measures   92
CONCLUSION   93
HOLDING A VARIABLE CONSTANT   94
Further Discussion   95

CHAPTER 7   Selection of Observations for Study   97

SAMPLING FROM A POPULATION OF POTENTIAL
 OBSERVATIONS   99
 Random Sampling   99
 Quasi-Random Sampling   101
 Purposive Sampling   102
 Selection of Cases for Case Studies   103
CENSORED DATA   104
 When Scholars Pick the Cases They're Interested In   104
 When Nature Censors Data   106
SELECTION ALONG THE DEPENDENT VARIABLE:
 DON'T DO IT!   107
SELECTION OF CASES FOR CASE STUDIES (AGAIN)   109
ANOTHER STRATEGY, HOWEVER: SINGLE-CASE
 STUDIES SELECTED FOR THE RELATIONSHIP
 BETWEEN THE INDEPENDENT AND
 DEPENDENT VARIABLES   110
Further Discussion   *111*

CHAPTER 8   Introduction to Statistics: Measuring
      Relationships for Interval Data   112

STATISTICS   113
IMPORTANCE OF LEVELS OF MEASUREMENT   113
WORKING WITH INTERVAL DATA   114
 Regression Analysis   114
 Correlation Analysis   123
 Correlation and Regression Compared   128
 Problem of Measurement Error   130
Further Discussion   *132*

CHAPTER 9   Introduction to Statistics: Further
      Topics on Measurement of Relationships   133

MEASURES OF RELATIONSHIPS FOR
 ORDINAL DATA   133
MEASURES OF RELATIONSHIPS FOR
 NOMINAL DATA   137
 Dichotomies and Regression Analysis   138
LOGIT AND PROBIT ANALYSIS   140
MULTIVARIATE ANALYSIS   142
CONCLUSION   147

CHAPTER 10   Introduction to Statistics: Inference,
or How to Gamble on Your Research   150

LOGIC OF MEASURING SIGNIFICANCE   151
EXAMPLE OF STATISTICAL INFERENCE   152
HYPOTHESIS TESTING   153
   Null Hypothesis   154
   Example: χ^2 155
   Sampling Distribution   157
   Importance of N 160
   Problem of Independent Observations   162
SIGNIFICANCE TEST: ALWAYS NECESSARY?   163
POLLING AND SIGNIFICANCE TESTS   164
USES AND LIMITATIONS OF STATISTICAL TESTS   165
CONCLUSION   165
Further Discussion   *165*

CHAPTER 11   Where Do Theories Come From?   167

SELECTED BIBLIOGRAPHY   170

INDEX   174

Foreword

I first met Phil Shively when he was an assistant professor and I was a graduate student at the same institution. I learned that he was a comparativist, with all the cross-cultural interests, historical perspective, and eye for important problems that come with that scholarly focus. Yet he approached his research questions with the same quantitative tools that most of us in American politics used. In the late 1960s, that was an unusual combination. Certainly it was a revelation to me. Phil combined all this scholarly acumen with great scientific honesty, an utter lack of pretension, and a gift for making friends.

Phil was soon off to the University of Minnesota. A few years passed. He became editor of the *American Journal of Political Science*. He used his talents to act as a real editor, shaping not-quite-ready manuscripts into professional publications and helping beginning assistant professors like myself convey research findings to a professional audience.

I had begun teaching undergraduate courses in research methods. Some of the material was strictly quantitative, and I used an introductory statistics text. But political science is not a branch of statistics. It has its own logic, a blend of quantitative reasoning, qualitative judgment, and political horse sense—what A. Lawrence Lowell, Harold Gosnell, and V.O. Key taught us to do. I needed another book, a text that would convey the importance of that unnamed something that distinguishes genuine intellectual achievement from mere technical expertise. One might call it "the craft of political research." It was not hard to see which text I needed. Phil's little volume conveyed precisely the intellectual range, sound judgment, and conceptual rigor my students needed. I have used and recommended this book in its many editions ever since.

The book's topical coverage is just what one hopes for in an undergraduate methods course. First, it is more theoretically engaged than most such texts, and the conceptual discussion is nonsectarian. Marx and Duverger make an appearance; so do Mancur Olson and Anthony Downs; so do Philip Converse and Robert Putnam. Students will learn that ideas matter, not the statistical software; and they will see that theoretical narrowness is the antithesis of good science.

All the standard "scope and methods" topics appear in the text, including reliability, validity, scales of measurement, and much else. Students need to know those ideas before they begin their own research, but they don't know that they need to know. Too often, they hope that they never need to know. Indeed, badly conveyed, the material can be stupefyingly dull.

Good teaching begins from where the student is. In this text, the classic concepts are enlivened by interesting political examples—arms races, congressional reapportionment, and the infamous *Literary Digest* election polls from the American Thirties. Thoughtful political science majors of all substantive interests will find themselves engaged.

Other crucial topics get lively treatment, too. In recent years, experiments—laboratory, field, and natural—have taken on greater importance in political science. It is gratifying to see that renewed emphasis reflected here in the central chapters of this book. Focusing the discussion on causality, Shively conveys what the shouting is about. And as always, important examples from recent political research bring the reader to the topic in a natural way, without slipping into the methodologist's occupational disease—hectoring the student about rigor and right thinking.

As Shively notes, not all important political research topics can be addressed with experiments. Observational data matter, too, and some of the deepest political research topics permit no other approach. Shively's final chapters address sampling, contingency tables, graphics, correlation, regression, and even a brief introduction to logit and probit analysis. The student gets a warning about measurement error, outliers, and selection bias at this early stage, which my own teaching experience suggests is much needed. The perils of comparing corrrelations across samples are also addressed. The fundamental idea that logit is essentially just regression on a different scale of measurement is skillfully conveyed.

All in all, this book's range of topics, discussed at its level, are just what is needed in an introductory undergraduate course. If the focus is research design, the book can stand on its own. In an introduction to statistics for political scientists, students will find this a beneficial (and very welcome!) companion to the statistics text.

Over the years, Phil and I have become co-authors and good friends. But my enthusiasm for this book predates all that. It is a pleasure to recommend it to a new generation of students, as well as to their teachers. Attentive readers will find, as I did with the latest edition, that ideas for research projects begin flowing spontaneously. And of course, spurring the reader's own thinking is what good teaching and good books on research design are meant to do.

CHRISTOPHER H. ACHEN
Roger Williams Straus Professor of Social Sciences
Princeton University

Preface

I wrote this little book in 1970, when I was an assistant professor at Yale University. In teaching a number of sections of Introduction to Research to undergraduates there, I had found that the students benefited from an introduction that emphasized the internal logic of research methods and the collective, cooperative nature of the research process. I could not find a book that presented things in this way at a sufficiently elementary level to be readily accessible by undergraduates. And so I wrote this book.

It has followed me through the rest of my career so far, and has given me enormous pleasure. It has always seemed to me that it fills a needed niche. There are many books that teach students how to gather and analyze data, and teach them the terminology we use in describing research design. But in this book, I especially aim to help them understand why we do things the way we do, and at the same time to convey the pleasure and excitement of original research. It has always been a thrill for me when students have told me that they have benefited from the book. A few years ago, a woman wrote to thank me as she graduated with a master's degree from a first-rate public policy institute. She had always wanted to go to a good public policy school, but had felt she would not be able to handle the mathematics. When she was assigned *The Craft* in an undergraduate class, she realized that she was indeed capable of understanding these things, and went on to success at the school she had been afraid was impossible for her. I believe that focusing on understanding along with technique can be especially helpful for students like her.

NEW TO THIS EDITION

While the general principles of good argument and investigation don't change, I have made a number of additions and deletions in this eighth edition:

- I have changed my presentation of types of research to make certain that I give engineering research its full due; I have always thought that the two types of empirical research are equally valuable and interesting, and I have made some effort in this edition to make sure that that is clear in the text.
- I have added a box on how to draw a random sample, to help make more clear to students just what is involved mechanically in doing this.
- I have changed my presentation of the Goodman-Kruskall gamma to make more clear that it is based on the relative numbers of concordant and discordant pairs in a table.

- I have also updated several examples, replacing classic studies with more recent ones, and have changed my terminology to refer to formal theory more accurately as "positive theory."
- In further updating, all examples using election survey data are based on the 2008 election.

I must also admit to a recent change of heart (or, perhaps, a return to an old love). Regular users of this text may recall that a few editions ago, under prodding from reviewers, I changed my example of elegant research from Philip Converse's "Of Time and Partisan Stability" to the more recent *Making Democracy Work*, by Robert Putnam. Putnam's book and the resultant research program on social capital are of course splendid, but I always regretted sacrificing Converse's article. It is still the most beautiful piece of political science research I know. And so I returned in the sixth edition—and continue here—to "Of Time and Partisan Stability" and include with it the same explication of Markov chains that I used in those earlier editions.

FEATURES

I believe the most distinctive feature of the book is that everything dealt with in it is presented, explained, and justified by how it helps us to develop theory. A unifying narrative runs throughout in which everything we do in research is tied to our central task of developing usable theories that allow us to understand causal relations. As for other features, I have tried to keep the book simple and short, with a strong emphasis on understanding the underlying principles of what we do. I include at the end of most chapters some suggested further readings, and a few provocative questions. And at various points, boxed sections explain certain distinct questions like "linear relationships" or the law of large numbers.

As you can no doubt tell from the tone of this preface, this is a book for which I have great affection. I hope you will enjoy it as much as I have enjoyed it.

SUPPLEMENTS

Longman is pleased to offer the following resource to qualified adopters of *The Craft of Political Research* and their students that will make teaching and learning from this book even more effective and enjoyable.

For Students

MySearchLab. Need help with a paper? MySearchLab saves time and improves results by offering start-to-finish guidance on the research/writing process and full-text access to academic journals and periodicals. To learn more, please visit www.mysearchlab.com <http://www.mypoliscikit.com/> or contact your Pearson representative. To order MySearchLab with this book, use ISBN 020571935X.

ACKNOWLEDGMENTS

Thanks to the following reviewers for their very helpful suggestions and comments: Terri Susan Fine, University of Central Florida; Garrett Glasgow, University of California at Santa Barbara; and Patrick James, University of Southern California.

W. PHILLIPS SHIVELY

CHAPTER 1

Doing Research

Scholarly research is exciting and is fun to do. Some students, caught in the grind of daily and term assignments, may not see it this way. But for people who can carry on research in a more relaxed way, for professors or for students who can involve themselves in a long-range project, research may be a source of fascination and great satisfaction.

> Francis's preoccupation with DNA quickly became full-time. The first afternoon following the discovery that A–T and G–C base pairs had similar shapes, he went back to his thesis measurements, but his effort was ineffectual. Constantly he would pop up from his chair, worriedly look at the cardboard models, fiddle with other combinations, and then, the period of momentary uncertainty over, look satisfied and tell me how important our work was. I enjoyed Francis's words, even though they lacked the casual sense of understatement known to be the correct way to behave in Cambridge. (Watson, 1968, p. 198)[1]

This is the way James D. Watson describes his and Francis Crick's search for the structure of the DNA molecule. *The Double Helix*, his account of their work, gives a good picture of the excitement of research. It is more gripping than most mystery novels.

Although research can be exciting in this way, the sad fact is that writing papers for courses is too often something of a drag. First of all, course papers are tied to all sorts of rewards and punishments—your future earnings, the approval of others, and so on. All of the anxiety associated with these vulnerabilities comes, indirectly, to lodge on the paper. Yet this is probably a lesser cause for frustration in student research. After all, each of these anxieties may also be present for professional scholars. A more important reason for the student's lack of enthusiasm is the simple fact that a paper is generally regarded, by both teacher and student, as a practice run,

---

[1]Reprinted with permission from Watson, James D. *The Double Helix* (New York: Atheneum, 1968).

going through the motions of scholarship. Usually, not enough time is allowed for the student to think long and seriously about the subject, especially with other papers competing for attention. And even when adequate time is allowed, there usually is a feeling on both sides that this is "just a student paper"—that it doesn't really matter how good it is, that a student will learn from doing the thing wrong. Students must have the chance to learn from their own mistakes, but this attitude toward the research work cheats them of the pleasure and excitement that research can bring, the feeling of creating something that no one ever saw before.

There is probably no way out of this dilemma. In a book such as this, I cannot give you the drama and excitement of original research. I can only give my own testimony, as one for whom research is very exciting. But I can introduce you to some selected problems you should be aware of if you want to do good research yourself or to evaluate the work of others. I also hope to make you aware of what a challenging game it can be, and of how important inventiveness, originality, and boldness are to good research.

SOCIAL RESEARCH

Social research is an attempt by social scientists to develop and sharpen theories that give us a handle on the universe. Reality unrefined by theory is too chaotic for us to absorb. Some people vote and others do not; in some elections there are major shifts, in others there are not; some bills are passed by Congress, others are not; economic development programs succeed in some countries, but fail in others; sometimes war comes, sometimes it does not. To have any hope of controlling what happens, we must understand why these things happen. And to have any hope of understanding why they happen, we must simplify our perceptions of reality.

Social scientists carry out this simplification by developing theories. A theory takes a set of similar things that happen—say, the development of party systems in democracies—and finds a common pattern among them that allows us to treat each of these different occurrences as a repeated example of the same thing. Instead of having to think about a large number of disparate happenings, we need only think of a single pattern with some variations.

For example, in his book on political parties, Maurice Duverger was concerned with the question of why some countries develop two-party systems and others develop multiparty systems (1963, pp. 206–280). The initial reality was chaotic; scores of countries were involved, with varying numbers and types of parties present at different times in their histories. Duverger devised the theory that (1) if social conflicts overlap, and (2) if the electoral system of the country does not penalize small parties, then the country will develop a multiparty system; otherwise, the country will develop a two-party system.

His idea was that where there is more than one sort of political conflict going on simultaneously in a country, and where the groups of people involved in these conflicts overlap, there will be more than two distinct political positions in the country. For example, a conflict between workers and the middle class might occur at the same time as a conflict between Catholics and non-Catholics. Then, if these groups overlapped so that some of the Catholics were workers and some were middle class, while some of the non-Catholics were workers and some were middle class, there would be four distinct political positions in the country: the Catholic worker position, the non-Catholic worker position, the Catholic middle-class position, and the non-Catholic middle-class position. The appropriate number of parties would then tend to rise, with one party corresponding to each distinct position.

However, Duverger thought that this tendency could be blocked if the electoral system were set up in such a way as to penalize small parties—by requiring that a candidate have a majority, rather than a plurality, of votes in a district, for instance. This requirement would force some of the distinct groups to compromise their positions and merge into larger parties that would have a better chance of winning elections. Such a process of consolidation logically would culminate in a two-party system. To summarize the theory: A country will develop a two-party system (1) if there are only two distinct political positions in the country, or (2) if despite the presence of more than two distinct political positions, the electoral law forces people of diverse positions to consolidate into two large political parties so as to gain an electoral advantage.

Having formulated this theory, Duverger no longer had to concern himself simultaneously with a great number of idiosyncratic party systems. He needed to think only about a single developmental process, of which all those party systems were examples.

Something is always lost when we simplify reality in this way. By restricting his attention to the number of parties competing in the system, for example, Duverger had to forget about many other potentially interesting things, such as whether any one of the parties was revolutionary, or how many of the parties had any chance of getting a majority of the votes.

Note, too, that Duverger restricted himself in more than just his choice of a theme: He chose deliberately to play down exceptions to his theory, although these exceptions might have provided interesting additional information. Suppose, for instance, that a country for which his theory had predicted a two-party system developed a multiparty system instead. Why was this so? Duverger might have cast around to find an explanation for the exception to his theory, and he could have then incorporated that explanation into the original theory to produce a larger theory. Instead, when faced with exceptions such as these, he chose to accept them as accidents. It was necessary for him to do this in order to keep the theory simple and to the point. Otherwise, it might have grown as complex as the reality that it sought to simplify.

As you can see, there are costs in setting up a theory. Because the theory simplifies reality for us, it also generally requires that we both narrow the range of reality we look at and oversimplify even the portion of reality that falls within that narrowed range. As theorists, we always have to strike a balance between the simplicity of a theory and the number of exceptions we are willing to tolerate. We do not really have any choice. Without theories, we are faced with the unreadable chaos of reality.

Actually, what social scientists do in developing theories is not different from what we normally do every day in *perceiving*, or interpreting, our environment. Social scientists merely interpret reality in a more systematic and explicit way. Without theories, students of society are trapped. They are reduced to merely observing events, without comment. Imagine a physicist—or a fruit picker for that matter—operating in the absence of theory. All she could do if she saw an apple falling from a tree would be to duck, and she would not even know which way to move.

Social theory, then, is the sum total of all those theories developed by social scientists to explain human behavior. Political theory, a subset of social theory, consists of all theories that have been developed to explain *political* behavior.

Types of Political Research

The way a particular political scientist conducts research will depend both on the uses that she visualizes for the project and on the way she marshals evidence. Political research may be classified according to these two criteria.

The two main ways by which to distinguish one piece of research from another are:

1. Research may be directed toward providing the answer to a particular problem, or it may be carried on largely for its own sake, to add to our general understanding of politics. This distinction, based on the *uses for which research is designed*, may be thought of as applied versus basic research.
2. Research may also be intended primarily to discover new facts, or it may be intended to provide new ways of looking at old facts. Thus, political research can be characterized by the *extent to which it seeks to provide new factual information* (empirical versus nonempirical).

A glance at Table 1-1 shows us the four types of political research based on different combinations of these two dimensions. *Normative philosophy* consists of arguments about *what should be* in politics. Probably the oldest form of political research, it includes among its practitioners Plato, Karl Marx, Ayn Rand, Paul Krugman, George Will, and others. It is applied research; that is, its goal is problem solving. This means that it is not intended so much to devise or amend political theories as to use what political theories tell us about society and politics as a basis for making political decisions. It is also nonempirical, in that it does not consist primarily of investigating matters of fact. It typically takes certain political facts as given and combines them with moral arguments to prescribe political action. A good example is John Stuart Mill's argument in *Considerations on Representative Government*, in which

TABLE 1-1   Types of Political Research

	Applied	Recreational
Nonempirical	Normative philosophy	Positive theory
Empirical	Engineering research	Theory-oriented research

he urges the adoption of democratic representative government because (1) the chief end of government should be to facilitate the development in each citizen of his full potential (moral argument), and (2) democratic government, by giving the people responsibility, will do this (factual assumption).

Like normative philosophy, *engineering research* is geared to solving problems. However, its stance is empirical; it is concerned with ascertaining the facts needed to solve political problems. Some examples would be measuring the effects of various reapportionment methods, trying to design a diplomatic strategy to effect disarmament procedures, and designing methods of riot control.

These two forms of applied research are important parts of academic political science, but they are also often pursued outside of academia. Political engineering is a thriving industry and many courses relevant to it are taught in political science departments, but research and instruction in it are also often found in special separate institutes like the Kennedy School of Government at Harvard or the Institute for Research on Poverty at the University of Wisconsin. Private corporations such as the Rand Corporation and the Gallup Poll also study engineering problems in politics.

Normative philosophy is taught extensively in political science departments, but often this means primarily the *history* of normative philosophy and its development, not the active formulation of normative theories. Much work in normative philosophy is done in political science departments, of course, but much is also done in law schools, or outside academia by writers in philosophy, or in publications like the *Weekly Standard* or the *Nation*.

At the other end of the continuum from applied research is recreational research. It is usually called "pure" or "basic" research, but this carries the unpleasant implication that applied research is either impure or of limited value. This type of research is really not as flippant as the choice of the term *recreational* might make it seem, for this is research carried on for its own sake, to improve political theory. Political scientists pursue this type of research for the twin pleasures of exercising their minds and increasing their understanding of things. In a high sense of the word, it is "recreation."

Positive theory, largely a post–World War II phenomenon, is the most recently introduced form of political research. Like normative philosophers, positive theorists posit certain facts about politics; but in contrast to normative philosophers, they posit facts as empirical conditions rather than as the foundation for moral arguments. And they distinctively operate by deriving further implications of the posited conditions by precise logical and mathematical operations. Their concern is to take the posited facts, or assumptions, and derive theories from them. Their end goal is to develop reasonably broad and general theories based on a small number of agreed-upon assumptions.

A good example of positive theory—indeed, a work by which many would date the emergence of positive theory as a distinct field in political science—is Anthony Downs' *An Economic Theory of Democracy* (1957). Downs builds a wide-ranging theory from a set of assumptions such as: (1) voters and parties behave rationally; (2) political conflict occurs on only one issue at a time; and (3) political events are not perfectly predictable. Some of the predictions generated from his theory are (1) in a two-party system, parties will tend to agree very closely on issues, whereas in a multiparty system, they will not; (2) it may be rational for the voter to remain uninformed; and (3) democratic governments tend to redistribute income. (Of course, one must recognize that excerpts such as these do even more than the usual violence to a rich net of theories.) It is important to emphasize that this sort of work is almost solely an exercise in deduction. All of the conclusions derive logically from a limited set of explicit assumptions. Downs' purpose in this is simply to see where the assumptions he started with will lead him. Presumably, if the assumptions produced an untenable result, he would go back and reexamine them.

The main use of positive theory, as in the example above, is explanation; a positive theory is used to construct a set of conditions from which the thing we wish to explain would have logically flowed. Such explanatory positive theories are then often tested empirically through theory-oriented research. But because positive theory consists of taking a set of assumptions and working out where they lead—that is, what they logically imply—it is also useful for developing and analyzing strategies for political action. That is, we can use positive theory to construct analyses of the following form: If we want to achieve X, can we devise a set of reasonably true assumptions and an action which, in the context of those assumptions, will logically lead to the goal we desire? Positive theory is used in this way, for example, to argue for various ways to set up elections, or for various ways to arrange taxes so as to get the outcomes we want. Flat-tax proposals are a good example. They originated in argument of the following form: (a) If we want to maximize investment and economic growth, and (b) if we assume that governmental investment is inefficient and that individual taxpayers act so as to maximize their income, then (c) can we deduce what sort of taxes in the context of the assumptions of (b) would best achieve (a)?

Like normative philosophy, positive theory interacts with empirical research. Positive theorists usually try to start with assumptions that are in accord with existing knowledge about politics, and at the end they may compare their final models with this body of knowledge. But they are not themselves concerned with turning up new factual information.

Good work in positive theory will take a set of seemingly reasonable assumptions and will show by logical deduction that those assumptions lead inescapably to conclusions that surprise the reader. The reader must then either accept the surprising conclusion or reexamine the assumptions that had seemed plausible. Thus, positive theory provides insights by logical argument, not by a direct examination of political facts.

Following from Downs, a great deal of positive theory in political science has based itself on the economists' core assumption of *rational choice*: the assumption that individuals choose their actions in order to maximize some valued object and minimize the cost expended in achieving it. (In economics, the valued object is generally taken to be money; in political science, it may be money—as in theories of why and how communities seek pork-barrel spending—but theories may also posit that the valued object is a nonmonetary policy such as abortion, or political power itself. Sometimes the object may even be left unspecified in the theory.)

A good example of positive theory that illustrates the rational choice assumption is Mancur Olson's *The Logic of Collective Action* (1965). The rational choice assumption pointed Olson to a question no one had asked before, and allowed him to stand received wisdom on its head. Olson wrote on the very basic question of political organization in society. Before his book, scholars had assumed that when interests existed in society—racial minorities, businesses, professions, groups with special concerns such as historic preservation—political organizations could be expected to emerge naturally to represent those interests.[2] We should thus expect to see a wide range of parties and interest groups engaged in politics. A whole school of political science, the *pluralist school*, was organized around the expectation that most of the time, most of society's interests would be actively organized.

Based on the rational choice assumption, however, Olson reasoned that there was nothing natural about organization at all. From the standpoint of any individual in a group with a shared object, he concluded, participation in the group is usually nonrational. Remember that the rational choice assumption states that individuals choose their actions in order to maximize a valued object, while minimizing the cost expended in achieving it. If I am a person concerned with historic preservation, I know that unless I have very unusual resources, my individual contribution to an interest group pursuing preservation will not make a measurable difference. Let us say there are 300,000 people around the country who share my interest; if each of us contributes $100 to the cause, the difference if I do or do not contribute is a budget of $29,999,900 versus $30,000,000. To the organization this amount would be trivially small, but to me $100 makes a real difference. If I contribute, I will have expended a significant cost without getting any more of my valued good, which is not rational. What is rational, instead, is to be a *free rider*, and let all those other people make the contributions. However, Olson pointed out, since every potential member of such an organization is in this same situation, the marvel should be that any interest organizations exist at all.

Olson laid out several conditions under which organizations might nonetheless arise. One such condition is that one potential member might have such large resources that she knows no organization is possible without her participation. The largest department store in town, for instance, knows that a Downtown Merchants' Association cannot function if it does not join and contribute. The Bijoux Tee-Shirt Shop on the corner, though, is not in that situation. Under these circumstances, we can count on an organization being set up, because rationally, the large store cannot get its valued good unless it takes the lead in setting up the association.

No theory can ever be all-encompassing, and in fact one function of theory may be that it highlights exceptions for closer examination. We know that many people do contribute to political organizations even though, as Olson has proved, it is irrational for them to do so. The virtue of Olson's theory in this case is that instead of viewing such contributions as "natural" and therefore ignoring them, we are forced to treat the contributions as a puzzle requiring further investigation.

However, in a wide array of settings Olson's theory predicts behavior rather well. The excruciating efforts of public television stations to get their viewers to join rather than be free riders ("Please! Only one in ten of our viewers is a member. If you join

---

[2]For example, Duverger (1963) assumed this in the theory I described on pp. 2–3.

KXXX-TV today we will send you this beautiful coffee mug!") bear testimony to the power of Olson's logic. In the next chapter, you will see that it may also help to explain why small nations typically do not pull their "fair" weight in international alliances.

Although positive theory is the fastest growing type of political research, most research and teaching in political science is still of the fourth type suggested in Table 1-1, *theory-oriented research*. This type of research is concerned with expanding our knowledge of what happens in politics and of why it happens as it does. Like political engineering, it is empirical; it is concerned with discovering facts about politics. But unlike engineering, which deals with facts for their usefulness in specific political problems, this research deals with them to develop new political theories or to change or confirm old ones. Accordingly, the most important activity in this research is the development of theories linking observed facts about politics. In engineering, facts are sought out if they are needed to solve a problem; here, they are sought out if they will be useful in developing theories.

Duverger's study of political parties is an example of theory-oriented research. Another good example is a test by Diehl and Kingston (1987) of the theory that arms buildups lead to military confrontations. They examined changes in military expenditure by major powers from 1816 to 1976 to see whether increases tended to be followed by involvement in war. No matter how they adjusted things—looking for delayed reactions, looking only at "arms races" in which two rivals simultaneously increased their military forces, and so on—they found no relationship. Military engagements were no more or less likely to occur following military buildups than under other circumstances. They concluded by exploring the implications of this finding, one of which is that arms expenditure must therefore be determined more by domestic political considerations than by the international situation.

Research Mix

Practically no research is a *pure* example of any of the types I have presented here. These are abstract distinctions, types of emphasis found in particular pieces of research. Generally, any specific piece of work is a mix of more than one of the types. Although one method will usually predominate, there will almost always be some interaction between the different types in any given work. Two examples may help illustrate this point.

First, let us look a bit more closely at normative philosophy, using Karl Marx's work as an example. Marx's theory of the dialectic is primarily a work in normative philosophy. His argument takes the same general form as that in Mill's essay on representative government: "Because _____ aspects of the human condition today are bad, and because the state and the economy function in _____ ways to produce these bad effects, we should strive to change the state and the economy in _____ ways, which will eliminate the bad effects." But Marx was less willing than Mill to simply *assume* the factual portions of his argument. Instead, he spent years of empirical research trying to work out the precise economic effects of capitalism.

It should be evident that anyone developing normative theories about politics must begin with some factual assumptions. A researcher may be relatively more willing to assume these facts from general experience and/or from the research of others, as Mill was; on the other hand, he may wish, like Marx, to conduct a personal investigation of this factual basis. Such activity will, of course, involve him to some degree in engineering research. It is characteristic of normative philosophy, however, that the researcher does not feel *required* to produce the full factual basis for his argument. In this respect, normative philosophy differs from the empirical types of political research.

The distinction is an important one. For one thing, the fact that normative philosophers are not required to provide evidence for all their assumptions leaves them free to devote more energy to other parts of the research task. More important, they often need to assume facts that cannot possibly be tested against reality. The normative philosopher must be free to imagine realities that have never existed before, and these, of course, cannot be tested. If normative philosophers were held to the same standards of factual evidence as empirical researchers, all utopian dreams would have to be thrown out.

As a second example of the way in which types of research are mixed in any one work, let us look at a case in which researchers working on a primarily engineering project found they needed to develop a theory to make sense out of their work. A group of sociologists led by Samuel Stouffer was employed by the Army to study the morale of American soldiers during World War II (Stouffer and others, 1949). Stouffer and his coworkers were puzzled by the fact that often a soldier's morale had little to do with his objective situation.

For instance, MPs were objectively less likely to be promoted than were members of the Army Air Corps. Of Stouffer's sample of MPs, 24 percent were noncommissioned officers (NCOs), compared with 47 percent of the air corpsmen. Paradoxically, however, the MPs were much more likely than the air corpsmen to think that soldiers with ability had a good chance to advance in the Army. This sort of paradox occurred a number of times in their study, and the researchers felt they had to make some sense of it if their efforts were to help the Army improve morale.

They did this by developing the theory of *relative deprivation* to account for their seemingly contradictory findings. According to this theory, satisfaction with one's condition is not a function of how well-off a person is objectively, but of whether her condition compares favorably or unfavorably with a standard that she perceives as normal.

The fact that so many air corpsmen were NCOs apparently made the corpsmen feel that promotion was the normal thing. Those who were not promoted were disappointed, and those who were promoted did not feel particularly honored. Among the MPs, on the other hand, promotion was sufficiently infrequent that *not* being promoted was seen as the norm. Those who were not promoted were not disappointed, and those who were promoted felt honored. Thus, paradoxically, the air corpsmen, who were more likely to be promoted, felt that chances for promotion in the Army were poor, and the MPs, who were less likely to be promoted, felt that chances for promotion in the Army were good!

I have mentioned these two examples to illustrate my point that most research work involves some mix of the four types of research. Indeed, a mix is so much the usual situation that when I tried to make a rough head count of the frequency of the different types of research in political science journals, I was unable to do so. I was simply unwilling to assign most articles to one or another of the categories. The various types of research interact in the work of every political scientist.

That most research involves a mix of the types does not preclude the importance of the distinctions, however. Generally, one type of research is dominant in any given piece of work, depending on the goals of the researcher. These goals have a lot to do with the way a study should be set up and the criteria according to which it should be judged.

Evaluating Different Types of Research

It is dangerous to set down simple standards for good research. Like any creative work, research should be evaluated subjectively, according to informal and rather flexible criteria. But I will risk suggesting two standards for research that will serve as examples of the way in which the type (or types) of research we are doing dictates the way we should conduct that research.

In the first place, in either form of empirical research, the researcher should be held responsible for *demonstrating the factual basis of his conclusions*. In either form of nonempirical research, this is not necessary, although a normative argument may be made more convincing, or an exercise in positive theory may be made more interesting by providing evidence for the factual basis on which its assumptions rest.

In the second place, good research of any sort should be *directed to an interesting problem*. But what sort of problem is "interesting" depends largely on the motivation of the study. For either sort of applied research, problems should be chosen that are of real importance for contemporary policy. Today, an argument about civil disobedience, for example, makes a more interesting problem in normative theory than a problem dealing with an argument about dynastic succession; a few hundred years ago, the reverse would probably have been the case. In other words, applied research should be *relevant*, in the common usage of the word.

Recreational research, on the other hand, requires problems that will have a substantial impact on existing bodies of theory. Many topics that are of considerable importance to an engineer show little promise for theory-oriented research. Similarly, many promising topics for recreational research are not directly relevant. For example, research on the difference between men's and women's voting in Iceland in the 1920s and 1930s would sound absurd from the standpoint of an engineer. But these voting patterns, occurring just after the extension of the vote to women, might be important for theories of how voting patterns become established among new voters. How to choose an interesting problem is one of the most challenging parts of empirical research. I will discuss this in some detail in Chapter 2.

In general, this book is concerned with empirical research, both applied and theory-oriented. Within empirical research, I devote somewhat more attention to theory-oriented research than to engineering, because it poses some special instructional problems. However, almost all of the material I present is equally important for either engineering or theory-oriented research.

ETHICS OF POLITICAL RESEARCH

Conducting research is an act by you. You must therefore be concerned about the ethics of your research, just as you are with all of your actions. There are two broad classes of ethical questions regarding our research. First, we must concern ourselves with the *effects on society of what we discover*. For instance, if you study techniques of political persuasion, it is possible that what you learn could be used by a political charlatan to do bad things. A colleague once published a study of the effects of electoral systems on representation, only to learn later that it was used by a military junta in a Latin American country to figure out how to produce a controllable "democracy."

Ethical questions of this sort are especially difficult because the results of our research are so hard to predict. Another colleague, in biology, was upset when he learned that his research on frogs' eyes turned out to have applications in the design of guidance systems for missiles! In the case of demeaning or dehumanizing research, a further problem arises, in that what seems "dehumanizing" to a person depends on what the person thinks "human" means—that is, it is very much a matter of personal beliefs and cultural context. The psychological research noted above may seem wholly appropriate, for instance, depending on one's view of humanness. As another example, the theory of evolution appears dehumanizing to many fundamentalist Christians but does not appear so to many other people.

One response to such difficulties might be to take a "pure science" approach, arguing that because it is so hard to judge the results of knowledge anyway, we should let the chips fall where they may. We should simply seek truth and not worry about its effects. As we will see throughout this book, however, the social scientist rarely deals in unquestioned truths. We work under sufficient difficulties, especially the fact that we usually cannot operate by experimentation (see Chapter 6), that our results are to some extent a subjective interpretation of reality. We operate within rules of evidence in interpreting reality, so we are constrained in what we can assert and cannot simply pull findings out of a hat; but still our results involve individual choices and judgment by us. We are not simply neutral agents of truth; we must take personal responsibility for the results of our research, difficult though these ethical questions may be.

A second class of questions, more specific than the ones described above but not necessarily easier to answer, deals with *our treatment of the people we are studying*. We are responsible to treat the subjects of our study fairly and decently. Particular problems arise in the following ways:

1. *Harm to subjects.* Harming the subjects of your study, either by doing harmful things to them or by withholding good things from them, should generally be avoided. Is it ethically right, for example, in evaluating the effects of a program that is intended to get people off the welfare rolls and into jobs, to withhold the program from some deserving people while administering it to others, in order to see how effective it is?
2. *Embarrassment or psychological stress.* You should avoid shaming people into participating in your study, or submitting them to embarrassing situations.

3. *Imposition.* You are asking your subjects to help you. Don't demand more of them than is reasonable. Public officials may get a hundred questionnaires a year; keep yours short. Dinnertime is a good time to reach people by phone, but it is also an annoying time if you have 15 minutes worth of questions to ask.

4. *Confidentiality.* Generally, the subjects of your study will wish to have their privacy protected. It is not enough just to withhold publishing their names. Relevant details you include in your report might make it easy to identify the subject (a member of Congress, female, from the South, the senior member of her committee, etc.). You should take care to truly mask the subjects who have helped you.

5. *Fooling or misleading the subjects.* As an overall rule, you should make certain that your subjects know exactly what they will be doing and what use you will make of them. As you will see in Chapter 6, the results of your study might well be more valid if the people you study are unaware that they are being studied. However, everyone has the right not to be fooled and not to be used without his or her consent.

The problems I have noted here pose difficult ethical questions of the "ends and means" sort. If research that will benefit society can be conducted only by mistreating subjects, should it be done? There is no clear answer. If the costs to subjects are slight (inconvenience, pain of which they are informed in advance) and the social benefits great, we would generally say yes, it should be done. But what if it puts subjects in danger of death, as may be true of political research that delves into racketeering or corruption?

The most horrible historic example of science gone bad is that of the Nazi doctors who killed prisoners by immersing them in ice water to see how long people could survive in freezing water. A painful ethical question today is whether even to use the results of that research, which was purchased at great human pain, but which may potentially help in saving lives and—we hope—will never be available again from any source. Does using the results of the research justify it? If so, perhaps we should destroy the results. But might that not lead to greater human pain for victims of freezing and exposure whom we might have helped?

The one firm rule, for me at least, is that people should never be coerced or tricked into participation and should always be fully informed before they agree to participate.

Political Theories and Research Topics

In this chapter, we look more closely at the nature of political theories and at the factors that influence the decision to do research on a particular theory. Along the way, I will discuss some standards to use in deciding whether a theory is weak or strong.

Although this chapter deals with political theories, you should not assume that it is important only for what I have called theory-oriented research. Indeed, as I pointed out in Chapter 1, the key to solving many engineering problems may be a political theory of some sort. To effect a change in some given phenomenon, you may need to develop a theory that accounts for several factors and allows you to manipulate them to produce the desired change. Much applied research on the problem of enriching the education of underprivileged children, for example, has had to concern itself with developing theories to explain why one child learns things more quickly than another. The Stouffer study, cited in Chapter 1, is another example of an engineering study in which it was necessary to develop a theory. In that case, Stouffer and his collaborators had to explain why MPs had higher morale than air corpsmen. This was necessary if they were to devise ways to raise the morale of Army personnel in general.

On the other hand, many engineering studies do not require that a theory be developed; they simply involve measuring things that need to be measured. Taking the U.S. census is one example of such engineering research. Others include the Gallup Poll, studies measuring the malapportionment of state legislatures, and comparisons of the relative military strength of various countries.

In sum, engineering research may or may not involve the development of political theories; theory-oriented research always does. Theory is a tool in one type of research; it is an end in itself in the other. But no matter which type of research one is currently engaged in, it is worth taking a closer look at the nature of theory.

CAUSALITY AND POLITICAL THEORY

In the social sciences, theories are generally stated in a causal mode: "If X happens, then Y will follow as a result." The examples we looked at in Chapter 1 were all of this form. In the Duverger example, *if* a certain configuration of political conflicts exists, and *if* the country adopts a certain electoral law, *then* the number of political parties in the country can be expected to grow or shrink to a certain number. In the Diehl and Kingston study, the authors tested a theory that *if* a country increases its military expenditure, *then* it might be expected to go to war.

A causal theory always includes some phenomenon that is to be explained or accounted for. This is the *dependent variable*. In Duverger's theory, the dependent variable was the number of parties. A causal theory also includes one or more factors that are thought to affect the dependent variable. These are called the *independent variables*. Duverger used two independent variables in his theory: the nature of social conflicts in a country and the country's electoral system.

All of these factors are called "variables" simply because it is the variation of each that makes it of interest to us. If party systems had not varied—that is, if each country had had exactly the same number of parties—there would have been nothing for Duverger to explain. If one or the other of his independent variables had not varied, that factor would have been useless in explaining the dependent variable. For instance, if all countries had had the same electoral system, the variations in party systems that puzzled him could not have been due to differences in the countries' electoral systems, inasmuch as there were no differences.

The dependent variable is so named because *in terms of the particular theory used* it is thought to be the result of other factors (the independent variables). The shape it takes "depends" on the configuration of the other factors. Similarly, the independent variables are thus designated because *in terms of the particular theory*, they are not taken as determined by any other factor used in this particular theory.

The same variable may be an independent variable in one theory and a dependent variable in another. For instance, one theory might use the social status of a person's father (the independent variable) to explain the person's social status (the dependent variable). Another theory might use the person's social status as an *independent* variable to explain something else, perhaps the way the person votes.

Thus, no variable is innately either independent or dependent. Independence and dependence are the two roles a variable may play in a causal theory, and it is not something about the variable itself. It all depends on the theory:

Theory 1: Democracies do not tend to initiate wars.
Theory 2: Countries with high per capita incomes are more likely to be democ-racies than poor countries are.

In theory 1, *democracy* functions as an independent variable; the tendency to wage war depends on whether or not a country is a democracy. In theory 2, *democracy* functions as a dependent variable; whether or not a country is likely to be a democracy depends on its per capita income.

WHAT DOES GOOD THEORY LOOK LIKE?

Three things are important if we are to develop good, effective theories:

1. *Simplicity*. A theory should give us as *simple* a handle on the universe as possible. It should use no more than a few independent variables. It would not be very useful to develop a theory that used 30 variables, in intricate combinations, to explain why people vote the way they do. Such a theory would be about as chaotic and as difficult to absorb as the reality it sought to simplify.
2. *Predictive accuracy*. A theory should make *accurate predictions*. It does not help to have a simple, broad theory which gives predictions that are not much better than one could get by guessing.
3. *Importance*. A theory should be *important*. However, what makes a theory important is different in engineering research than in theory-oriented research, so we shall consider them separately.

In *engineering* research, a theory should address a problem that is currently pressing. This is a subjective judgment, of course, but before you begin your research, you should try to justify your choice of topic, not only to yourself but also to your audience. Your research report should include some discussion of the importance of the problem and of possible applications for your findings. It may seem unnecessary to point this out, but it is an important part of the engineering research project, one that is often carried out sloppily and in an incomplete way. Students have been known, for example, simply to turn in a computer printout as a paper, because "the applications are obvious." True, the *obvious* applications are obvious, but an imaginative researcher who sits down and thinks about it for awhile may be able to point up additional, more varied ways in which the results can be used.

In *theory-oriented* research, the theory should give a handle on as big a portion of the universe as possible; that is, it should apply broadly and generally. It is easy to develop a trivial theory. A theory of the organization of borough presidencies in New York City, for example, might predict quite accurately for that specific situation. But inasmuch as the borough presidents have little power, it would not help us very much to reduce the chaos of New York City politics, let alone the chaos of politics in general.

When we say that a theory should apply "broadly" and "generally," we are referring not only to how large a selection of items from reality the theory deals with, but also to how great a variety of preexisting theories are affected by the new theory. A theory can attain great generality rather economically if it helps to recast older theories, each of which involves its own portion of reality. Thus, a theory of electoral change might take on importance partly from the phenomena it explained directly—changes in people's votes; but it would be a more valuable tool if it could be shown to have significant implications for other areas of social theory—democratic theory, general theories of attitude change, or whatever. In effect, it would perform two simplifying functions: It would not only give us a handle on the rather limited portion of our environment that it sought to explain directly, but it would also shed light on the wider universe dealt with by the other theories.

In the example just cited, a theory to explain the organization of borough presidencies in New York City, the theory accrues so little importance directly as to look absurd. But it might be possible, if the borough presidencies were taken as examples of some broader concept in urban politics, then the study would borrow importance from this underlying phenomenon. The borough presidencies might, for example, serve as a useful microcosm for studying the workings of patronage.

If a theory can succeed reasonably well at meeting these three criteria— importance, simplicity, and predictive accuracy—it will be useful as a tool for simplifying reality. Such a theory is sometimes described as *elegant*.[1] One difficulty in creating an elegant theory is that trying to meet any one of the three basic criteria tends to make it harder to meet the other two. In the example of Duverger's theory, we saw that he might have improved the accuracy of his theory's predictions by bringing in additional explanatory variables; but this would have reduced the simplicity of the theory. Similarly, an attempt to make a theory more general often will cost us something in either the simplicity of the theory or the accuracy of its predictions.

Aside from its utility and simplicity, there is also an element of "beautiful surprise" to elegant research. A piece of research that goes against our expectations, that makes us rethink our world, gives us a special kind of pleasure. Political scientists often jokingly refer to this element as the "interocular subjectivity test" of research—Does it hit us between the eyes?

A good example of research with beautiful surprise is a study of the impact of "get-tough" policies against illegal immigration across the United States–Mexican border. In the late 1980s and early 1990s, the U.S. Immigration and Naturalization Service added extra guards and imposed punishments on employers found to be hiring illegal immigrants. One thousand extra border patrol officers were then added each year for several years afterward. Douglas S. Massey and Kristin E. Espinosa (1997) found that since the border crossing had been made tougher, illegal immigrants who originally would have come to the United States for only a few months of seasonal labor now stayed year-round because they knew it would be hard to get back into the United States if they went home to Mexico. The end result was that the number of illegal immigrants present at any given time was increased, not decreased, by the stepped-up enforcement.

It appears to be particularly hard to achieve elegant research in the social sciences, compared with other scientific areas. Human behavior is more complex than the behavior of physical objects—in fact, some think it may be largely beyond explanation. On the other hand, it may be that human behavior can be understood, but that we have not yet come up with a social theory that could show the true potential of our field. At any rate, it is rare for theory in the social sciences to achieve elegance. If a theory's predictions are reasonably accurate, it is usually because the scope of the theory is restricted or because many of the exceptions to the theory have been absorbed into it as additional variables, making it very complex.[2]

---

[1] The choice of this word typifies the aesthetic pleasure—and the vanity—with which researchers approach their work.

[2] Another reason for the difficulty of attaining elegance in social research is simply that most social science terms are imprecise and ambiguous. This problem is addressed in Chapter 3.

The fact that most social science theory is not very elegant does not mean that it is not good. The real test of a theory's value is whether its subject matter is important and how close it has come to elegance, *given* that subject matter. If it is important to understand humankind's behavior, it is important to try to develop theories about it, even if things do not fall as neatly into place as we would like.

I am always amused when people say of a question that is being made to look more difficult than it really is, "This shouldn't be that hard; what the heck, it's not rocket science"—implying that rocket science is the essence of difficulty and complexity. Not to take away from the difficulty of rocket science, but plotting the trajectory of an object in a vacuum is far simpler than understanding the motivation of a human being. Perhaps one day the old saw will become, "This shouldn't be that hard; what the heck, it's not social science."

Example of Elegant Research: Philip Converse

In his article "Of Time and Partisan Stability" (1969), Philip Converse came about as close to developing an "elegant" theory as one can commonly do in the social sciences. His study is worth looking at in some detail.

Converse took as his dependent variable the strength of the "party identification" of individuals—their sense that they are supporters of one or another of the political parties. In an earlier study, he and Georges Dupeux had found that, whereas about 75 percent of Americans who were polled identified with some political party, a similar poll conducted in France showed that less than 45 percent of the respondents did so (Converse & Dupeux, 1962). Other studies had shown high levels of party identification in Britain and Norway and lower levels of party identification in Germany and Italy. Because the overall extent to which citizens of a particular country felt bound to the existing parties seemed likely to have something to do with how stable politics in that country would be, Converse wanted to know why the level of party identification varied as it did from country to country.

At the time of their earlier study, he and Dupeux had found that the difference in percentage of party identifiers between France and the United States seemed to be explained almost wholly by the fact that more Americans than French had some idea of what party their fathers had identified with. As we can see in Table 2-1, within each row there was practically no difference between the French and American levels of party identification. In both countries, about 50 percent of those who did not know

TABLE 2-1   Percent Having Same Sort of Party Identification

	USA	France
Know father's party	79.4	81.6
Do not know father's party	47.7	50.7

their father's party expressed identification with some party themselves.[3] About 80 percent of those who *did* know their father's party were political party adherents. Thus, the difference between the two countries was a result of the fact that the Americans knew their father's party so much more frequently than the French did.

At the time, Converse and Dupeux accepted this as an interesting finding and did not elaborate on it. But in "Of Time and Partisan Stability," Converse used the earlier finding to suggest a general theory of the process by which countries developed stable patterns of party preference.

In doing so, he brought two strands of theory together. First, he reasoned that the difference between France and the United States could be explained easily if the previous generation in France had indeed included very few voters who identified with a party. It could have been, of course, that the difference was due to the fact that the French did not talk to their children about politics as much as the Americans did. But for the purposes of argument, Converse chose to assume that this was not the case. He then showed that if his assumption about the previous generation's low level of party identification were true, one could expect the next generation in France to be much more like the Americans. Also, if the assumption were true, France must be moving toward the level of party identification found in the United States, Britain, and Norway. (This development can be seen in the box, "Markov Chains," on p. 19)

Converse further reasoned that the 80 percent and 50 percent figures might be universally true. (He *knew* only that they held for France and the United States.) If this were so, then both France and the United States might simply be examples of a general process that all countries undergo when their citizens are first given the vote. In the first election, scarcely any voters in a given country would identify with a party, but 50 percent of second-generation voters would express identification. (Since of those whose fathers had not identified with any party, 50 percent developed an identification of their own.) Thus, gradually party adherence would reach a stable level. According to this scheme, the relatively low level of party identification in France must have resulted because the vote was extended later and less completely there than in America. (French women, for one thing, were first given the vote in 1945.) Thus, France must be at an earlier stage of the process than America.

The second strand of theory came into play when Converse tied his theory of national development to some older findings on individual voters in the American electorate. Voting studies commonly had shown that within an individual's life span, the older he was the more likely he was to identify strongly with a party. Moreover, this had been shown to be a result of how long he had been exposed to the party by being able to vote for it, rather than of his age itself (see, for example, Campbell et al., 1960, pp. 161–164).

Working from these two angles, Converse developed a simple theory that predicts the strength of a voter's party identification from just two things: (1) the number of years the person has been eligible to vote (which is a dual function of age and how long elections have been held in his/her country); and (2) the likelihood

---

[3]Remember that this was an early study, done in 1962. It was not long before further work showed similar effects for mothers!

that the individual's father had identified with a party (which in turn depends on what portion of the father's adult life elections were held in which he was eligible to vote). The first of these derived from the earlier research on individual development, the second from the comparative study of France and the United States by Converse and Dupeux. Thus, essentially, party identification is predicted from the individual's age and the length of time that the country has been holding elections.

A few examples of predictions from his theory are (1) at the time elections are first held in a country, the pattern we typically observe in Europe and America (the young being weakly identified, the old strongly) should not hold; all should identify at the same low levels; (2) if elections were interrupted in a country (as in Germany from 1933 to 1945), levels of party identification should decline at a predictable rate; (3) *if* the transition rates for all countries were roughly the same as

MARKOV CHAINS

Converse's reasoning is based on some cute, simple mathematics that you can play with for yourself. If the rates of transferring identifications are in fact the same in two countries, then even though the countries differ greatly in the level of identification at present, we would expect them to converge rapidly. For example, Converse and Dupeux estimated for France and the United States that about 80 percent of those whose fathers had identified with a party developed an identification of their own, and that, of those whose fathers had not identified with a party, about 50 percent developed an identification of their own. Given these figures, and assuming that party identifiers have the same number of children as nonidentifiers, then if 30 percent of the population of country A presently identify with a party, and 90 percent of the population of country B presently identify with a party, in the next generation we would expect to see

$$(0.8 \times 30\%) + (0.5 \times 70\%) = 59\%$$

of country A having an identification, and

$$(0.8 \times 90\%) + (0.5 \times 10\%) = 77\%$$

of country B having an identification. In the next generation after that, we would expect to see

$$(0.8 \times 59\%) + (0.5 \times 41\%) = 67.7\%$$

of country A having an identification, and

$$(0.8 \times 77\%) + (0.5 \times 23\%) = 73.1\%$$

of country B having an identification. Thus, in two generations the two countries, which had started out being quite different, would have moved to similar levels of party identification. The process involved here, called a "Markov chain," is described in J. Kemeny, J. Snell, and G. Thompson, *Introduction to Finite Mathematics* (Englewood Cliffs, N.J.: Prentice-Hall, Inc., 1957), pp. 171–178.

for France and the United States, then party identification levels in all electoral democracies should converge over the next few generations toward a single value of about 72 percent.

Thus, although Converse's theory was quite simple, it was applicable to a wide variety of questions. It simultaneously explained individual behavior and characteristics of political systems. It implied a more or less universal form of political development at the mass level—with a prediction of initial, but rapidly decreasing, potential for electoral instability in a new electorate. And it included the startling suggestion of a convergence of "mature" electorates to a common level of party identification approximately equal to that of Britain, Norway, or the United States.

The theory was simple, and it was broadly applicable. What was more, it seemed to predict fairly accurately, thus fulfilling the third criterion for "elegance." Using data from Britain, Germany, Italy, the United States, and Mexico to test the theory, Converse found that the theory predicted quite well for all five countries.

Over the years after it appeared, the Converse article stimulated a great deal of further research, which is what one would expect of elegant work. His findings served as assumptions for further theoretic work (Przeworski, 1975). They also stimulated researchers to investigate whether in fact the transition probabilities on which the Markov chain is based are the same in all industrialized countries (Butler & Stokes, 1969, p. 53), and to test whether new electorates actually behave as Converse's theory predicts they would (Shively, 1972; Leitner, 1997; Tilley, 2003; Dalton & Weldon, 2007). It is in this way that a good piece of theoretical work feeds, and becomes enmeshed in, the whole body of theoretical exploration.

To Quantify or Not

A side issue in the question of how to develop elegant theory is the old chestnut: Should political science be "quantitative" or not? There has been much rhetoric spilled over this. As long ago as 1956, James Prothro called the dispute "the nonsense fight over scientific method," but it has not cooled sufficiently in the intervening decades.

It is a bit hard to pin down what the term *quantitative* means, but generally, research that pays a good deal of attention to *numerical* measures of things, and tends to make *mathematical* statements about them, is considered quantitative. Research that is less concerned with measuring things numerically, and tends to make *verbal* statements about them, is considered relatively less quantitative.

Anything in political science can be stated with varying degrees of quantification. To give a crude example: "The length of service of members of the U.S. House increased from 1880 to 2005 on the average by 0.78 years every decade; the rate of increase was 0.68 years per decade before 1922, and 0.86 years per decade after 1922," says approximately the same thing as "From 1880 to 2005, representatives served a steadily increasing length of time in the House; the change proceeded a bit more rapidly in the latter half of that period." The first form of the statement gives more precise information, but the sense of the two statements is the same.

Each approach involves costs and benefits for research. Most people would agree that precise information is more useful than imprecise information, all other things being equal. But it may be that the time and attention spent in gathering precise data make it difficult for the researcher to appreciate the larger aspects of a theory. Also, because some kinds of data by their very nature are more amenable to precise formulation, there is the danger that overconcern with precision may restrict our choice of research to those variables we can more easily quantify. It is striking, for instance, how little the U.S. presidency is studied by political scientists. This oversight may well be due to the difficulty of getting "hard" data on what goes on in that office.

I deal with the issue of proper levels of precision in Chapter 5. For our purposes here, the important thing is to see what relationship degrees of quantification bear to elegance in research.

First of all, the particular subject we are studying affects the extent to which it is possible for us to quantify. In election studies, there is considerable scope for quantification. Records from earlier elections are usually kept in fairly good order; the results of many attitude surveys are also available, and most voters do not regard their actions as something about which they need to maintain secrecy. Thus, the quantitative researcher is able to do a great deal. On the other hand, in Chinese studies, or in studies dealing with the U.S. presidency, sources of quantitative data are quite restricted, and most research must be relatively nonquantitative.

In virtually every field of political research, however, work can be conducted in either a primarily quantitative or a primarily nonquantitative mode. It is probably best that studies with *varying degrees of quantification* be carried on in any given field of political research, for the different levels of quantification complement each other. Typically, less quantitative research provides greater breadth, greater openness to totally new theories, and a greater awareness of the complexity of social phenomena. On the other hand, studies employing more quantitative data are more likely to produce simple, usable theories; and they are certainly more likely to give us a clear idea of how accurate a theory's predictions are. Thus, each approach has its own costs and benefits, and it is well to remember that no particular degree of quantification has a corner on elegance.

CHOICE OF A TOPIC

The choice of a research topic is intimately bound up with the elegance of what comes out of the research effort. In selecting a topic, of course, the first step is to choose a general area that is interesting and significant for you. By choosing to study political science, you have already begun to narrow the field, and you certainly will narrow things more before you are ready to begin. There is no difficulty in this; you simply follow your interests.

But once you have chosen a general area to work in, picking a particular topic to research is difficult. This is the critical decision in doing research. It is also the most difficult aspect of research to teach anyone. It is at this step—seeing that a problem exists and that there is a good chance you can provide new insight into it—that originality and talent are most critical.

The important thing in choosing a topic is to pick one that shows promise of giving you new and elegant results. This implies two things: (1) You want to formulate your topic question so that your results will be likely to alter existing opinion on a subject, and (2) you want your results, as much as possible, to attain the three criteria for elegance: simplicity, predictive accuracy, and importance.

Engineering Research

Choosing a topic is somewhat simpler in engineering research than it is in theory-oriented research. Here, it is primarily a question of using your time and talents efficiently. To yield elegant results, the topic should be one that deals with a pressing problem and one on which you think you are likely to come up with findings that are both accurate and simple enough to be useful. At the same time, you will want to state your thesis so that your results will not duplicate an earlier study, or at least point up where that work produced mistaken results. There is no sense in wasting your time running over ground that has already been worked unless you think you are likely to discover discrepancies.

One difficulty in choosing the topic is that you probably will have to compromise among your goals. You may decide that for the problem nearest your heart, there simply is not enough material available to let you study it satisfactorily. Many topics relating to defense or to the executive are of this sort. Or, it may be that a topic interests you not because it deals with the most pressing problem you can think of, but because you have seen some research on it that you think would be rather easy to correct.

The main thing to do in looking for a topic is to read. You should read so that you are certain you are picking an important problem, and you should read to find out how likely it is that your topic will yield useful results. Finally, you should read to see what other work has been done on the problem, or on similar problems, so that you will see where you are most likely to produce results that are new.

Theory-Oriented Research

Choosing a topic that will produce important results for theory is undoubtedly more difficult than formulating a question that may yield important practical applications. You will recall that if theory-oriented research is to be important, it should have a broad and general effect on theory. This effect can be achieved either directly through the phenomena it explains or indirectly through the variety of other theories it affects. Similarly, to be "new," the research results must either produce totally new theories or lead to some change in the status of older theories.

This means that in framing any topic for research, you are involved at once in the full body of political science theory, for a single piece of research may simultaneously affect many different theories. Research on how a congressional committee reaches its decisions, for example, can affect theories about power in Congress, general theories about committees and organizations, theories about executive–congressional relations, theories about elite political behavior, and so on.

Thus, what the researcher in this area must do is to decide which research topic is going to produce the greatest change in the status of existing theories. This task requires not only that she be familiar with as broad a range of existing theories as possible, but that she also have some idea of where an existing body of research is weakest and most needs to be supported or changed.

Deciding where you are likely to produce theoretical results that are simple and predict accurately requires the same sort of guessing as in engineering research, but in theory-oriented research it is harder to decide how important the results of a study are likely to be. You must juggle all of these decisions around so as to get the best mix—a topic that will produce results that are as new and as elegant as possible. This is not something for which rules can be laid down—it is an art.

DEVELOPMENT OF A RESEARCH DESIGN

It may be true, as I say, that choosing a topic is not something for which rules can be laid down. But it is certainly something for which rules *have* been laid down. Because of an exaggerated fear of *ex post facto* argument, some social scientists have developed a very restrictive procedure to serve as a standard in carrying on research.[4] According to this procedure, the researcher should first frame a theory, stating it in the form of a set of hypotheses to be tested. These hypotheses presumably are based on work others have done in the past. The researcher should then gather fresh data with which to test the theory. Finally, having tested the theory, the researcher should either reject it or enshrine it *solely on the basis of those new data*. It is true that this procedure erects formidable barriers to protect us from *ex post facto* argument, but it has a number of serious drawbacks.

In the first place, it lends an exaggerated significance to the results of the new study. Even in cases where a variety of previously existing evidence favors a particular theory, that evidence presumably is to be ignored if the new test gives contradictory results. Second and more important, the usual procedure deters researchers from casting about creatively for research topics and theories. Because it requires that hypotheses be fixed firmly at the beginning of the research process, it effectively reduces the research task to a selection of obvious hypotheses. It offers researchers no encouragement to think about their theories once research has begun. Researchers are not supposed to remold theory as they go along, learning more about the subject. They are merely supposed to react to old theories and concepts rather than to think up entirely new problems for explanation. In short, this approach encourages the researcher to function as a clerk.

The epitome of this type of thinking is the *research design*—a common student exercise in which students are instructed to frame some hypotheses (presumably based

---

[4]*Ex post facto* argument results when an investigator forms a theory on the basis of certain evidence, then uses that evidence to affirm the theory. If a political scientist formed a theory of congressional committees on the basis of intimate experience with the House Appropriations Committee, for example, and then carried out a study of the House Appropriations Committee to test the theory, this would be *ex post facto* argument. The danger in this is that any given situation has certain unique aspects, and these are likely to be included in any theory based on it. If the same situation is then used to test the theory, it will look as if the unique aspects are indeed general, whereas if a different test situation had been used, those parts of the theory would have been found wanting.

on their reading) and show how they might gather data to test those hypotheses. A doctoral candidate whom I once talked with seemed to me the perfect example of repeated exposure to exercises such as these. He needed to find a topic for his dissertation and he thought that a good way to do this would be to look through a book laying out theories of elections, pick a few propositions about voting behavior, and test them with some data.

This is how we train people to do research, but most of us have better sense than to follow our own precepts. A search of articles in political science journals will turn up only a few that report research that follows the rules. One of the better-kept secrets in political science is that good political scientists generally do not draw up research designs before they start to work on a topic. Nor do they usually "frame hypotheses" in any formal sense before they start to work, although they usually have some operational hunches about what they expect to find. And they most certainly do not ignore older evidence, even the evidence that suggested a theory to them in the first place.

Their procedure is much less formal than the one they prescribe for students. They play with data, immerse themselves in what other people have written, argue with colleagues, and think. In doing so, they grope for interesting theories, theories that are elegant and give a new slant to things.

Although I have condemned the formal procedure for designing research, I hasten to add that it should not be rejected completely. One of its advantages is safeguarding against *ex post facto* argument. Furthermore, even though the research design undoubtedly stifles initiative and creativity, it is more methodical and easier to apply for the beginning researcher. Because students usually operate under stricter deadlines than other researchers, it may make sense for them to work with specific goals in mind so that they can estimate accurately at the beginning of a project when it will be completed. Also, it is hard to teach someone to grope for interesting topics and theories. Perhaps a good way to learn is by starting with the more clear and obvious procedures, then gradually loosening up as experience is gained.

Observations, Puzzles, and the Construction of Theories

One way to look at choosing topics and developing theories is with the realization that they are at heart very commonsensical processes, based on our daily experiences. This is often lost in the forest of scholarship, in which scholars frequently deal with abstractions (and with each other's rival abstractions). But at heart all theory-oriented research in the social sciences is of the following sort:

1. Something in our lives puzzles us, and we try to think of an explanation to account for it.
2. To account for it, we put it in a broader, general category of causal relationships (i.e., a theory).
3. To test whether the broader theory is valid as an explanation, we draw other specific predictions from the theory and test these to see whether the theory's predictions are generally true. If they are, the theory qualifies as a plausible explanation of the thing we are trying to explain.

As an example, consider the puzzle that the United States has always contributed proportionally more than almost all other members of the NATO military alliance, especially as compared with the smaller members of the alliance, as seen in Table 2-2.

The small allies all appear to varying degrees to ride on the coattails of the United States. One way to explain this would be to treat it as a specific instance of a more general relationship—that in any voluntary cooperative group the member with the greatest resources always tends to make disproportionate contributions. That is, a member who sees that the group would fail without her contribution will come through strongly; a relatively insignificant member will see that the group would do about equally well whether or not she contributes and will tend to sit back and be a free rider. In the NATO example, if the United States does not contribute vigorously, the alliance languishes, but little Estonia hardly makes a difference one way or another.

A lot of the political scientist's creativity will then come into play in devising other, testable predictions from the theory to see whether it is generally valid. In this example, we might examine chambers of commerce to see whether the biggest merchants in town usually carry most of the freight. Or we might look at trade union–supported political parties such as the Labour Party of Great Britain to see whether the largest unions carry a disproportionate share of the burden. If the theory holds up well across a variety of such tests, it will be a plausible potential explanation for the disparity in spending in NATO—and it will also have yielded us an interesting theory, with broad applications.[5]

Lest working out a theory or a puzzle should seem too easy or too pat from these examples, let me review for you a puzzle currently in real play, to show the uncer-

TABLE 2-2   U.S. Defense Spending, Compared with the Seven Smallest Members of NATO

	Gross National Product (billions of $)	Defense Spending as Percentage of Gross National Product
United States	15,664	4.0
Luxembourg	49	0.7
Slovenia	45	1.6
Bulgaria	40	2.1
Lithuania	38	1.2
Latvia	27	1.6
Estonia	21	1.6
Iceland	20	0.3

Source: International Institute for Strategic Studies, *The Military Balance*, 2009.

[5]The theory used in this example derives from the broader theoretical structure of Mancur Olson's *The Logic of Collective Action* (1965), which was discussed in pp. 6–7. The structure of argument discussed in this section—see a puzzle, frame an explanation based on a more general principle, devise other unrelated predictions from the general principle in order to test it—is presented skillfully by Charles A. Lave and James G. March in *Introduction to Models in the Social Sciences* (1975), especially in the first three chapters.

tainty and the progression of steps by which scientific discussion of a puzzle usually proceeds in real life.[6] A great deal of attention has been directed over the past decade to the so-called democratic peace—the observation that no democracy has ever been observed to initiate war with another democracy. It is extremely rare in the social sciences for any relationship to be as invariant as this one, and the relationship is also of great importance in the assessment of democracy, so it is not surprising that this has attracted the attention of some very good minds.

First of all, a number of scholars have questioned whether the observation is as infallible as it is claimed to be. Both "democracy" and "war" are subject to a certain amount of interpretation. Since no country is a pure democracy, how much democracy is enough to have the country count as democratic? When the NATO alliance attacked the Yugoslavian government of Slobodan Milošević in 1998 (a government which had been elected, but in an election without much real competition), was that a case of democracies attacking another democracy? Similarly, "war" is not always a black-and-white concept. When the U.S. Central Intelligence Agency gave covert support to a military coup against democratically elected President Allende of Chile, was that war?

Granting the gray areas of definition, however, most political scientists consider the democratic peace to be an enduring relationship of quite unusual regularity. This observation, then, poses the puzzle: Why is it that democracies do not attack one another?

There have been two primary explanations offered. First, many scholars argue that democracies share a number of values in common, such as respect for individual liberties and a high value on competition. They also share an international norm of compromise and bounded resolutions to conflicts. These characteristics, it is said, make democracies unlikely to wage war on those with whom they agree in so many areas.

Alternatively, a number of scholars point to the institutional structure of democracies as the explanation. People generally do not want to fight wars, and in democracies the wishes of the broad populace count for more than in nondemocracies. Accordingly, the chance that two democracies will enter a war, if in both of them the people's concerns count for a good deal, is low.

But beyond these two broad positions, as the diffuse scientific "conversation" has proceeded, many subtly nuanced theories have been developed. As one example, Bueno de Mesquita et al. (1999) point out that both of the broad explanations are hard to reconcile with the fairly strong willingness of democracies to initiate wars of conquest or empire. In the late nineteenth century, for instance, democratic France and Great Britain frequently sent armed forces to help acquire additions to their empires. And in the early twentieth century, the democratic United States enthusiastically engaged Spain in a war intended to lift some parts of the Spanish Empire such as Puerto Rico and the Philippines. These were not wars waged on democracies, but it was certainly the case that democratic values, and the influence of "the people" in these democracies, did not prevent these countries from entering into warfare rather happily.

---

[6]The discussion that follows draws heavily on the useful review of the democratic peace literature in Bueno de Mesquita et al. (1999).

Bueno de Mesquita and his coauthors propose instead a slightly complicated explanation based on rational choice theory.

1. In a democracy, a leader must satisfy a fairly large number of people in order to stay in power; in an autocracy, leaders typically need satisfy only a small number—the army, for instance—or a single party.
2. A war involves costs, but also benefits if won. A democratic leader needs a higher ratio of potential benefits to costs to justify going to war than an autocrat does, because the democratic leader has to reward more people. (See [1.] above.) Therefore, the stakes are higher for democratic leaders. An autocrat might lose a war yet stay in power. (Saddam Hussein of Iraq was an example, continuing in office after he lost the first Gulf War in 1991; he was ousted only later by direct action of American troops in 2003.) It is hard to imagine a democratic leader losing a war and not being voted out of office.
3. Since the stakes are higher for democratic leaders, they will be more careful about entering wars than will autocrats; and once involved in wars, democratic leaders will fight them more determinedly.
4. Given reasonably good information about each other, it is unlikely that either of two democrats involved in a conflict will think that he or she has a preponderant chance of winning a war; and each will know that the other (because it is a democracy) will fight very determinedly if there is a war. Therefore, the countries can be expected to try to negotiate their disputes rather than go to war over them.

This is a good explanation, but it certainly has not represented the last word in political scientists' collective effort to work out an explanation of the puzzle. (A good exercise for you would be to frame rebuttals of the rational choice explanation from the standpoint of the first two explanations—the "shared values" explanation and the "institutional role of the people" explanation.)

Note that throughout this discussion of puzzles and explanations, I have said that what is produced is a *plausible potential explanation*. It typically is the case that more than one plausible potential explanation can be produced for anything needing explanation. It then becomes the task of the scholar to decide among them on the basis of how broadly they apply, how simple they are (remember, a theory that is as complicated as the reality it is meant to explain has not gotten you very far), how accurately they predict, and so on. But the basic building blocks of political explanation are plausible potential explanations, derived in just the way that I have outlined here.

MACHIAVELLIAN GUIDE TO DEVELOPING RESEARCH TOPICS

There are really no guidelines that I can give you for developing a research topic other than to remind you once again that you are working toward results that are both *new* and *elegant*. Perhaps if we view the development task from the perspective of political research in general, however, we will gain some clue as to its place in the entire scheme.

Implicit in this chapter is the view that scholarly research represents a loose cooperative effort among many people. I mentioned earlier the pleasure that researchers feel in creating something that no one has seen before. This is mixed, however, with a sense of pride in being part of an ongoing tradition. One's work is something brand new, but it also draws on Karl Marx, or Emile Durkheim, or Robert Putnam, and *modifies the meaning of their work.* Scholars involved in developing theory form a kind of priesthood—admittedly sometimes run less on faith and more according to the laws of laissez-faire and caveat emptor—focused on the common goal of perfecting elegant theories. As we have seen, the celebrants carry on this process by developing new theories and adapting old ones, fitting these theories to the real world to see how accurately they predict things, and feeding the results of such research back into the body of theory.[7]

From this description of the process of research, we can derive a set of rules to guide the individual researcher. If empirical research is motivated by a desire to affect the state of theories, either by confirming them or by working changes in them, you will be doing your best job when you maximize your effect on theory with a given investment of time and money. To do this, you must:

1. **Maximize the generality of the theory you intend to examine.** This is basically a restatement of the first criterion for elegant research. Note, though, that this rule is not something absolute, for any phenomenon can be examined at different levels of generality. One person may be hit on the head by an apple and form a theory of falling apples; another may have the same experience and form a theory of universal gravitation. The physical activity of the "study" is the same in both cases; the difference lies solely in the level at which the researcher works.

   As an example from political science research, consider the variety of studies done on the presidency. The narrowest range of theory is found in biographies of particular presidents. The researcher in such a biography generally is concerned only with explaining what happened during a particular president's life, especially during his term in office. A broader range of theory is aimed at in studies of the U.S. presidency, which may analyze the nature of the office, the sources of executive power, the way in which presidents' personalities can influence their behavior in office, and so on.[8] A still broader range of theory is seen in studies that use the U.S. presidency as an example of sovereigns in general and seek to explain the sources and limitations of sovereign power. Richard Neustadt's *Presidential Power and the Modern Presidents* (1991), for instance, often operates at this level of generality.

2. **Pick a weak theory to work on.** The weaker the previous confirmations of a theory have been, the greater your contribution will be. Of course, you have a

---

[7]Needless to say, it is not quite as neat as this. For one thing, a given person usually does not handle all these aspects of a particular problem. One person may work simply at clarifying theories, another may do a descriptive study of a particular case, and a third may relate the new evidence to the body of older theory. Most researchers can expect to carry on any or all activities at any time.

[8]For example, a study of the nature of the presidential office (such as Koenig, 1968), a study of presidents' political personalities (Barber, 1972), or an analysis of presidents' leadership (Greenstein, 2000).

greater probability of refuting a weak theory. But also, if your research does confirm the theory, your work will again be more significant than if the theory already had a good deal of confirming evidence.

Obviously the best way to use the strategy of picking a weak theory would be to state a new, original theory yourself. In this case, your hypotheses are necessarily in need of proof, and any evidence you can buttress them with will be important. Remember, though, that "new, original theories" that are also elegant are hard to come up with.

Another way to follow this strategy is to pick an anomaly—that is, a question on which previous research has been contradictory. An early example of research stimulated by an anomaly is the study by Sidney Tarrow (1971) of the political participation of French peasants. Tarrow was struck by the fact that although French peasants regularly responded to surveys by stating that they were not very interested in politics, they also regularly turned out to vote in greater numbers than did the urban French.

This anomaly led Tarrow to probe more deeply into what political involvement means to the French, so as to resolve the apparent contradiction. His conclusions led to the rejection of the traditional "interest in politics" measure. They also shed new light on the nature of French voters' attachment to political parties. On this hinged the apparent contradiction, since French peasants were fiercely independent and understood "interest in politics" to imply some sort of approval of the existing parties. Though they were in fact interested in politics, they denied this because of their antipathy to the parties.

A current anomaly, on which political scientists are now working, is the "paradox of participation".[9] In general, the more highly educated people are, the more likely they are to vote. (In the 2008 presidential election, for instance, 79 percent of college graduates voted, 55 percent of high school graduates did so, and only 39 percent of those with less than a high school education went to the polls.[10]) So one would expect that as the citizens of a country became better educated, voter turnout would rise. But while the American population became dramatically better educated after World War II, participation in elections stagnated. In 1940, for instance, 76 percent of Americans had less than a high school education, a number which had dropped to 14 percent by 2007; but in 1940, 59 percent of eligible adults voted in the presidential election, a figure only slightly below the 64 percent turnout in the 2008 election.

Another example of a nice anomaly just waiting to be analyzed is the fact that in the 2008 election, the lower voters' incomes were, the more likely they were to vote for Barack Obama. But if you look at the "blue states"—the states he carried—they are on the whole well-off states with high average incomes (California, Connecticut, Vermont, New York, etc.). What sort of theory might you devise to explain this?

[9]The paradox is reviewed in Dalton and Klingemann (2007).
[10]U.S. Census Bureau, "Voting and registration in the election of November 2008."

Anomalies like these are hard to come by, because earlier investigators generally have noticed them already and have tried to resolve them. If you can find an anomaly having to do with a significant area of political theory, however, you can be certain that any plausible efforts at resolution will be interesting.

Besides anomalies, you might choose a problem you believe has just not been sufficiently researched, perhaps one in which all variables have not been covered. Thus, you might replicate a study in a different context from the original one. Arthur A. Goldsmith (1987) tested a well-known theory of Mancur Olson (1982) that prolonged political stability produces rigid social and economic structures and that these in turn retard economic growth. Goldsmith noted that Olson's conclusions were based mostly on the experiences of the West and Japan. The Third World would provide a laboratory of less-developed countries with a wider range of cultures and economic circumstances. And in fact, Goldsmith found that examination of these countries did not support Olson's theory, though he hastened to add that his measure of "instability" was questionable and might have been a source of the disparity. The most likely reason, at least to my taste, is that the context is different. Olson's theory relies on the negative economic effects of organized interest groups. Such groups are strong and active in the countries Olson studied, but not in the Third World context that Goldsmith studied. Goldsmith's negative results thus point up the importance of organized interest groups in Olson's theory.

3. **Make the connection between the general theory and your specific operations as clear as possible.** This really just boils down to making sure you say what you think you are saying. It involves such things as the accuracy of your deductions from the theory to the specific situation, the accuracy with which you have measured things, and so on. Much of the rest of this book focuses on such problems.

You may have noticed that these three rules resemble the criteria for elegance fairly closely. You also may have noticed that the basic philosophy behind them—"Do research that makes as big a splash as possible"—reads like a guide for ruthless and hungry assistant professors. But each of the rules, derived from my underlying Machiavellian outlook, also has a beneficial effect on the field as a whole. If individuals choose those problems of theory that have so far had the weakest verification, for example, the entire field will benefit from an examination of those theories most in need of investigation.

Needless to say, these guidelines should remain flexible enough to allow different mixes of research strategy. There is no one "scientific method" involved here. One person may find a tool that measures a variable better than had been done before and then simply apply it to sharpen previously examined relationships. Another may note an anomaly in a theory and organize an experiment to resolve the problem. A third may look over previous research findings and place a new, broader, or simpler interpretation on them. All are following the rule of maximizing their impact on theory.

4. **Present your theory as clearly and vividly as possible.** A Machiavellian researcher wants to influence as many people as possible, so it makes sense to make your reader's life easier and your message more compelling. This means, write well and present any graphic information well. People often think *how* you say

something is separable from *what* you say, but that is simply not true. If the purpose of theory is to change people's understanding of the world, then the way the theory is communicated to them is an integral part of the development of the theory.

How to write well and design graphic displays well are beyond the scope of this book; each really requires a book in its own right. Fortunately, I can suggest three truly good books that will help you. For writing, I recommend William Knowlton Zinsser's *On Writing Well: The Classic Guide to Writing Nonfiction* (New York: Harper Collins, 1998). Another introduction to writing, more focused on political science papers, is Gregory M. Scott and Stephen M. Garrison, *The Political Science Student Writer's Manual*, 5th ed. (New York: Longman, 2006). An excellent introduction to good graphic presentation is Edward R. Tufte's *The Visual Display of Quantitative Information* (Cheshire, Conn.: Graphics Press, 1983).

▪▪ Further Discussion

An intriguing book relevant to this chapter is Arthur Koestler's *The Act of Creation* (1969). An excellent introduction to building elegant theories is found in the first three chapters of Lave and March (1975). Two books outside political science that are very good examples of seeing and solving puzzles (and great reads, as well) are Steven Levitt and Stephen J. Dubner, *Freakonomics* (2005) and Thomas Eisner, *For Love of Insects* (2005).

Some questions you might consider are:

1. Presumably, work in normative philosophy or in positive theory could be evaluated in terms of elegance, just as empirical research is. What changes would this require in the definition of elegance?

2. This chapter has implied that the usual way to come up with a theory is to focus on a body of observations and look for regular patterns in them. Although this is the usual procedure, it is neither the only nor necessarily the best approach. What drawbacks might it involve? In what alternative ways might one develop a theory?

3. I stated in this chapter that most social science theories are causal. What would a noncausal theory look like? Under what circumstances would it be likely to be used? (*Hint:* Consider Einstein's famous theory, $E = mc^2$.)

Importance of Dimensional Thinking

In Chapter 2, I argued that flexibility and originality—in a word, freedom—are important in doing good research. In this chapter, I shall stress the need to state theories in a clear, unambiguous way—a form of self-discipline that must accompany such freedom.

In particular, we shall be concerned with framing theories in terms of concepts that cannot easily be subdivided into further distinct meanings, either denotative or connotative—in other words, very simple concepts whose meaning is unequivocal. I shall call such simple concepts *unidimensional,* in contrast to concepts whose meaning may vary from reader to reader and even from time to time, that is, *multidimensional* concepts.

Consider the following example: As a description of climates, "temperature" is a unidimensional concept. Temperature can vary along only one dimension, from hot to cold. Therefore, if a theory states that a temperature below x degrees causes the spotted ibex to stop breeding, that statement will mean the same thing to every reader. "Good weather," on the other hand, is a multidimensional concept that involves among other things temperature, wind velocity, humidity, amount of precipitation, and degree of cloud cover. If there is a variation along any one of these separate dimensions, the "goodness" of weather varies. If the theory stated that "bad weather" caused the spotted ibex to stop breeding, the meaning of that theory would be left to the reader's judgment. Is it rain that discourages the ibex's ardor? Or do high winds make him think of other things? Is it the heat? The humidity?

As we can see from this example, it is preferable to frame theories in terms of unidimensional rather than multidimensional concepts. The English language does not always make this easy, however. In this chapter, we shall look at the English language in general and at the varied theories that may be hidden in ordinary language.

ENGLISH AS A LANGUAGE FOR RESEARCH

I have assumed so far that if political research is to be useful, a minimal requirement is that its results should mean the same thing to any two different readers. Unfortunately, the English language is badly designed to function as a medium for stating research results clearly and without ambiguity. Most English words can take on a variety of meanings, depending on the context and on the mood of the reader. To use an everyday example, the statement, "The welfare bill failed in the House because the administration did not fight for it," might mean:

1. A welfare bill was passed, but not the one the writer wanted.
2. No welfare bill passed at all.

Whichever of these is the case, the failure could have resulted from any number of other events, for example:

3. The administration privately passed the word to its supporters to undercut the bill.
4. The administration wanted the bill, but did not campaign as hard as it usually does for bills it wants.
5. The administration campaigned as hard as it usually does for bills it wants, but not as hard as the writer would have done.
6. The administration went all-out for the bill, but failed to get it passed—and the writer is in the opposing party.

Note that in these statements there are many additional phrases that are ambiguous: "pass the word," "undercut the bill," "want the bill," "campaign for the bill," "go all-out."

As another example of a multidimensional concept, consider *political party*. This concept can be broken down into at least six component dimensions: those people who vote for the party in a given election, those people who are registered with the party, those people who identify themselves in their minds with the party, those people who do voluntary work for the party at some given time, the officers of the party, and those who are running or elected as candidates under the party label. When researchers write about "the political party," they may be referring to any or all of these various dimensions of the term. Thus, unless political scientists specify which dimensions apply, they may merely succeed in creating confusion. A few further examples of multidimensional terms are *power, enjoyment, conservative, economic development, intelligent,* and *love*.

Debates in political science sometimes resolve themselves into the fact that participants are using the same term in different ways. The word *liberal*, for instance, has many dimensions, some of which are probably even inconsistent. Just to look at one of its dimensions, it often connotes "free-spending," although in its original usage, which is still fairly current in Europe, it means "favoring a limited role for government." Since the term *liberal* has generally unpopular connotations in the United States and is multidimensional in complex ways, it is natural to use this flexible word as a club in describing candidates. In the election of 1996, for instance, the late Senator Paul Wellstone of Minnesota was described by his opponent as "embarrassingly liberal" for his vote against a bill reducing welfare payments. He responded that his vote was actually "deeply conservative" because it reflected the moral values of Minnesotans. Was Wellstone's vote "liberal" or "conservative"? The argument proceeded almost irrespective of its merits.

The strategy I am introducing here, framing theories in terms of unidimensional concepts, can help us to keep clear the meanings of the words we use and to avoid this kind of confusion.

Ordinary Language

As we have just seen, many English words involve more than one dimension, and these component dimensions are rarely specified in ordinary language. Multidimensional concepts are valuable and useful in ordinary language, as is indicated by their popularity. The connotations accruing to a word that means many different things simultaneously add richness to our language. Art and rhetoric could not be restricted to unidimensional vocabularies.

But in the social sciences, we pay a high price for this benefit. Rich connotations, which are so important to art, get in the way of analytic thinking. A poet is pleased if she chooses a word whose meanings give the reader pause for thought; it is the poet's job to create a rich confusion of varied nuances. The job of the social analyst, however, is to bring order out of social chaos by means of simple theories.

Multidimensional words hamper social scientists in at least three ways:

1. *Poor communication.* Because a reader can never be certain what meaning an author intended, multidimensional words hamper communication.
2. *Difficulty with measurement.* Whenever social scientists want to measure a variable, they confront an impossible task unless they have defined the variable in such a way that it consists of a single dimension. For example, consider a political scientist who wanted to measure the "amount of interaction" between various nations. Now, "interaction" involves a number of dimensions: alliances, volume of trade, tourism, exchanges of mail, and so on. Suppose that this political scientist discovered the following things about countries A, B, and C:

Between Countries	Volume of Trade/Year	Items of Mail/Year	Alliance
A and B	$10 billion	20 million	Yes
B and C	$5 billion	30 million	Yes
A and C	$20 billion	10 million	No

Between which two countries is there greater interaction? A and C trade together a great deal but are not allies; B and C exchange a great deal of mail but do not trade together as much as A and B. Clearly, "amount of interaction" is not a unidimensional variable. Had the investigator chosen three separate measures—trade, mail flow, and alliance—there would have been no problem in comparing the countries. We can confidently state, for instance, that A and C share the greatest trade, followed by A and B and by B and C. We return to such problems of measurement in Chapter 4.

3. *Ambiguous associations.* From the standpoint of the social scientist, another fault in multidimensional words is that each such word is itself a theory of sorts. By associating several distinct things with a single term, a multidimensional word implies the theory that these things go together. *But unless its component dimensions are made explicit, it is a poorly articulated and poorly controlled theory.*

For example, the word *wise* has long connoted (1) broad practical knowledge, (2) a highly developed understanding of relationships, (3) a contemplative bent, and (4) a background of long practical experience. Among other things, it has implied the theory that the older (and thus the more experienced) one got, the better one understood things. So, if I use the word *wise* rather than *intelligent*, my reader picks up this little theory subliminally embedded in my statement.

Theories such as this, embedded in multidimensional words, change as common usage reflects changed moods and new experiences. But the process by which they change is not a very satisfactory one; it is a process that gives us little confidence in the new theories that are produced. It may be an unarticulated dislike for the theory implied by the word *wise*, for example, which has led to diminished use of the word in egalitarian America and its degradation in such slang as "Don't get wise with me!" and "wise guy." It is in just such a way that word usage gradually changes, reflecting different views of the world. The polite substitution of the term *developing nations* for *underdeveloped countries* in the 1950s and 1960s is another example. This change in usage reflected the changed status of the Third World and at least some hopeful thinking about what was happening there.[1]

This process of theory development is uncontrolled. In a sense, it is very democratic—probably more democratic than we would like. Everyone who uses a particular word takes part in the process, and a person's influence is more or less proportional to the number of people who hear her use the word. There is no provision made for greater influence on the process by those who know more about the subject. Dictionaries, by codifying word usage, serve to slow down the process of change, but they do not affect the *quality* of the change.

Another problem with the process is that these changes often proceed at a snail's pace. Thus, theories that are embedded in multidimensional words survive practical refutation much longer than if they were made explicit. The words *liberal* and *conservative* are a case in point. Because such attitudes as a desire for activist government, concern for the legal rights of individuals, pacifism, and internationalism often seemed to go together when one looked at the political elite in the United States, the term *liberal* came to denote their presence and *conservative* their absence. (The words were borrowed from a European context, but their meanings were considerably changed, which only added to the subsequent confusion.) The implied theory—that these attitudes tended to coincide—was never very accurate

---

[1]Today, of course, reality has caught up with rhetoric in the explosive economic growth of countries like China, India, and South Korea.

as a description even of the elite and it has proved to be quite inaccurate in describing people in general. It turns out, for example, that people who are liberal on individuals' rights are often conservative on economic issues.[2]

Thus, while changes in usage do produce changes in the theories implied by multidimensional words, the process by which these changes are made is capricious; this is presumably not the way we want to develop social theory. Social scientists should be uncomfortable if hidden away in their statement of a theory are additional little theories that are implicit and uncontrolled.

Let me sum up the argument thus far: Social scientists should use unidimensional language for three reasons:

1. The meaning of a theory is not unambiguously clear if it is couched in multidimensional words.
2. Variables cannot be measured unambiguously if they have been defined in a multidimensional way.
3. Inclusion of multidimensional words in a theory confuses that theory with additional theories that are implied by the existence of the multidimensional words themselves.

Despite our prescription, however, we must acknowledge the fact that the English language contains many words that hold a rich variety of meanings and connotations. These are to be valued in their own right, yet social scientists often must create their own vocabulary. If ordinary language does not provide unidimensional words for the things social scientists want to say, they must invent the words themselves. This is one reason that social science writing so often strikes readers as flat and cold. What most people mean by "social science jargon" is the unidimensional vocabulary invented by social scientists for their use in analytic research.

Writing from which the richness of varied connotations has been removed is flat. This is simply one of the costs we must pay to write analytically. Of course, this is not meant to excuse poor writing in the social sciences or anywhere else. Unidimensional language is a minor handicap under which social scientists operate, but it need not prevent them from writing clear and graceful prose.

Actually, writers in any analytic field suffer the same handicap. Natural scientists must create their own vocabularies, too. But somehow the loss of richness seems more painful in the social sciences than in other fields. The physicist may describe a body's motion in terms of "mass," "velocity," and "acceleration" rather than saying that it "hurtles through space," and the mind does not rebel. But when the political scientist describes politics as consisting of "system inputs," "system outputs," and "feedback loops," the mind does rebel. This is because the social scientist deals with *people*,

---

[2]Another example of meanings of words being slow to change, an amusing one, is offered by the old saying "the exception that proves the rule." Taken at face value—as it usually is—this phrase is idiotic. An exception does not prove a rule, but should cause us to reconsider the rule. The secret is that centuries ago "to prove" meant to submit to a test; in fact, the word has the same root as "proof" and was used in phrases such as "submit to a proof by fire." The phrase about exceptions has continued, with "proof" included in it, even though the changed meaning of the word has rendered the phrase meaningless.

the thing we care most passionately about. It does not bother us when a physicist tries to reduce the complex motion of a particle to unidimensional concepts, but when social scientists try to simplify the complex reality of politics, the family, or of protests, we are disturbed.

PROPER USE OF MULTIDIMENSIONAL WORDS

I have argued that we should try to use only indivisible dimensions as concepts in political science. But there is another side to the question, which leads me to temper that stance somewhat. Although it is always necessary to think and work with unidimensional concepts in the social sciences, it may be convenient to put separate dimensions together in *explicit* multidimensional combinations.

"National integration" may provide an example of such a concept. There are many dimensions implied in the term: political consensus within the nation; widespread communication and personal interchanges within the nation; a feeling, among the nation's people, that they all belong together; legal integration; and so on. It would be possible to do without the term *national integration* and work directly with these dimensions, but it would be awkward. There are a great number of dimensions involved, and they may combine in odd ways. At the same time, there *is* a widespread feeling among political scientists that these things tend to go together to constitute a general process. This process might not be at all easy to discern if we were forced to work simultaneously with the large number of unidimensional concepts involved in it. Accordingly, political scientists over the last few decades have explicitly developed the term *national integration*, composed of these various dimensions, to refer to the general process. The result has not been fully satisfactory, but there does appear to be a need for such a summary term.

The use of an explicit combination of separate dimensions such as this has some of the advantages of both "ordinary language" and unidimensional language, as well as some of the disadvantages of each. Such summary constructs may add grace and interest to the presentation of your results and ideas. They may add clarity, too, if you are working with so many dimensions simultaneously that readers would have difficulty keeping track of them. And they help to keep your theory parsimonious.

Such explicit combinations of dimensions have the advantage, as compared with ordinary language, that you have built your own juxtaposition of dimensions into the word. However, these contrived concepts retain many of the disadvantages of ordinary language. A reader cannot tell, for example, when faced with a high score on a variable that combines dimensions A, B, and C, whether this means that A and B were high and C low, or that B was high and A and C were low, or whatever. Although explicit multidimensional words are more useful than ordinary language, you should not use them casually.

I have used as my "bad" examples words from ordinary language rather than words specifically designed for use by scholars. In general, as I have indicated, when scholars design terminology it is a good deal tighter than ordinary language. However, even scholarly vocabulary is often not as tight as it could be. It may happen, for instance, that several scholars working independently of each other devise related unidimensional words, each set up for one particular research use. When these related words are taken as a group, they may produce confusion as great as that resulting from ordinary language. In one study, Kroeber and Kluckhohn (1952) counted several hundred different ways in which the word *culture* was used by anthropologists.

Accordingly, explicit dimensional analysis of a body of scholarly work, even if it is already at a quite abstract level, can help us to clarify the meaning of the whole body of work and may point up new directions for theoretical development. Conceptual analysis of this sort is terribly important to research. Perhaps the most frequent failing in research is that this part of the work is done casually and sloppily. The following analysis of different ways of using the concept *power* is an extended example of how such dimensional analysis might proceed.

Example of Dimensional Analysis

The basic building block of all political science analysis is the concept of power. But this concept is multidimensional and notoriously difficult to pin down. Major debates of the last few decades can be clarified by dimensional analysis.

Robert Dahl led off the modern debate over the nature of power with a study of power in local politics in New Haven, Connecticut (Dahl, 1961). He noted that on different issues, different sorts of people were involved, so he concluded that local political power was not concentrated in an elite but was widely distributed. Bachrach and Baratz (1962) responded that the true essence of power lay not in participation in decisions but in being able to lay out the agenda for what questions were to be discussed. Despite the fact that a wide range of people had participated in New Haven discussions, it might be that a small group of powerful figures had determined what issues would be open for discussion. The question of the city government taking over the public utilities had not been on the table, for instance; nor at that time had there been any interest in the relative situation of women vis-à-vis men.

In 1974, Steven Lukes added a further complication. True power lay not in the mechanics of decision making, either in the decision itself *or* in setting the agenda. Rather, true power lay in the ability to define for people what their interests were. If one could convince white workers in New Haven that the most important thing to them was education for their children rather than defending whites' prerogatives against blacks—or if you did the reverse of this—you would have already pretty well determined the political outcomes.

As a final hook, Peter Digeser (1992) drew on the work of Michel Foucault to suggest that *real* power consists not of determining what people will see as in their interests but rather in determining what leads them to define their very identity. If the New Haven workers can be led to identify themselves as whites rather than as workers, that determines all that follows.

Although the scholars involved in these arguments have generally viewed their own version of power as ruling out one or more of the others, dimensional analysis can show how they all work together. Each of these conceptualizations actually emphasizes a different dimension of power: Dahl emphasizes *whether one has partici-pated in a decision*; Bachrach and Baratz, *whether one has helped set the agenda for public decisions*; Lukes, *whether one has influenced people's understanding of their interests*; and Digeser, *whether one has influenced people's political identities*.

Figure 3-1 lays these out as four dimensions of power. The power any person holds in a particular political decision may be analyzed in terms of her position on the four dimensions. On a question of park policy, for instance, a newspaper editor may have been involved in the setting of identities, in influencing people's under-standing of their interests, and in determining the agenda of issues facing the city but may not have been involved in the actual decisions. A member of the city park board may have been involved in the decision but may not have exercised power in any of its other dimensions. An elementary school teacher may have been involved in the process of forming identities but may not have exercised power in its other dimensions; another school teacher, interested and active on park questions, may have been involved in the process of forming identities and may have participated in the decisions, but not have exercised power in the other two dimensions.

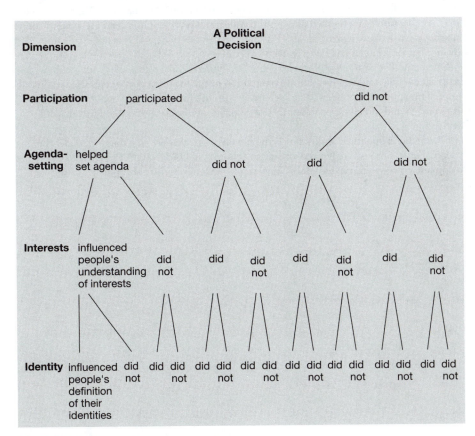

FIGURE 3-1   Four Dimensions of Power

Dimensional analysis of this sort allows us to see the interrelations of various approaches to a question and can also give us a rich framework with which to apply a multidimensional concept. It also allows us to compare the importance of the dimensions. Implicit in each later scholar in the discussion sketched above was the idea that his notion of power was deeper and more basic than those that went before. A dimensional analysis gives us a structure within which we can address this question.

▚ Further Discussion

Formal treatment of dimensional analysis was introduced by Allan H. Barton, "The Concept of Property-Space in Social Research" (1955). Philip E. Jacob's "A Multi-dimensional Classification of Atrocity Stories" (1955) furnishes a good example of dimensional analysis in practice.

Some examples from political science are Chapter 11 of Robert Dahl's *Political Oppositions in Western Democracies* (1966), a first-rate analysis of the relevant dimensions for classifying "opposition"; Harry Eckstein's *Pressure Group Politics* (1960), especially pp. 15–40, in which he classifies pressure group activities; and the third chapter of his *Division and Cohesion in Democracy* (1966), an excellent dimensional analysis of "political division"; Hanna Pitkin's *Representation* (1969), a collection of various writings on the concept of representation, among which Pitkin's own essay is particularly insightful; also Pitkin's *The Concept of Representation* (1967); and Giovanni Sartori's *Parties and Party Systems* (1976).

One branch of political philosophy is the "analytic political philosophy" approach, which seeks to study political ideas by a close examination of the meaning of concepts used to describe politics. This approach is reviewed in Richard Bernstein's *Restructuring of Social and Political Theory* (1978) and in Felix Oppenheim, "The Language of Political Inquiry: Problems of Clarification" (1975).

One branch of political philosophy is the Finally, as an exercise, you might consider the conceptual problems involved in the well-worn aphorism of Lord Acton: "Power tends to corrupt and absolute power corrupts absolutely." How would you analyze this conceptually? *Can* it be analyzed?

Problems of Measurement:

Accuracy

In this chapter, I explore problems of accurate measurement. These are problems that arise when we try to relate the actual operations in a piece of research—that is, measures of things—to the concepts that form the basis of our underlying theory. Concepts, of course, exist only in the mind. One necessary assumption, if we are to claim that a piece of research has tested a given theory, is that the things measured in the research correspond to the things in the theorist's mind.

This is often a difficult assumption to make. In the preceding chapter, you saw one kind of problem that can stand in the way of it. The political scientist who wanted to measure the amount of interaction between nations found that there was no single satisfactory indicator of "interaction." A number of things—trade, mail exchanges, alliance, and so on—partook of "interaction," but no one of them alone was synonymous with the mental construct.

In the social sciences, only rarely are we able to measure our concepts directly. Consider, for example, the concepts "social class," "respect for the presidency," and "power in the community." Any variables we would choose to measure these concepts correspond only indirectly or in part to our mental constructs. This is the basic problem of measurement in the social sciences.

Consider the concept "social status." Among social scientists there are two popular versions of this concept: "subjective social status," the class that individuals consider themselves as belonging to; and "objective social status," an individual's rank with regard to prestige along social hierarchies such as education, income, and occupation. Neither version of the concept can be measured directly.

In the case of "subjective social status," we cannot measure directly what individuals feel about their status. We know what they report, but their replies to our inquiries may not be what we are looking for. They may not know what they "really" feel, for instance; or they may misunderstand the question and give a misleading answer. Then again, a person may feel differently from one day to the next, in which case the measure of his status will depend on our rather arbitrary choice of day.

41

In the case of "objective social status," again we cannot measure the variable directly. "Objective status" has something to do with income, education, occupation, and various other hierarchies, some of which we may not know about. None of these provides a sufficient measure in itself. For example, if we tried to use occupation alone as a measure of social status, we would be faced with the difficult question of whether a plumber who made $40,000 a year was really of lower social status than a bank teller who made $25,000 a year. Similarly, if we tried to use income alone as a measure, we would be faced with the problem of what to do with a retired teacher, whose income might be near the poverty level. "Social status" in this case is a concept that is related to a number of measurable things but is related only imperfectly to each of them. The best we can do in measuring it is to combine the various measurable indicators into a pooled measure that is roughly related to the concept "objective social status."

We encounter similar problems in measuring the other concepts I have cited as examples. Like many other variables in political science, these concepts are of considerable interest and use in theories but are by their nature impossible to measure directly. The general problem posed by such variables is presented schematically in Figure 4-1.

As you saw in Chapter 2, in political research we are commonly interested in relating concepts through a theory. This is always true in theory-oriented research, and it is true most of the time in engineering research as well. If we cannot measure directly the concepts we wish to use, we find ourselves in the position depicted in Figure 4-1. We want to say, "Concept A bears a relationship of thus-and-so form to concept B." But all that we can observe is the relationship between measure A and measure B. Whether what we say about the measures is an accurate statement of the relationship between the concepts depends on the unobserved relationships between concept A and measure A and between concept B and measure B. We can only assume what these relationships are. Like the theory itself, these relationships cannot be observed.

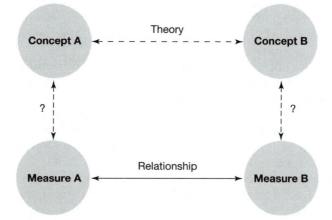

FIGURE 4-1   The Problem of Measurement

As an example, suppose you want to assess the theory tested by Diehl and Kingston, that countries that are increasing their armaments tend to engage in aggressive international policies (see Chapter 1). You might be faced with the following relationships:

1. *Relationship between the concept "increasing armaments" and the measure of "increasing armaments."* You clearly cannot measure increases in a nation's armaments directly; only a national intelligence apparatus has the facilities to do that, and even then, the result is imperfect. Therefore, you might take as your measure the country's reported expenditures on armaments. Now, a country that is not preparing to launch an aggressive military venture would have less reason to lie about an arms buildup than would a country (such as Germany in 1933), that is consciously preparing for aggression. Therefore, the relationship between concept and measure in this case might be: When a country is not building up its armaments, or when it is building them up in order to launch an aggressive action, its reported expenditures on arms will not increase.
2. *Relationship between the concept "increasing armaments" and the concept "aggressive international policies."* Let us assume, for this example, that countries that are increasing their armaments do tend to engage in aggressive international policies.
3. *Relationship between the concept "aggressive international policies" and the measure of "aggressive international policies."* Let us assume, for this example, that we are able to develop a measure that corresponds almost perfectly to the concept "aggressive international policies." (In practice, of course, this would be a difficult variable to measure, and it certainly would be necessary first to analyze the varied dimensions involved in "aggression" and "policies" in order to state more clearly just what was meant by the concept.)

We now find ourselves in the position depicted in Figure 4-2. Here, because of peculiarities in the relationships between the concepts and the measures of these concepts, the relationship you can observe between the measures turns out to be the opposite of the true relationship between the concepts. Worse yet, inasmuch as the two measures and the connection between them are all that you can observe, you would have no way of knowing that this was happening. This is why I have called indirect measurement of concepts *the* problem of measurement.

One solution to the problem might be to measure variables only directly. Some concepts are directly measurable. A few examples are people's votes if an election is nonsecret and you tabulate the result yourself; statements you hear made on the Senate floor; a bomb you see dropped or thrown.[1]

---

[1] It is reasonable, also, to include here reliable observers' accounts of such events. Even though the measurement of these things is technically indirect, if you accept another observer's account of them, you should be able to achieve a very tight fit between the concept "event happens" and the measure "reliable observer says that event happens."

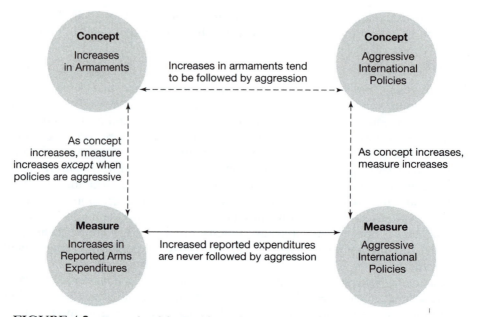

FIGURE 4-2   Example of the Problem of Measurement

The difficulty with such a solution is that concepts that can be measured directly are usually trivial in and of themselves. They are too idiosyncratic to use in general, interesting theories. I would hate to say that particular statements by U.S. senators lead nowhere, but as far as political theory is concerned, it is true. Any given statement can apply only to itself. It takes on a general meaning only if it is placed in a category, so that it can be compared with other statements. For instance, Senator_____'s statement, "The president's policies are bankrupting the people of my state," is not intrinsically of theoretical interest. It can be placed in various categories, however: "statements of opposition to the president," "statements of concern for constituents' needs," "bombastic statements." Placing it in one of these categories allows us to compare it with other senatorial statements and to develop theories about the causes and effects of such statements.

Note, though, that by placing it into a category, we have used the statement as an indirect measure of the concept which the category represents. No given statement is a perfect case of the "bombastic statement" or of the "statement of opposition to the president." Rather, a number of statements *approximate* each category, and we choose to use these statements as indirect measures of the abstract concept we cannot measure.

To sum up the argument thus far: For a concept to be useful in building theories, it usually must be an abstraction, which cannot be measured directly. Further, of those interesting concepts that *are* in principle directly measurable (how individuals vote in an election, for example), many cannot be measured directly for practical reasons (the elections are held with a secret ballot). Therefore, most of the time we must work with variables that are indirect measures of the concepts in which we are interested. This means that there are interposed, between our (concrete) operations and the (abstract) theory we want to work on, relationships between our concrete concepts and their abstract measures.[2] This is the situation illustrated graphically in Figures 4-1 and 4-2. *The chief problem of measurement is to ensure, as much as possible, that the relationships between concepts and measures are such that the relationship between the measures mirrors the relationship between the concepts.*

Problems we may encounter in trying to achieve this correspondence between measures and concepts fall under two headings: problems of measure *reliability* and problems of measure *validity*.

RELIABILITY

A measure is reliable to the extent that it gives the same result again and again if the measurement is repeated. For example, if people are asked several days in a row whether they are married, and their answers vary from one day to the next, the measure of their marital state is unreliable. If their answers are stable from one time to the next, the measure is reliable.

The analogy of measuring with a yardstick may help make the meaning of reliability clear. If an object is measured a number of times with an ordinary wooden yardstick, it will give approximately the same length each time. If the yardstick were made of an elastic material, its results would not be so reliable. It might say that a chair was 20 inches high one day, 16 the next. Similarly, if it were made of a material that expanded or contracted greatly with changes in temperature, its results would not be reliable. On hot days it would say that the chair was shorter than on cold days. In fact, the choice of wood as a material for yardsticks is in part a response to the problem of reliability in measurement, a problem certainly not confined to the social sciences. Wood is cheap, rigid, and relatively unresponsive to changes in temperature.

There are many sources of unreliability in social science data. The sources vary, depending on what kinds of data are used. Official statistics, for example, may be unreliable because of an unusual number of clerical errors or because of variability in how categories are defined from one time to the next. ("Votes cast in an election," for instance, may mean "all votes, including spoiled ballots" at one time, "all valid votes" at another.) Attitude measures may be unreliable because a question is hard for respondents to understand, and they interpret it one way at one time, another way the next. Or the people entering their responses into the computer may make mistakes.

---

[2]Technically, these relationships are called *epistemic correlations*. "Correlation" means relationship, and "epistemic" has the same root as "epistemology"—the study of how we know.

As an illustration, let us list the various sources of unreliability that might be involved in tabulating responses even to a simple question about whether a person is married:

1. The question might be phrased badly, so that respondents sometimes interpreted it to mean, "Are you now married?" and sometimes, "Have you ever been married?" It might not be clear how people who were separated from their spouses, but not divorced, should answer.
2. Respondents might be playing games with the interviewer, answering questions randomly.
3. Dishonest interviewers might be playing games with the researcher by filling out the forms themselves instead of going through the trouble of getting the respondents to answer them.
4. Respondents' answers might depend on their mood. Perhaps they would answer "yes" when they had had a good day, or "no" when they had had a bad day.
5. Respondents' answers might depend on the context of the interview. A person might say "no" to an attractive interviewer and "yes" to everyone else.
6. There might be simple clerical errors in copying down the answers, either by the interviewer on the spot or by the person who transcribes the interviewers' copy into a computer.

Admittedly, some of these possibilities are far-fetched. The example itself is a bit strained, inasmuch as straightforward informational items like this one can usually be measured with reasonable reliability. But the same sorts of conditions affect the reliability of less straightforward survey questions, such as "What do you like about candidate X?" "What social class do you consider yourself to be a member of?" and "Do you feel people generally can be trusted?"

A few examples from a classic study of reliability (Asher, 1974) will help give you a sense of the magnitude of this problem, at least in American survey research. Even on attributes that should be relatively easy to measure reliably, such as gender and race, some errors appeared when the same respondents were interviewed at two-year intervals by a well-administered survey. On the average, the reported gender of respondents changed 0.5 percent of the time from one interview to the next, whereas race did not change at all. Characteristics on which it is somewhat easier to be vague or mistaken showed substantial unreliability. For example, the report of respondents' educational background showed *lower* education two years later (which is logically impossible), an average of 13 percent of the time. Presumably, questions that permit a considerable degree of interpretation, such as attitudinal questions, would show even more unreliability.

Reliability as a Characteristic of Concepts

Thus far, I have treated the unreliability of a measure as if it were a result of unpredictability in the relationship between the concept and its measure. An additional source of unreliability in the measure is variability in the "true value" of the concept. In our previous example, perhaps some people got married, or divorced, from one time to the next. This source of unreliability would be easily distinguishable from others, however, because it would show up as a recognizable pattern of stable answers up to a certain point, followed by changed, but once again stable, answers.

A more interesting case is presented when the true value itself varies randomly. This situation sometimes provides the basis for interesting theories. In one study, Converse (1964) noted that on many standard questions of political policy, people's attitudes appeared to vary randomly across time. He concluded that on certain issues, the mass public simply did not form stable opinions; and he went on to draw interesting comparisons between elite and mass opinion, based on that conclusion.

Note that to reach this conclusion, Converse had to assume that he had effectively eliminated other sources of unreliability, such as interviewer error and confusion about the meaning of questions. Having first eliminated these sources of unpredictability in the relationship between concept and measure, he could then treat the unreliability in his measure as a reflection of unreliability in the concept. Christopher Achen (1975) later challenged Converse's conclusions on just these grounds.

Testing the Reliability of a Measure

Although unreliability may sometimes spur on further theoretical research, as it did in this case, it is usually a barrier we want to eliminate. Careful work is the best way to achieve reasonable reliability—double-checking all clerical work, trying out the questionnaire on a small pilot study in order to catch and correct unclear questions, and so on.

We often wish to know how successfully we have reduced unreliability. A number of tests have been developed to help researchers check the reliability of a measure. I shall describe two of them briefly.

The *test-retest check for reliability* simply consists of repeating the measurement a second time, allowing for a suitable interval of time between the two measurements. If the second measure strongly resembles the first—that is, if the measure is stable over the elapsed time—it is considered relatively reliable. One problem with this test, of course, is that there is no way to distinguish instability that stems from "real" unreliability in the concept being measured, from instability due to problems in the measurement process.

Another test, the *split-half check for reliability*, avoids this problem. It is particularly useful whenever a measure is multidimensional—for instance, a measure of "social status," which is made by combining such items as an individual's income, occupation, education, house size, and neighborhood into a single summary measure; or a measure of "welfare policy expenditures," comprising such disparate items as welfare payments, unemployment relief, hospital subsidies, and school lunch programs.

In the split-half test, the researcher randomly divides these assorted items into two groups and then composes a summary "measure" out of each of the groups.

Because all of the items are taken to be measures of the same thing, the two summary measures should tend to be the same. A measure of how close they are to each other provides a check on how reliable the total summary measure is.

As an example, consider a state-by-state measure of "welfare policy expenditures." It might be that one particular item—disaster relief, for instance—varies greatly from state to state and from one year to the next in any one state. In one year, there might be no natural disasters; in another, there might be floods or a hurricane. That particular item would be a source of unreliability in the overall measure. It also should cause the split-half test to show a relatively low reliability, for its erratic variation would make the score based on the group in which it was included less likely to equal the score based on the group that did not include it.

These two checks for reliability complement each other. The test-retest check is appropriate for any sort of measure that can be replicated. It checks for *all* sources of unreliability, but this often includes changes in the true value of the concept rather than only the instability that is due to the measurement process.

The split-half check is appropriate for measures comprising a group of subitems. It checks only for those sources of unreliability that do not operate over time, inasmuch as all of the subitems presumably are measured at the same time. Accordingly, it can miss some sources of instability in the measurement process, such as the effect of the length of time since payday or of changes in the weather, on respondents' answers to an interview question. But this is actually an important benefit: If we are able to screen out true change over time in the concept, we will have a much better idea of any instability due to the measurement process.

VALIDITY

Reliability has to do with how dependably a measure mirrors its concept. In thinking about reliability, we assumed implicitly that the measure tended to mirror the concept faithfully and that the problem of reliability was simply that this tendency may be a rather loose one. We assumed, in other words, that if the concept were measured a large number of times, the average of those measures would reflect our "ideal" concept. The problem in reliability is that since the measures vary, at any given time one of them could be rather far from the true value of the concept.

A more serious failing of our measurements, however, could result if they lack *validity*. A measure is valid if it actually measures what it purports to measure. That is, if there is in principle a *relationship of equivalence* between a measure and its concept, the measure is valid. A measure cannot be valid if it is not reliable. But it can be reliable and yet still not be valid. If it gives the same result repeatedly, the measure is reliable, but it could distort the concept in the same way each of these times, so that it does not tend to mirror it faithfully. In effect, it would be "reliably invalid."

The relationship between the measure "increases in reported arms expenditures" and the concept "increases in armaments" in Figure 4-2 is an example of invalid measurement. The relationship between the concept and the measure is such that when "increases in armaments" are high, "increases in reported arms expenditures" may be either high or low, depending on the reason for the arms buildup. The measure might be reliable (a country that reported low increases in one year, for instance, should be likely to report low increases the next year also), but it would still be invalid, because the measure does not mirror the concept accurately.

The relationship between validity and reliability can be clarified by introducing the notion of *random error* and *nonrandom error*, which will also be important when we look at measuring the strength of relationships in Chapter 8. Random error is the sort of error we have addressed in discussing reliability. If in the long run, on the average, the measures of a concept tend to be true, we can assume that any error in the measure is random. In measuring education, for example (see p. 46), we encountered a good deal of random error; people tended to report their level of education differently from one time to the next. There was no reason to expect that people were deliberately misrepresenting their educational level, however, so we would expect that in the long run, accidental reporting errors would cancel each other out and the average of many such reports would give a true measure of the concept for a particular group of people.

By contrast, nonrandom error is systematic error that tends in the long run, on the average, to distort a given measure of a concept. Thus, if we asked people whether they had a prison record, it is likely that there would be a good deal of nonrandom error in the measure, as people systematically tried to suppress their prison records. Even in the long run, on the average, this measure would not give an accurate estimate of the true value.

Quite simply, a measure is valid to the extent that it is free of both sorts of error. A measure is reliable to the extent that it is free of random error alone. Thus, reliability is a necessary but not a sufficient condition of validity.

The two sorts of error are presented visually in Figure 4-3. Think of an archer who is trying to produce "valid" shots, that is, shots at the center of a target. The shooting may suffer from either random error (the archer is erratic) or nonrandom error (the archer has some systematic problem—perhaps there is a wind from the left, and the archer has not yet learned to correct for it), or both. These two sorts of error result in the four possible combinations shown in Figure 4-3. The archer achieves "reliability" on both targets B and D but achieves "validity" only on target D.

Some Examples

A few examples are in order. There are many ways that a measure can be invalid. We have already discussed several instances of random error, so we will confine ourselves here to examples of nonrandom error.

One common source of invalid measures is extrapolation from a sample to a population that is not really represented by that sample. Using letters to the editor as an indicator of public opinion would be unwise, for instance, because the people who write such letters are not an accurate cross section of the public as a whole. Their opinions would not be a valid measure of "public opinion."

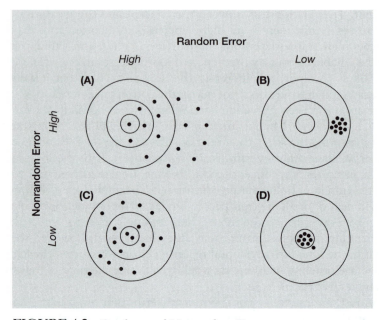

FIGURE 4-3   Random and Nonrandom Error

A comic case of sampling problems from the early days of opinion polls is the *Literary Digest* poll. The *Literary Digest* was a giant magazine in the United States in the early part of the twentieth century. Starting in 1924, the *Digest* ran an ambitious poll in presidential election years. Virtually everyone who owned a car or a telephone was reached by the poll, which was sent out to a mailing list obtained from telephone directories and state automobile registration lists. Only about 20 percent of the sample ballots mailed out were returned, but even at that, the *Digest* had over 2 million responses each time.

The *Digest* sample distorted the U.S. population in two ways. First, it essentially sampled only the upper and middle classes, inasmuch as those who did not have a car or a telephone—at a time when cars and telephones were far less universally owned than today—did not get onto the mailing list. Also, it sampled only those who were interested enough and energetic enough to return the sample ballot. Because only 20 percent of those who received the ballot returned it, this seems to have been a rather select sample.

In 1924, 1928, and again in 1932, the *Digest* poll was very successful, coming within a few percentage points of the actual outcome in each of those elections. By 1932, the poll had become an institution; it was attacked in the *Congressional Record* and featured in *New Yorker* cartoons. Thus it was a shock when the poll's prediction of a landslide victory for Landon in 1936 was gainsaid by FDR's decisive victory. When the *Literary Digest* went out of business the next year, it was thought that the shock and loss of reputation from having called the election so badly was a factor in the magazine's demise.

Apparently, the interested, middle-class sample the *Digest* drew upon did not vote much differently from the rest of the country from 1924 through 1932. Accordingly, its sympathies were a valid measure of the way the country was going to vote in those elections. Between 1932 and 1936, however, Roosevelt initiated the New Deal, which broadened his support among the poor and drove the middle class to the Republicans. After 1936, the sympathies of the middle class were no longer a valid measure of the way the country would vote.

A questionnaire item may also result in an invalid measure when respondents attach a significantly different meaning to the question than was intended by the researcher. It had always been thought, for example, that French farmers were essentially apolitical. When asked in surveys "How interested are you in politics?" they had generally responded, "Not at all." At the same time, it was striking that voting participation was higher among farmers than among most groups in the French population. If they were not interested in politics, why did they vote?

In a study designed to explore this paradox (see p. 29), Sidney Tarrow discovered that the innocent question about political interest had been spreading confusion. French farmers apparently interpreted "interest in politics" to mean commitment to some particular party, with many of them vehemently rejecting political parties. Thus, many farmers who were interested in politics but considered themselves independents responded "Not at all" to this invalid measure of "interest in politics."

Checks for Validity

Taking precautions. Our problem in checking the validity of a measure is similar to the general problem of measurement, depicted in Figure 4-1. We say that a measure is valid if it is a true measure of its concept. *But the general problem of measurement is precisely the fact that usually all we can observe is the measures.* We cannot know what the relationship between a concept and its measure is. How, then, can we assess the validity of the measure?

The answer, of course, is that there is no pat way to do so. Part of the "craft" in the craft of political research is cleverness and care in developing measures that appear likely to be valid. Some techniques are available to help in developing valid measures.

These deceptively simple strategies consist of taking various precautions against invalidity during the construction of a measure. The most important thing is to think through the measurement process carefully and to be on guard against any way in which the relationship between concept and measure might be distorted.

For example, we now know that drawing a sample in certain ways (drawing a random sample, for instance) guards against a fiasco like that which destroyed the *Literary Digest* poll. Also, in determining the final form of a questionnaire that you hope to use in a study, you should ask a few people to answer your questions and then to relate their understanding of the questions themselves. This may alert you to questions that mean something different to your respondents than they mean to you. Such preliminary testing of one's measures is called a "pilot study." Similarly, in using official documents, you should go thoroughly into the background of the things reported there—how they were developed, what the terms mean, how broadly they are intended to apply, and so on.

These techniques simply require the investigator to think ahead to problems that could occur in the relationship between concept and measure and act either to prevent these or to check to see whether they are present. At the most general level, the strategy I have suggested here requires only that the investigator consider carefully how plausible it is that the measure mirrors the concept.

Test of validity. Thus far, our strategies have not actually provided a test of the validity of the measure. Such a test can be made, although it is necessarily subjective and open to varying interpretations. Let us say that we want to decide whether measure α is a valid measure of concept A. If there is some measure β that we are certain is strongly related to concept A, we can check to see whether measure β is related to measure α. If it is not, *and* if our assumption of a relationship between β and A is true, then α cannot be a valid measure of A.

The study by Tarrow cited earlier provides an example of this logic. Tarrow's initial conclusion that the usual question "How interested are you in politics?" was providing an invalid measure of "political interest" among French farmers came from his observation that farmers had in fact one of the highest levels of electoral participation among French citizens. Because he could not conceive of high electoral participation occurring in the absence of high political interest, he concluded that the conventional measures, which had showed low political interest coinciding with high participation, must not have been measuring political interest validly.[3]

As another example of this kind of test, consider a measure of nations' hostility to each other—based on content analysis of the nations' newspapers (α). If we found that two of the nations went to war against each other (β) yet the measure did not show an accompanying increase in feelings of hostility between the two, we would be suspicious of the validity of the measures.

Such an indirect test of validity is possible only when a researcher is quite certain that β must go along with A. That kind of certainty is uncommon and may not be shared equally by every observer. Thus, this test is not always, or even usually, possible; and it is always rather subjective. But assessing the validity of measures is so important that an indirect test, when it can be used, will greatly strengthen your findings.

The most general test of validity is what is called *face validity*. This is just a fancy term for whether a measure looks right to you. Is it valid "on its face"? After all, you have considerable experience with politics and must judge for yourself whether the measure does what you want it to do. If you think it does (and people who read your work agree with you), it has face validity.

---

[3]In this example, "political interest" corresponds to A, farmers' responses to the question on political interest correspond to α, and farmers' electoral participation corresponds to β.

IMPACT OF RANDOM AND NONRANDOM ERRORS

It should be obvious that the best measure is one that is fully valid, that is, one that has in it neither random nor nonrandom errors. Because social scientists often operate with measures that include some amount of one or the other sort of error, however, it is worth considering what happens under those circumstances. As it happens, the two sorts of error have different effects on the development of theory.

The effect of nonrandom error is simple and severe. If a measure is systematically invalid, there is no reason for us to expect any correspondence between the relationship we actually observe from our measures and the idealized relationship we wish to investigate.

The effect of unreliability (if the measures are otherwise valid) is more subtle. To the extent that measures are unreliable, the relationship at the measure level will tend to be looser and weaker than the true relationship. It will parallel the true relationship but will appear weaker than is actually the case. If the measures are sufficiently unreliable, the basic relationship can be so weakened that it will appear, from what we can observe, as if there is no relationship at all.

This is illustrated in Table 4-1. Each set of two columns tabulates the closeness of elections in ten congressional districts, as well as their representatives' seniority. It is apparent from the figures in the first set of columns (True Values) that there is a relationship between the two, inasmuch as representatives from safe districts tend to have greater seniority than those from marginal districts. The relationship is also quite strong; seniority increases without exception as the representatives' margins of victory increase.

TABLE 4-1   Safe Districts Related to Seniority, Using Simulated Data

True Values		Less Reliable Measures		Very Unreliable Measures	
Seniority	*Margin of Victory (%)*	Seniority	*Margin of Victory (%)*	Seniority	*Margin of Victory (%)*
32	18	32.0	21.6	12.8	9.0
24	12	19.2	12.0	12.0	12.6
23	11	11.5	12.1	30.2	8.8
20	11	22.0	4.4	22.4	6.6
14	8	14.0	5.6	21.2	12.0
11	6	11.0	6.0	13.1	3.6
10	6	9.0	10.8	2.5	0.1
6	4	3.6	4.0	13.8	2.8
5	3	4.5	3.6	21.3	1.5
2	1	2.4	0.5	0.2	12.9

In the third and fourth columns, random error, such as might occur from clerical errors or other sources of unreliability, has been added to the original measures; this makes them less reliable. In the fifth and sixth columns, an even greater degree of random error has been added. Note that the relationship becomes weaker in the second set of data (there are more exceptions to the general tendency) and virtually disappears in the last. If we were to test the relationship between safe districts and seniority and had only the data from the last two columns in hand, we would probably conclude that there was no relationship.

IMPORTANCE OF ACCURACY

Inaccuracy in measurement is a critical problem whose potential for mischief does not yet seem well enough understood by political scientists. Because the variables we work with are difficult to measure, we have in many cases come to accept measures that we know full well are inadequate. Much of survey research tends to fall into this category. The loose acceptance of cross-national indicators (for instance, using "newspapers read per 1,000 population" as a measure of the political awareness of various electorates) is another example of this problem.

To the extent that our measures are not valid, what we do with them is irrelevant. This simple fact has tended to be forgotten in a general ethos of making do with poor measures. Fortunately, political scientists are now becoming more aware of the problem of measurement, but its importance must be constantly underscored.

Let me reemphasize the important pitfalls to be careful of in measurement:

1. *Be sure that the measures you choose fit the relationship among concepts that you wish to examine.* Often, an interesting question is lost through mistakes in setting up empirical operations to parallel the theoretical question.

   Stephen Ansolabehere, Alan Gerber, and James M. Snyder, Jr. (2002) demonstrated this problem in a paper showing that three decades of research on whether electoral reapportionment affected public policy had been subtly misdirected and had, as a result, reached exactly the wrong conclusion. In the wake of the *Baker* v. *Carr*[4] decision, scholars had looked to see whether taking away the unfair overrepresentation of rural counties had led to an expansion of state spending. The implicit assumption was that rural areas would have preferred to keep spending down, so if they lost influence on policy, spending should have risen. When they found that spending levels after reapportionment were no higher than they had been before reapportionment, scholars

---

[4]*Baker* v. *Carr* 369 US 186 (1962). In this decision, the Supreme Court ruled that it was unconstitutional to have state legislative districts with widely varying populations. Prior to the decision, many states had done no legislative redistricting for half a century, so backward rural areas that had not experienced much growth in their populations were hugely advantaged relative to rapidly growing cities and suburbs. For instance, in Florida, before the Court's decision, Jefferson County, with a population of 9,543, had had one seat in the state senate and one seat in the state house of representatives. Miami's Dade County, population 935,047, had had one seat in the state senate and three seats in the state house of representatives.

concluded that changing the electoral rules had had no impact on public policy. The reason was pretty clear: Under the bad, old system both Republican suburbs and Democratic cities had been disenfranchised, while rural areas, which had benefited, were not all that clearly either Democratic or Republican. So redressing the imbalances was approximately a wash in terms of party strength.

Ansolabehere and his coauthors pointed out, though, that the true test of whether electoral institutions affected policy was not the effect on the two parties, or on the overall spending level of the state, but whether counties that gained fair representation thereafter got a more equal share of state expenditures. In other words, the true test of whether equality of representation affected policy was not whether the level of spending rose—it was pretty obvious why it did not—but whether it was distributed more equally as a result of more equal representation. When the researchers tested the effect in this way, they found dramatic policy effects from reapportionment. Three decades of research and commentary had missed the point.

2. **Test your measures for possible inadequacies.** Even when a measurement problem is not so central as to nullify the results of a study, recurrent nagging inadequacies in the chosen measures may debilitate a theory so that it becomes almost a trivial exercise. Consider a test for the simple theory: "To the extent that they understand politics, if people's need for public services is relatively great, they will be more liberal." A political scientist might operationalize the three variables of this theory in a way such as the following:

1. "Understanding of politics" indicated by *years of education*. This would seem reasonable; at least, understanding should be fairly closely related to education.
2. "Need for public services" indicated by the *size of the person's family*. Again, although this is a rough measure, it would seem that the more dependents a person had, the more that person would depend on a variety of public services.
3. "Liberalism" indicated by *voting Democratic*.

Now, the empirical analog of the theory becomes: "The more educated a person is, the stronger the relationship between the size of that person's family and the probability that the person will vote Democratic." This statement is ridiculous. I have exaggerated here slightly, but only slightly, the extent to which unimaginative scholars will allow moderate errors of measurement to accumulate in a statement until the statement loses much of its meaning. The cure for this problem is simply to use care and imagination in developing measures.

In this chapter, I have discussed problems in the accuracy of measurement. These problems turn out to be of two basic types, depending on whether they stem from flux in the measure (the problem of reliability) or from a basic lack of correspondence between measure and concept (the problem of nonrandom error). In the next chapter, we look at another aspect of measurement, the question of how precisely a measure should be calibrated. In Chapter 8, we will return to tackle the problem of measuring relationships when random or nonrandom error is present.

▪▪ Further Discussion ▪▪

A delightful book with a unique approach to handling certain problems of validity is *Unobtrusive Measures*, by Eugene J. Webb, Donald T. Campbell, Richard D. Schwartz, and Lee Sechrist (1966). The ideas presented in the book are both creative and sound, and the text itself is filled with interesting and highly unusual examples. Frederick Mosteller's article "Errors," in the *International Encyclopedia of the Social Sciences* (1968), is well worth reading. Mosteller details a variety of possible sources of invalidity and unreliability. Herbert Asher (1974) presents some good examples of reliability problems, with a rather technical discussion of ways to handle them. See also Kirk and Miller, *Reliability and Validity in Qualitative Research* (1985).

Several good examples of specific measurement problems are Niemi and Krehbiel (1984), "The Quality of Surveying Responses About Parents and the Family"; Hammond and Fraser (1984), "Studying Presidential Performance in Congress"; Feldman (1983), "The Measurement and Meaning of Trust in Government"; and Converse and Pierce (1985), "Measuring Partisanship."

A useful exercise would be to list as many factors as you can that would lead to random or nonrandom error for each of the following measures: intended vote (in surveys); strength of armed forces; agreement with the president (in congressional voting); tribalism; unemployment; hierarchical control in an agency; and personal income.

Problems of Measurement: Precision

The preceding chapter dealt with problems of the reliability and validity of measures. Those problems concerned the relationship between a measure and the concept that measure is intended to mirror. In this chapter, we deal with the "quality" of the measure itself—how precise it should be, or how finely calibrated, if it is to be useful.

In a study of Norwegian politics, Harry Eckstein felt that it was necessary to apologize for the fact that some measures he would use were subjective intangibles ("warmth in social relations," for instance, and "sense of community") rather than precise numerical quantities.

> [M]any of the indicators used in the text may not be readily recognized as such by contemporary social scientists. By an indicator we usually mean nowadays a precisely ascertainable quantity that stands for some imprecise quantity (as GNP may indicate level of economic development, or as the number of casualties in revolutionary violence may indicate its intensity). I do use such quantities in what follows. More often, however, readily observable "qualities" are used as indicators of not-so-readily observable qualities. This strikes me as both defensible and desirable, for quantitative indicators are not always as "indicative" of what one wants to know as other observations, nor always obtainable. In overemphasizing quantities we sometimes miss the most telling data—in any case, data that may be reliable in their own right or used as checks on the inferences drawn from quantitative data. I conceive of all social behavior as a vast "data bank," only some of which is quantitatively aggregated in yearbooks and the like, and much of the rest of which may speak volumes to our purposes, if used circumspectly. (Eckstein, 1966, footnote pp. 79–80)[1]

---

[1]From Eckstein, Harry, *Division and Cohesion in Democracy: A Study of Norway* (Copyright 1966 by Princeton University Press). Reprinted by permission of Princeton University Press.

It is wrong that Eckstein should have felt the need to apologize. This should have been an unnecessary justification, but unfortunately, precise measurement has become enough of a fetish in political science that it is no doubt always possible to find someone who will dismiss a piece of work because it is not "quantitative." In this chapter, I sort out just what kinds of precise quantification are helpful in political research.

The cardinal rule of precision might read: *Use measurements that are as precise as possible, given the subject you are studying; do not waste information by imprecise measurement.* One theme of this chapter will be that this rule is as susceptible to violation by "quantifiers" as by "nonquantifiers." To discuss it further, I must first distinguish between two kinds of precision with which we shall be concerned. I call the first of these *precision in measures* and the second *precision in measurement.*

PRECISION IN MEASURES

Precision in measures corresponds roughly to our colloquial use of the word *precision*—that is, keeping the units of measurement relatively fine. For example, reporting a person's income in dollars is more precise than rounding it off to the nearest thousand dollars, and rounding income off to the nearest ten thousand dollars is still less precise. Similarly, reporting a person's religion as "Presbyterian," "Reformed Jewish," "Greek Orthodox," and so on is more precise than reporting it as "Protestant," "Catholic," and "other."

Although as a general rule, precision in measures is obviously a good thing, its importance can be overrated. First, the degree of precision we need is determined by what we wish to do with the data. If we were registering voters, for instance, any precision in measuring age that went beyond labeling people "under 18" and "over 18" would be unnecessary and possibly a nuisance as well. Generally, though, in theory-oriented research, we are not able to limit the necessary level of precision in this way. Instead, we are interested in looking at the entire range of variation and have no particular cutoff point in mind.

Sometimes, even in theory-oriented research, too much precision in measures can be a nuisance. Consider Figure 5-1, which shows the relationship between age and participation in the 2008 presidential election. The figure is so chaotic that it is hard to decipher a relationship.

Given the limited number of individuals (about 2,100) consulted in the poll, there is only a small number of respondents for each particular age. This means that the percent voting will fluctuate a good deal from one age-group to the next (see the box "Law of Large Numbers," p. 61). Thus, in the ensuing, largely random fluctuation of percent voting, it is difficult to pick out a systematic pattern in the relationship between age and participation in elections, although we can see that participation generally rises with age.

One way to handle this problem, of course, would be to expand the study by considering more individuals in each category. But this usually is neither practical nor in many cases possible. If we study U.S. presidents, for example, we are limited to a population of 44.

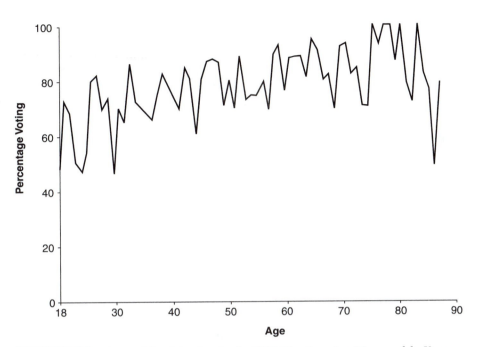

FIGURE 5-1   Age and Participation in the 2008 Election: Age Measured *by Years*

Source: 2008 Presidential Election Survey, National Election Study. Data provided by the Interuniversity Consortium for Political and Social Research.

Another way to handle the problem is to decrease the precision of the measure, creating a smaller number of categories with a larger number of cases in each.[2] This has been done in Figure 5-2, with age measured to the nearest half-decade rather than to the nearest year. With the larger number of cases in each age class, the measures of percent voting fluctuate less and the form of the relationship between age and participation becomes clearer, with increases coming in the first couple of decades, and a drop-off among the very aged.

If it is true that sometimes we may be better off with less precision in our measures, then it appears likely that this sort of precision is not so important that research should be judged solely, or even largely, on how precise its measures are. On the other hand, although there are situations in which we may want to back off from precise measures, one should not conclude that precision is not helpful or important. To continue with the example of age and participation, if age were measured still less precisely than in Figure 5-2, we could again lose some of the pattern that appeared there. If age were measured in units of 35 years, for example, we would find that 73 percent of those in the first unit (18–52) voted, and that

---

[2]Reducing precision in this way to eliminate random noise in the data is appropriate only for chart making, visual presentation, and comparing percentages. Data analysis techniques such as regression analysis handle random noise in their own way. Reducing precision in measures is thus unneccessary when one is *analyzing* data, and it may cause such techniques to give systematically inaccurate results. (See Chapter 8 for a description of regression analysis.)

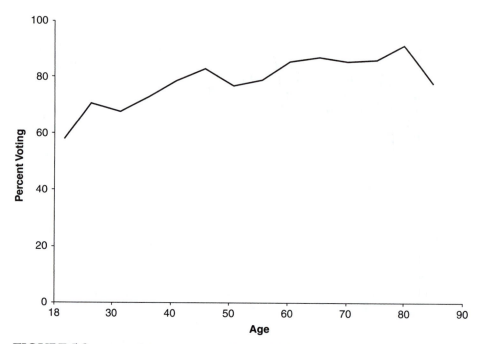

FIGURE 5-2   Age and Participation in the 2008 Election: Age Measured by Half-Decades

84 percent of those in the second unit (53–87) voted. Although we would still see a strong relationship in these figures, much of the interesting detail of Figure 5-2 would be lost.

The time to ensure that your measures will be as precise as you want is when you are gathering data. A number of precautions are in order. First, make sure that you include as large a number of cases as is practical, so that you will not have to reduce the precision more than you would like. For example, if your study concerns a specific group within the population, it makes sense to get an adequate number of the group into your study, even if the resultant data are not "typical" of the entire population. This sort of selection is known as drawing a *stratified sample*. Thus, if you wanted to study the effects of different kinds of discrimination, you might draw up a sample consisting of equal numbers of WASP,[3] white ethnics, blacks, Puerto Ricans, and Chicanos. Had you simply drawn a random sample of the population, you probably would have drawn too few Puerto Ricans and Chicanos, and you would have had to lump them together with either the blacks or the white ethnics.

Another pitfall to avoid at the data-gathering stage is casually throwing away precision that might later prove useful. When asking people their age, record the

[3]WASP is the acronym for white, Anglo-Saxon Protestant.

LAW OF LARGE NUMBERS

The fact that the smaller the group of individuals sampled, the more any measure based on that group will deviate from its norm is one part of the law of large numbers. (This law forms the basis for a great deal of statistics.) The fact is intuitively obvious. If a research team selected groups of 1,000 people randomly and calculated the percentage male, they would expect to get very nearly the national figure in all of them. With groups of 100, they would get increasingly erratic measurement. (It would not be unlikely for there to be 60 males in 100 people, for example.) With groups of 10, there would be wild fluctuation; and with groups of 1 (the smallest possible "group"), all groups would be either 0 or 100 percent male.

number of years old, not "under 30," "30–40," and the like. You can always group the data later if you want to; at this point, you should save all the information you get. If you ask people their religion, write down "Presbyterian," "Roman Catholic," and so on—not "Protestant," "Catholic," or "Jewish." In short, do not group the information you have until you have finished gathering it. You will have a better idea then of how fine a grouping you want to end up with.

If it is true, as the cardinal rule states, that it is important to be as precise as possible and not to waste information, these suggestions will help meet that rule. But the rule also states that we should be as precise as we can, *given the subject we are studying*. Because of the limitations imposed by a specific research topic, we must be careful not to overemphasize the importance of precision in measures. Many questions in political science simply do not admit of great precision of this type. Eckstein's study, which he defended in the quotation given at the start of this chapter, is a case in point. He wanted to study the degree of "community" in Norway. That concept did not lend itself to finely calibrated measures.

It would be foolish to give up such studies on this account. Precision in measures is important, but not indispensable. No one should stop studying the presidency because the number of cases is limited; or stop studying past historical periods because data are limited and many kinds are "pregrouped" in inconvenient ways; or stop studying political corruption because many facts are hidden or grouped together.

PRECISION IN MEASUREMENT

The sort of precision discussed in the preceding section, precision in measures, can be overemphasized. But the next sort, precision in measurement, cannot. "Precision in measures" referred to keeping distinctions as fine as was possible and practical. But we also find varying levels of information in the process of measurement itself. There are basically three different ways to measure, each of which is qualitatively different from the others, in that it contains information not included in the others.

The most primitive way to measure a variable is simply to assign the individuals being studied to categories of that variable. This is called *nominal* measurement. For example, to measure religion, we may label people "Catholic," "Protestant," "Jew," or "other." To measure nationality, we may label them "British," "German," "Russian," and so on. Nominal measurement places individuals into distinct categories of a variable, but it does not tell us anything about how the categories relate to each other.

If, in addition to assigning categories, we can rank the categories according to "how much" of the variable they embody, we have achieved *ordinal* measurement. In such measurement, we have some idea of a scale that might ideally represent the variable, and the scores we assign to individuals show whether they fall higher or lower than others on such a scale. Examples are (1) social status, measured in some way, such as "lower/working/middle/upper"; and (2) party identification, measured as "strong Democrat/weak Democrat/independent/weak Republican/strong Republican."

Further precision in measurement is possible if in addition to ranking the scores according to "how much" of the variable they represent, we can say how great the differences between the scores are. To do this, we must have some common unit of measurement for our scale. Note that such a unit was lacking in the two examples of ordinal measurement. We could not say whether the difference in status between "working" and "middle" was greater than that between "lower" and "working," nor could we say whether the difference between "weak Republican" and "strong Republican" was greater than that between "independent" and "weak Republican."

If units exist by which we can measure the intervals between scores like these, we have achieved *interval* measurement. Some variables commonly measured in intervals are income (with the unit expressed in dollars), percent voting by districts (with the unit expressed in percentage points), governmental expenditure on a program (with the unit expressed either in dollars or in percentage points if measured as a percentage of the budget), air power (with the unit expressed in kilotons of bombing coverage, number of planes, or whatever), body counts (with the unit expressed in number of dead people), and so on.

It is clear that these levels of precision comprise a nesting progression, as shown in Figure 5-3. All interval measurements are also ordinal measurements and nominal measurements, and all ordinal measurements are also nominal measurements. That is, if we had an interval measure but chose to ignore our knowledge of the distances involved between scores, we would still have scores on an ordinal measure. And if we had scores on an ordinal measure but chose to ignore our knowledge of the relative ranking on the variable, we would still have a nominal measure, a set of distinct classes to which individuals were assigned.[4]

---

[4]A further refinement in precision is possible if in addition to measuring the length of intervals along a scale. We can assign a score of zero to some point on the scale. We are then said to have "ratio" measurement (because we can then take one score as a multiple of another score, which is not possible if there is no zero point). I have not included ratio measurement in my discussion here because it has not, as yet, figured importantly in data analysis in the social sciences. All of the interval scales I noted above could in fact be treated as ratio scales. Generally, however, this is ignored and they are treated simply as interval scales.

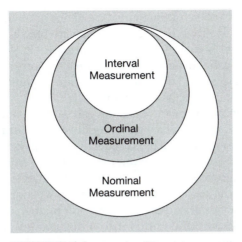

FIGURE 5-3   Levels of Precision

To put it a little differently, if two individuals have different scores on a variable, then (1) if the variable is measured nominally, we know that the two differ on the variable; (2) if the variable is measured ordinally, we know that the two differ on the variable *and* which one has the higher score; and (3) if the variable is measured intervally, we know that the two differ on the variable, which one has the higher score, *and* how much higher that score is than the other person's.

The three major levels of measurement, then, are nominal, ordinal, and interval measurement. As a definition of "precision in measurement," we can say that measurement is relatively precise insofar as it operates at a level that is relatively informative. Interval measurement is more precise than ordinal measurement, which is in turn more precise than nominal measurement.

Innate Nature of Levels of Measurement

Obviously, the level at which we measure things is not just a choice we make; if it were, we would simply measure everything at the interval level. Some measures are *continuous*; that is, they consist of gradations which, in principle, can be subdivided infinitely. An example is income, which can be expressed in thousands of dollars but which could be subdivided into hundreds of dollars, into dollars, into cents, into tenths of a cent, and so on. All continuous measures lend themselves naturally to interval measurement because their infinite divisibility requires that there be some unit of measurement that can be divided.

Measures that are not continuous are called *discrete*. These consist naturally of separate points that cannot be further divided. There are a few discrete measures that are interval. Elections, for example, are periodic events that cannot be subdivided. We could use the number of elections that a person had experienced as a measure of his political exposure, which would produce an interval measure, with "five elections" being two units higher than "three elections." The measure would be interval but would not be continuous; we could not subdivide elections into half-elections, or anything like that. For most discrete variables, however, such as "race," "religion," "region," or "social class," no unit presents itself by which categories (such as "African American" and "white") can be compared. Thus, with a few exceptions, such as "elections," discrete variables are by their nature either ordinal (if they have an ordering to them) or nominal.

We see, then, that all continuous measures can be expressed as interval measures, whereas almost all discrete variables are naturally either ordinal or nominal. As a result, the level of measurement we use is generally not a personal choice but inheres in the thing we are measuring. There are two caveats to this statement, however: (1) We could always ignore information we have about a measure, and treat it as a lower-level measure (the next section, "The Sin of Wasting Information," argues against this); and (2) *sometimes* we can add other information or theory to a naturally nominal or ordinal measure and enrich it to a higher level than its natural level: this is discussed in the section after next, "Enriching the Level of Precision in Measurement."

The Sin of Wasting Information

Time and again, data collected at a higher level of precision are collapsed to a lower level to simplify handling the data, writing reports, and so on. Age is often grouped into categories such as "youngest," "younger middle-aged," "older middle-aged," and "oldest"—an ordinal measure. Or income is grouped into "low," "middle," and "high."

Aesthetically, of course, it would seem better to know more about a subject rather than less. This alone should be enough to justify our cardinal rule: *Use measurements that are as precise as possible, given the subject you are studying; do not waste information by imprecise measurement.* This aesthetic consideration applies both to precision in measures and to precision in measurement. But inasmuch as I argued earlier that for practical purposes precision in measures might sometimes be sacrificed, it appears that an aesthetic consideration is not compelling, in and of itself.

A more important reason for following the cardinal rule, one that applies only to precision in measurement, arises if we are interested in using the measures to study a relationship between two or more variables. In this case, we can do qualitatively different things with data measured at different levels of precision. With more precise measurement, we can do a greater variety of things with our data and thus have more of an opportunity to develop interesting theories. It is for this reason that precision in measurement is more important than precision in measures. Let me provide an example.

In Figure 5-4, the relationship between age and percent voting, which we looked at earlier, is presented in three forms, accordingly (A) age is collapsed to a nominal measure and all knowledge of ranking and unit distance in it is lost; (B) age is collapsed to an ordinal measure and the knowledge of unit distance in it is lost; and (C) age is maintained at an interval level of measurement.

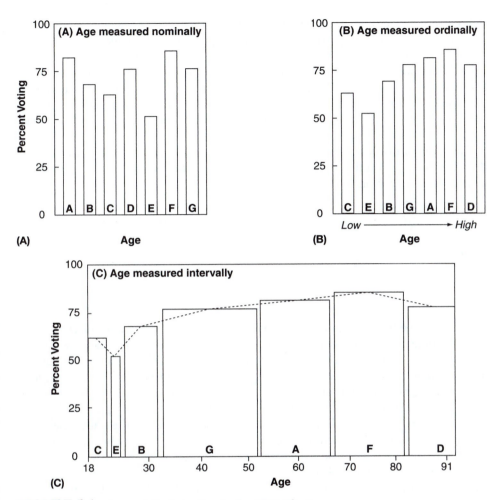

FIGURE 5-4   Age and Participation in the 2008 Election

In the first case, with age measured nominally, we can see that there is a relationship between age and participation in elections. This is indicated by the fact that different age-groups participate at different rates. Only 52 percent of the individuals in category E vote, for instance, as compared with 87 percent of those in category F. If age and participation were not related, we would expect about the same percentage of individuals in each category to vote. With nominal measurement, this is all we can say—*that the variables are or are not related.*

In the second case, with ordinal measurement, we can say a good deal more. We now know the ranking of the different categories of age: C is youngest, E the next to youngest, and then come B, G, A, F, and D. In addition to seeing whether or not the variables are related, we can see *the pattern of the relationship*. In this case, that pattern is one of increasing participation with increasing age up to some point, and then a reversal, with participation decreasing at the highest age.

If age were measured intervally, we could say still more about the relationship. Interval measurement adds information about the magnitude of differences in age expressed by the categories. If age were measured intervally, we could see whether or not there was a relationship, we could see the pattern of the relationship, and we also could see *the rate at which one variable changed in response to changes in the other variable*.

In Figure 5-4(C), the bars in the graph have been stretched to take into account the added information that the categories represent the following age-groups, measured in a common unit, years:

C   18–20
E   21–23
B   24–30
G   31–50
A   51–64
F   65–80
D   81–91

We can now see that the most rapid increases in participation occur in the early years, and that there is a big jump over about the next ten years; and that participation peaks around age 80, after which there is a decline. The dashed line tracing the path of the bars approximates the pattern we have already seen in Figure 5-2. This suggests an interesting combination of processes: Learning and acquiring the habit of voting during the first years of eligibility causes participation to rise most rapidly in the early years, but there are further slow increases up to about age 80. As these increases level off, there follows a decline, perhaps due to enfeeblement. This is a richer description of the relationship than we could have gotten using the ordinal measurement.

Notice that in Figure 5-4 (C), greater precision in *measures* also would have been useful, especially a finer breakdown of ages above 40. With the greater precision in measures of Figure 5-2, we can see that the peak occurs around age 89.

However, the information lost through the low precision in measures in part C is slight compared with the information lost by lowering the precision in measurement in parts A and B. *Preserving a high level of precision in measurement deserves a strong priority in research.*

Enrichment of the Level of Precision in Measurement

So far, I have argued that we should try not to drop data carelessly to a lower level of measurement. By a similar argument, we should always try to *raise* data to a higher level when this is possible. Given a certain amount of boldness and ingenuity, we may sometimes be able to do this.

Often, we can enrich our data in this way if we know something more about the data than is reflected in our measurement—in other words, if we have information about the data that would otherwise be wasted. This information may not be enough to provide neat, clean measurement at the higher level. If it were, we probably would have measured at the higher level in the first place. Generally, though, untidy measurement at a higher level is better than neat measurement at a lower level. A few examples may be the best way to show how measurement can be "enriched" in this way, by raising the level of measurement.

Examples of Enrichment

Example 1. You are studying the relationship between the colonial experience of new nations and the stability of democratic institutions in those nations. That is, you want to compare the stability of democratic institutions in former French, British, Dutch, and American colonies, for example. One way to do this would be simply to treat the problem as one of a relationship involving nominal measurement.

But it is likely that you have in mind some underlying scale along which the colonial experience varied, depending on which country had done the colonizing, and that you are really interested in the relationship between this scale and the stability of democratic institutions. If you can array the different mother countries along this scale, you can use them as an ordinal or interval measure of the scale.

You might, for example, be interested in whether or not the colonizing country tried to assimilate the native population to its own culture and the effect this had on the stability of the resulting institutions. On the scale "level of assimilation," the British colonial experience would rank low and the French quite high. The Dutch and American experiences would fall somewhere between these, with the United States possibly lower than the Dutch. For this particular purpose, then, the colonizing countries comprise at least an ordinal measure of the level of assimilation. If you could make a reasonably informed guess at the relative differences (such as Dutch rather close to the French; large gap between British and American), you might even be able to bring your data up to the level of rough interval measurement.

Further, you well might want to use a given nominal measurement twice or more in the same analysis, as a measure of different underlying scales. Thus you might be interested in predicting the stability of democratic institutions from two variables simultaneously: (1) the level of assimilation at which the colonizer aimed, and (2) the extent of oppression and violence during the colonial period. The colonizers would be arrayed differently along these two scales, and thus each would represent a different mix of the two variables. The United States, for example, probably would fall above the middle in assimilation, but low in oppression; France, high in assimilation and toward the middle in oppression; Belgium, low on assimilation but high on oppression; and so on.[5]

---

[5]Notice that the manner in which measurement of nominal variables has been enriched in these examples parallels the "dimensional analysis" that I urged in Chapter 3. Like vague, multidimensional concepts, nominal classifications involve an infinite number of dimensions. The various types of colonial experience we cited vary on degree of assimilation, extent of oppression, speed of economic development, geopolitical position, or what have you. Abstracting the appropriate ordered variable(s) from a nominally measured variable is much the same as abstracting the appropriate dimension(s) from a set of multidimensional concepts.

Example 2. You are studying the relationship between religion and political alienation. Religion could simply be measured nominally (Jewish, old-Reformation Protestant, Roman Catholic, etc.). Perhaps, however, you have in mind an underlying dimension that causes you to expect a relationship between the two variables. You might be thinking in terms of the extent to which one's religion promotes an apocalyptic view of the universe. If so, then as in Example 1, you could take the different religions ranked by their apocalyptic content as an ordinal or interval measure of this scale. Jews would fall near the bottom of such a scale and fundamentalist Protestants, near the top.

Alternatively, your theory might be that religious groups, simply as social organizations, build involvement among their members. In this case, you could array the different religions in terms of the size and "closeness" of their congregations, how democratic their legal structure is, or whatever. Note that the "right" ordinal or interval arrangement of the nominal categories depends on which underlying scale you want to tap. Thus, Jews would fall low on the "apocalyptic" scale but high on the "closeness" scale.

In working with ordinal variables (either "enriched" nominal variables or variables which obviously are ordered from the outset), a common unit may appear immediately, and you can treat the variables readily and directly as interval measures. For instance, abstracting the degree of "closeness" from religious affiliation suggests one ready interval measure—average size of congregations—although this admittedly would be only a rough measure whose validity would be questionable. Often, to enrich ordinal data, we must use a good deal of ingenuity, as in the next example.

Example 3. You want to measure the extent to which different educational programs tend to encourage pro- or antimilitary attitudes. You can distinguish three types of educational programs: military academy; general university, with participation in ROTC; general university, without participation in ROTC. These form an ordinal measure of "militariness" readily enough, with the military academy highest and the non-ROTC program lowest. Can you make an interval measure out of this ranking?

Fortunately, you might have some additional information on the subject. In a study of Annapolis midshipmen, ROTC, and non-ROTC students, for instance, it was found that 39 percent of the midshipmen thought the American military budget was too small; 10 percent of the ROTC students agreed, as did 4 percent of the non-ROTC students (Karsten and others, 1971). If you were willing to assume that at that time the Naval Academy was typical of the military academies and that there was a linear relationship between the promilitary orientation of an educational program and the percentage of its students who believed that the military budget was too small, this information would have allowed you to reconstruct the interval measure implicit in the ordered variable. (For an explanation of "linear relationship," see the box on p. 71)

If the degree of promilitary orientation in ROTC programs increased support of higher budgets by 6 percentage points over non-ROTC students, but the Naval

Academy increased budget support by 29 percentage points over ROTC students, then (given your assumptions) the interval between military academies and ROTC must have been 4.83 times as great as the interval between ROTC and non-ROTC. This is demonstrated geometrically in Figure 5-5.

Here I have drawn two of the many possible linear relationships between the "military content" of education and support for the defense budget. It should be clear that the same principle would hold for any linear relationship. Because you know the scores on budget support for non-ROTC, ROTC, and the Naval Academy, you can project across the graph to see where they should fall on the line

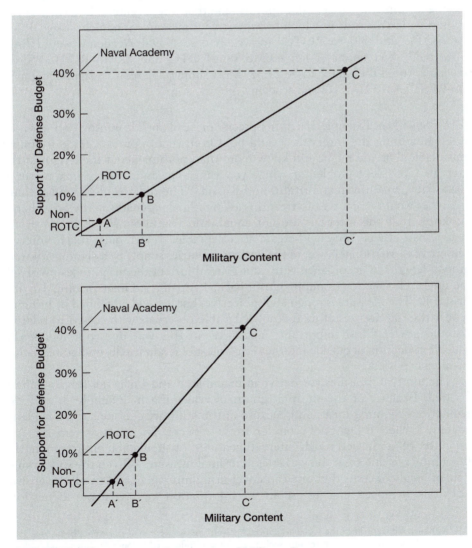

FIGURE 5-5   Enriching the Measure of Military Content

showing the relationship. Non-ROTC falls at A, ROTC at B, and the Naval Academy at C. Now look down the graph to see what scores on "military content" must be associated with positions A, B, and C on the line. These scores are A´, B´, and C´. Of course, you do not have units in advance by which to measure military content, but it is apparent that whatever units you conceive of, and whatever linear relationship between the two variables exists, the distance from B´ to C´ must be approximately five times the distance from A´ to B´. (To be exact, the ratio of the distances is 4.83.)

This gives you all you need to construct an interval measure—that is, an estimate of the relative differences (intervals) between scores of the measure. Because an interval measure does not assume that a zero point is known, you can arbitrarily pick the unit in which to express your measure. You might assign 1.0 to non-ROTC and 2.0 to ROTC, in which case Naval Academy would have to be 6.83. You might assign 4.0 to non-ROTC and 8.0 to ROTC; Naval Academy would then have to be 27.32. Most simply, the scores assigned might be non-ROTC, 4; ROTC, 10; and academy, 39.

Example 4. In Example 3, a rather precise piece of outside information was used to tell how long the intervals should be. Often such a precise guide is simply unavailable, but you might still know more than nothing about the length of the intervals. Consider a problem in which you want to measure the national power of Costa Rica, Spain, Great Britain, and Russia.[6] The *order* is clear, and a timid researcher would be content to treat this as an ordinal variable. On the other hand, you know that the intervals are not equal, and you know which intervals are greater than others. You could create an acceptable, though quite rough, interval measure of the national power of the various countries simply by assigning arbitrary interval lengths in accordance with your general idea of the magnitudes involved. You might choose, for example, Costa Rica, 1; Spain, 7; Great Britain, 10; and Russia, 40. The measure is rough and subjective, but it could be refined by bringing to bear the impressions of more knowledgeable observers with regard to relative national power. Most important, measuring in this way does not ignore the valuable collection of outside information—most of it admittedly undigested—that you already possess.

The interval measures you derive in Examples 3 and 4 may not leave you fully satisfied. Because of the indirect chain of reasoning in Example 3, and the assumptions required for it, and because of the arbitrary decisions to be made in Example 4, there is plenty of room for errors to occur. The question remains: Are you better off with such rough interval measures, or should you opt to ignore the size of intervals and treat the variables as ordinal measures? Given the wider range of theoretical concerns that one can cover using interval data, I think the answer is obvious. It makes sense to use all the information we have about a question,

---

[6]Although I have dubbed the variable "national power," for most purposes this would be broken down more profitably into component dimensions, such as "diplomatic influence," "economic power," and "military power."

even if we must supplement that information with assumptions and hunches. The alternative is to ignore a portion of what we know. Taking the "safer" course allows us to state our results with more confidence but reduces the importance of what we have to say.

Enriching measurement in this way is a research technique for which the researcher's creativity and ingenuity are critical. One mark of a good researcher is that she boldly seeks out all chances—not just the obvious or safe ones—to raise the level of measurement in her work.

LINEAR RELATIONSHIP

A relationship between two variables is *linear* if one variable changes by a constant amount with a change of one unit in the second variable, regardless of the value of the second variable. The relationship in graph A is linear; *y* increases by one-half unit when *x* changes by one unit, no matter what value *x* starts with. The relationship in graph B is nonlinear. Here, if *x* is high, a unit change in *x* produces relatively little change in *y*; if *x* is low, a unit change in *x* produces relatively great change in *y*.

Thus, the relationship in graph A can be expressed by a straight line, inasmuch as the relationship is the same at all values of *x*. The relationship in graph B must be expressed by a curve which tilts differently at different values of *x*, inasmuch as the relationship between the two variables is different for different values of *x*.

Quantifiers and Nonquantifiers Again

This discussion of precision in measures and precision in measurement has centered on the work of "quantifiers" (those who work by preference with objective data, especially with numerical data), simply because it was more convenient to introduce it in that way. But the same general conclusions hold for "nonquantifiers" as well.[7] To return to the quotation from Eckstein with which I introduced this chapter, it is clear that he was interested in doing the same things as quantifiers do, but in a different way. He wanted to measure variables and to assess relationships between those variables. His subject matter, however, rarely allowed him to use objective or numerical measures. For many variables in which he was interested, he could use only vague descriptions, such as "rather strong sense of community," "highly

---

[7]Let me repeat my earlier admonition. Being a "quantifier" or "nonquantifier" is not an either/or question. The extent to which a researcher uses objective data is generally not a matter of personality but rather of the subject she is studying and the data available for that subject.

developed team spirit," and so on. Most of these descriptions had to depend on his subjective judgment rather than on impersonal outside indicators.

Can this sort of work be described in terms of precision in measures and precision in measurement? Do the rules I have prescribed in this chapter hold for this sort of work as they do for more quantitative studies? First, we may note that measuring variables nonquantitatively requires the same sort of boldness that I urged in enriching data to a higher level of measurement. More important, we can see that this is primarily a problem of precision in measures, not of precision in measurement. A nonquantifier can measure things only approximately, but there is no particular reason why such research cannot approximate interval measurement.

For example, a student of Chinese politics might suggest that the higher a Chinese politician rises in the hierarchy, the less likely he is to press for the interests of his region. This statement approximates a relationship between two variables measured at the ordinal level ("height in the hierarchy" and "likelihood of lobbying"). Working more boldly and imaginatively, another student might approximate interval measurement. She might state, for example, that the higher a Chinese politician rises in the hierarchy, the less likely he is to press for the interests of his region; that this shift occurs very sharply as he moves from some particular level of the hierarchy to another; that the shift continues from there on up the hierarchy at a diminished rate; and finally, that near the top of the hierarchy, the process reverses itself, with the men at the top feeling secure enough to concern themselves more than those immediately below them with the interests of their regions.[8] This is certainly a richer statement than the earlier version, but it is no more "quantified" than the other. It is still based on subjective descriptions, made in the absence of objective indicators. The only difference is that in the second case the researcher enriches the level of measurement at which she is working.

▦ Further Discussion

A readable presentation along the lines developed in this chapter is Edward R. Tufte's "*Improving Data Analysis in Political Science*" (1968–1969). You should note that in this chapter I have presented a fairly radical position in favor of upgrading levels of measurement, a position that would not be accepted by all social scientists. To the extent that one is worried about measurement error, either random or nonrandom, one should be concerned about the possibility that "enriching" a level of measurement may insert either sort of error into the new measure. Personally, I think the risk is often justified; however, many scholars believe that the costs in carrying out such "enrichment" are greater than the benefits. A fairly technical paper that urges researchers to take seriously the risk of inserting measurement error by treating ordinal variables as if they were interval (an extrapolation similar to enrichment but riskier and less well thought out) is that by Wilson (1971). Another excellent article, a bit technical, is by Carter (1971).

---

[8]I have no idea whether this is a reasonable theory. I have constructed it merely as an example of the wide applicability of pseudo-interval measurement.

Two questions you might consider are:

1. Why would the technique in Example 3 not be appropriate if the relationship between "military content" and "support for defense budget" were nonlinear? What might you do in this case?

2. "Ratio" measurement is interval measurement for which, in addition to being able to measure the relative interval between different values of the measure, it is possible to assign the value zero to some point on the measure (see footnote 3). One difference between interval and ratio measurement is that whereas it is possible to add and subtract interval measures, it is possible to add and subtract, *multiply*, and *divide* ratio measures. It is possible to say that a given score is twice as great as another score, given ratio measurements; this is not possible with simple interval measurement. Fahrenheit temperature is an example of an interval measure that is *not* a true ratio measure, even though "zero" is arbitrarily assigned to one point on the scale. It is not true, for example, that a temperature of +20°F is half as "hot" as +40°F. In this chapter, I pointed out that the different levels of measurement were important because it was possible to make a greater variety of statements about relationships between variables that were measured in "advanced" ways. What statements might be made about relationships between ratio-measured variables that could not be made about relationships between interval-measured variables?

Causal Thinking and Design of Research

Thus far, everything we have looked at in this book has been justified in terms of how useful it is in establishing relationships between variables. It is time now to look more closely at what a "relationship" is, and how we interpret it.

Two variables are related if certain values of one variable tend to coincide with certain values of the other variable. Thus, social class and party vote are related in the United States, because those who vote Republican tend to be from the middle and upper classes. We have seen many such examples of relationships in earlier chapters.

If, in addition, we consider that the values of one variable *produce* the values of the other variable, the relationship is a *causal relationship*. The example of class and voting, noted above, is an example of a causal relationship. We feel that there is something about a person's social class that makes that person more likely to vote in a certain way. Therefore, we say that social class is a "cause" of party vote. It is not merely true that the two variables tend to coincide; they tend to coincide *because values of the one tend to produce distinct values of the other*.

Empirical, theory-oriented political research is almost exclusively concerned with *causal* relationships. As I pointed out earlier, a theory in its simplest form usually consists of three things: independent variables (those we think of as doing the "producing"), dependent variables (those we think of as being "produced"), and causal statements linking the two (refer again to p. 14).

In this chapter, we first discuss the idea of causation, and then follow this up with some ideas on research design. Research design—the way in which we structure the gathering of data—strongly affects the confidence with which we can put a causal interpretation on the results of research.

CAUSALITY: AN INTERPRETATION

The most important thing to note about causal thinking is that it is an interpretation of reality. In this regard, the assertion of a *causal relationship* differs from the mere assertion of a *relationship*, which is a rather objective statement. In the example of social class and the vote, for instance, there is objective evidence for the existence of a relationship, but a causal interpretation of this relationship is much more subjective. It might be argued, for instance, that class does not produce the vote, but that both are produced by something else—the ethnic, religious, and racial conflicts that have surfaced often in American politics. Thus someone could argue—and it would not be an unreasonable argument—that class is not a cause of the vote. Rather, that person might say, certain ethnic groups tend to vote for the Democrats; and these same groups, simply by accident, also tend to be working class. Therefore, the coincidence of class and party votes is just that—a coincidence. Distinguishing between this version of the relationship and the more common version is at least partly a matter of judgment.

Almost every situation in which we wish to make causal statements is similar to this example. The question of whether or not there is a relationship is objectively testable. The question of whether the relationship is a causal one, and of which variable causes which, requires an interpretation. Generally speaking, all that we know directly from our data is that two variables tend to occur together. To read causality into such co-occurrence, we must add something more, although as you will see, it is possible to design the research in ways that can help us significantly in doing this.

Consider two further examples: If we see that people who smoke regularly have a greater incidence of heart disease than nonsmokers, we might conclude that smoking causes heart disease. If we see that those U.S. senators who conform to the informal rules of the Senate tend to be the ones whose bills get passed, we might conclude that conformity is rewarded in the Senate. In both cases, we observe that two phenomena tend to occur together (smoking and heart disease, conformity and success). Our interpretation of this is that one of the phenomena causes the other. This interpretation is a subjective one.

We cannot always make a causal interpretation when two phenomena tend to coincide. The notion of cause involves more than that. Winter does not cause spring, although the one follows the other regularly. Similarly, hair color does not cause political party preference, although it is probably true in the United States that blonds, who are relatively likely to be white and Protestant, are more apt than brunettes to be Republicans. To qualify as a "causal" relationship, the coincidence of two phenomena must include the idea that one of them *produces* the other.

A good example of the difficulty of ascribing causal direction is the relationship between central bank independence and inflation. In general, political scientists think that if central banks (such as the Federal Reserve in the United States) are relatively independent of political control, they will use monetary policy more aggressively to fight inflation. Certainly, where central banks are independent, inflation is low. In a 1993 study, the three countries with the most politicized banks had averaged almost 8 percent inflation from 1955 to 1985; the three countries whose central banks were most independent had averaged only about 3.75 percent inflation.[1]

We see, then, that there is a relationship between the two; but is it true, as the economists believe, that bank independence causes low inflation? Batalla (1993) suggests that the opposite causal interpretation may be true. Reviewing the history of the 1920s and 1930s in Latin America, he notes that many countries had established autonomous central banks by the late 1920s, but that when high rates of inflation hit in the mid-1930s, most of them took away that autonomy. That is, low inflation rates allowed governments to tolerate independent central banks, while high inflation rates led the governments to pull the banks under their control. So, which causes which? Do independent central banks give us low inflation, or does low inflation give us independent central banks?

If ascribing *cause* to the coincidence of two things is so tricky, why do we bother with the notion of causation in our theories? What difference does it make whether class causes voting for a certain party, or whether the coincidence of class and party is due to something else that causes both of them? Remember that the ultimate purpose of theories is to give us levers on reality, some basis for choosing how to act. If A and B coincide but A does not cause B, changing A will not change B. Coincidence without cause gives you no lever.

ELIMINATION OF ALTERNATIVE CAUSAL INTERPRETATIONS

A causal interpretation is something that cannot come solely from our observations. But by setting up a study in certain ways and by manipulating the data appropriately, we can settle *some* of the problems in making causal interpretations. In our previous example of hair color, for instance, we might have looked only at WASPs and compared blonds and brunettes. If we then found that blond WASPs did not tend more often than brunette WASPs to be Republican, we could infer that hair color did not cause party preference.

In general, where we think that a third variable is causing two other variables to coincide accidentally, as in this hair color example, we can use our data to test the relationship. By *holding constant* the third variable, we can see whether it has led the original two variables to coincide in such a way as to resemble a causal relationship. Thus, if we artificially hold social position constant by looking only at WASPs, and now blonds and brunettes no longer differ in their politics, we can infer that the difference in voting was due not to the difference in hair color (which was merely a coincident variable) but to the difference in socioethnic background. We can then conclude that hair color does not cause political preference.[2]

---

[1] *The Economist*, November 20, 1993, p. 94.
[2] The technique of holding constant is discussed in greater detail at the conclusion of the chapter.

Thus there are techniques by which we can manipulate our data to eliminate *some* of the alternative causal interpretations of a relationship. But there is always one question about causation that remains ultimately subjective and that cannot be resolved completely by any techniques of data handling. Given that two variables are causally related, which of the variables causes which?

Suppose that two phenomena coincide and that there appears to be a causal relationship between them. Only you can decide which is the cause and which, the result. One useful convention in Western culture—but it is only a convention, even though it is so well established that it seems "natural" to us—is that causation works forward in time.[3] Accordingly, if we can establish that change in one of the variables precedes change in the other, and if we are sure that there is causation between the two, it is clear which variable must be the cause. We assume that pulling a trigger causes the shot that follows, rather than vice versa.

Although this convention frequently simplifies things for the researcher, there are many instances in which it cannot be used. Survey research, in which variables usually are measured just once and in a single interview, is a case in point. If voters who like the Republican party also tend to oppose welfare programs, which causes which? We might think that voters choose the party that offers the policies they prefer, but it might also be that voters choose the Republican party for other reasons, such as foreign policy, and then are influenced by the party's leaders to adopt its position on welfare programs as their own.

Summary

Let me pull together the argument to this point. It generally is not enough for us to note that two phenomena coincide. We generally also want to interpret *why* they coincide. There are three interpretations available to us, and our choice from among them is ultimately subjective.

1. **Causation is not involved at all.** The phenomena coincide because of logical necessity; that is, their coincidence is tautologically determined. Thus, by definition, spring follows winter, yet we do not think of winter as producing spring. A slight variation of this often occurs in the social sciences. It often happens that two slightly different measures of the same concept coincide. We would expect them to coincide, simply because they measure the same thing; we do not think of either of them as causing the other. For example, members of Congress who vote to increase aid to education tend also to support increases in welfare spending. This is not because their votes on one issue *cause* them to vote the way they do on the other. Rather, both votes are an expression of their general disposition to spend money on social programs. We must decide from outside the data at hand whether a coincidence of two phenomena is of this type or whether it involves causation.

[3]An example of a cultural tradition in which causation does not necessarily work forward in time is that of the Old Testament, whose writers believed that some people could prophesy what was to come in the future. In effect, the future event caused the prior prophecy to occur.

2. *The relationship we observe is a result of outside factors that cause the two phenomena at hand, and thus neither of these phenomena causes the other.* The study of hair color and party preference was an example of this. By setting up the study appropriately, we can control for various outside factors in order to concentrate on the relationship in question. In the hair color example, such a control was used. To this extent, we can see *from the data* whether the coincidence of the phenomena is of this sort. But we are still not exempt from making assumptions, for we must first have assumed the outside factor(s) causally prior to the two coincident phenomena. This is not always an easy decision to make. If it is possible to set up a true experiment (described in the next section), we can eliminate this possibility. But this is often not possible in "field" social sciences such as political science or sociology.

3. *One of the phenomena causes the other.* Here we have a true causal statement. We are still not finished making assumptions, of course, for we must decide which of the phenomena is the cause and which the effect. That is ultimately a subjective decision, though often we are aided in making it by the convention that causation must run forward in time.

As I have said so often in this book, one of the pleasures of research is that nothing in it is automatic. Even the most "quantitative" techniques do not take away our obligation and our right to be creative and imaginative. The fact that causal analysis is ultimately subjective may trouble us—objectivity always seems more comforting than the responsibility imposed by subjective judgment—but in a way it is also a great comfort, inasmuch as it keeps us, and what we do with our minds, at the heart of our research.

A FEW BASICS OF RESEARCH DESIGN

It should be evident from the discussion so far that the basic problem in causal analysis is that of eliminating alternative causal interpretations. Whenever two variables vary together (are related, coincide), there is a variety of causal sequences that might account for their doing so. A might cause B, B might cause A, both A and B might be caused by something else, or there might be no causation involved. Our task is to eliminate all but one of these, thus leaving an observed relationship, together with a single causal interpretation of it. Some of these alternatives can be eliminated only if we make assumptions from outside the actual study. But we also can design the study in such a way that certain alternatives are impossible. This will leave an interpretation that is dependent on fewer subjective assumptions and can thus lend a greater measure of certainty to the results.

Consider these examples:

1. *Agency study.* An organizational analysis of a government agency is made in which workers keep track of their output for a week. The organization is then restructured to decentralize decision making. After the reform, another week's tabulation shows increased output. Conclusion: Decentralized decision making increases output.

2. **Reagan's victory over the Soviet Union.** During the Reagan administration (1980–1988), the United States steadily increased its military spending. Over the three years from 1989 to 1991 the Soviet Union collapsed, which conservatives hailed as a victory for Reagan's policies. Conclusion: The economic strain of matching Reagan's military buildup had been too much for the Soviet system and had led to its collapse and the end of the Cold War.

3. **Organizing the poor.** In anticipation of a major campaign to organize the poor of a city, a survey is taken among them to measure their interest in politics. At the end of the organizing campaign, the same people are asked the same questions a second time. It turns out that those who were contacted by the campaign workers have indeed acquired an increased interest in politics, compared with those who were not. Conclusion: The campaign has increased the political awareness of the poor.

4. **Tax-reform mail.** The *Congressional Quarterly* reports the proportion of each senator's mail which favored tax reform. Comparing these figures with the senators' votes on a tax-reform bill, we see that senators who had received relatively favorable mail tended to vote for the bill, whereas those who had received relatively unfavorable mail tended to vote against it. Conclusion: How favorable a senator's mail was on tax reform affected whether or not she voted for it.

5. **Presidential lobbying.** In an attempt to measure his influence over Congress, the president randomly selects half the members of the House. He conducts a straw vote to find out how all the members of the House intend to vote on a bill important to him. He then lobbies intensively among the half he has randomly selected. In the final vote in the House, the group that he had lobbied shifted in his favor compared with what he could have expected from the earlier straw vote; the other half voted as predicted from the straw vote. Conclusion: His lobbying helped voting for the bill.

Let us look at the design of these studies to see how many alternative causal interpretations each can eliminate.

Designs Without a Control Group

In the first two examples, the design is of the form:

1. Measure the dependent variable.
2. Observe that the independent variable occurs.
3. Measure the dependent variable again.
4. If the dependent variable has changed, ascribe that to the occurrence of the independent variable.

Thus, in "Agency Study," (1) the workers' output is tabulated; (2) the organizational structure is decentralized; (3) the workers' output is once again tabulated; and (4) the conclusion is reached. This kind of design operates *without a control group*. As a result, there are a number of alternative causal sequences that might have produced the same result.

For example, a plausible alternative explanation for the increased productivity might be that the initial measurement of production, in which each worker kept track of output for a week, focused the workers' attention on productivity in a way that had not been done before, leading them to improve their productivity. In other words, it was not the decentralization of the agency, but the study itself, which caused productivity to rise.[4]

Had the study included a second agency as a control (see the next section), one in which output was measured at the same times as in the first agency but in which there was no decentralization, the alternative explanation would not have been plausible. That is, if the increased productivity in "Agency Study" had been due simply to the act of measuring, productivity in the control agency (in which the same measurements were taken as in the first agency) also should have increased. Accordingly, if we found that productivity increased more in the reorganized agency than in the control agency, we would know that this could not have been because of the act of measuring, for both agencies would have undergone the same measurements. That particular alternative interpretation would have been eliminated by the design of the study. In conducting the study without a control, the alternative interpretation can be eliminated only by assuming it away, which seems very risky.

"Reagan's victory over the Soviet Union" provides an example of another sort of alternative explanation that may be plausible in studies without a control group. It is quite possible that other things that occurred between the measurement of the two events (1980–1988 and 1989–1991) were the cause of the Soviet Union's collapse. Reform in Communist China, the growth of Muslim minorities in the Soviet Union, feuds among Soviet leaders—all might be proposed as alternative causes of the Soviet Union's collapse. If it were possible to find as a control group a similar system that went through the same other factors but was not engaged in an arms race with the United States, then these alternative explanations could be tested and perhaps eliminated. But of course, no such system exists.

This is a good example of how difficult it may sometimes be to include a control group in a design. Some circumstances just do not yield parallel cases that can be compared. As another example, consider that the existence of the United Nations has affected the foreign policy of every country in the world since 1945. How can a student of international politics distinguish its effect on foreign policy from the effects of the Soviet–American rivalry, the development of atomic weapons, the liberation of former colonies, and so on, all of which have happened at the same time? One cannot, of course. It is simply not possible to provide a control group of contemporary countries for which the United Nations has not existed.

---

[4]A famous example of this sort is the Hawthorne study, in which an attempt was made to measure how much productivity increased when factories were made brighter and more pleasant. As it turned out, the groups of workers who were placed in better surroundings did show major increases in productivity. But so did control groups whose surroundings had not been improved. The novelty of taking part in an experiment, the attention paid to the workers, and increased social cohesiveness among those groups chosen for the experiment—all these raised productivity irrespective of the experimental changes in physical working conditions that were made for some (but not all) of the groups. If a control group had not been used, the investigators would probably have concluded, mistakenly, that brighter and more pleasant surroundings led to greater productivity. See Roethlisberger and Dickson (1939).

The same general alternative explanation (that other things happening at the same time could have been the true cause) also might have applied to "Agency Study." If something else had happened between the two measurements of productivity—the weather improved, Christmas came, the president urged greater productivity, or whatever—this might have been the true cause of the increased production. Again, using a second agency as a control could eliminate such alternative explanations.

Studies without a control group pop up all the time. On January 4, 2004, the *Minneapolis Star Tribune* headlined a front-page story: "State Sex Ed Not Working, Study Finds." The story reported a study by the Minnesota Department of Health, which in 2001 had asked students in grades 7 and 8 of three schools that had adopted an abstinence-only sex education curriculum (not teaching contraception or safe sex, but rather providing materials to encourage students to abstain), whether "at any time in your life have you ever had sex (intercourse)?" They then came back in 2002 and repeated the question for the same group of students, now in grades 8 and 9. From 2001 to 2002, the number saying that they had ever had sexual intercourse rose from 5.8 to 12.4 percent. The conclusion of the article was that the abstinence-only curriculum had failed.

An abstinence-only curriculum might or might not fail to reduce sexual intercourse, but we cannot tell from this study whether it does. Students of that age, as they grow a year older, are in any case probably more likely to have sexual intercourse than when they were younger. A control group of students of the same age who had had a different curriculum for sex education would have been easy to add to the study, but without it we have no idea whether the students with the abstinence-only curriculum initiated sexual activity at a greater rate than they would have done without the curriculum, at a lesser rate, or at the same rate. We simply cannot tell whether the abstinence-only curriculum resulted in reduced sexual intercourse.

(The problem of interpreting results was also exacerbated in this case by the question, which asked students whether at any time in their life they had ever had sexual intercourse. The 5.8 percent who answered affirmatively in 2001 must have answered affirmatively again in 2002, so the percent responding "yes" in 2002 could have only risen or stayed the same; it was not possible for the percentage to decline. So, apparent failure of the program was baked into the study from the start. A better question wording, which would have been more sensitive to the impact of the new program, would have been: "During the past year, have you had sex [intercourse]?")

Use of a Control Group

The natural experiment. "Organizing the Poor" is an example of a design in which a control group has been added to handle the sorts of problems we just encountered. It is a *natural experiment*, a design in which a test group (i.e., a group exposed to the independent variable) and a control group (a group *not* exposed to the independent variable) are used, but in which the investigator has no control over who falls into the test group and who falls into the control group. In "Organizing the Poor," the matter of who was contacted by the campaign workers was decided by the workers' own choice of whom to contact and by the extent to which different people made themselves available for contact by the campaign workers. The natural experiment design is of the form:

1. Measure the dependent variable for a specific population before it is exposed to the independent variable.
2. Wait until some among the population have been exposed to the independent variable.
3. Measure the dependent variable again.
4. If between measurings the group that was exposed (called the *test group*) has changed relative to the control group, ascribe this to the effect of the independent variable on the dependent variable.

Thus, in "Organizing the Poor," (1) a number of poor people were surveyed as to their interest in politics; (2) the campaign occurred; (3) the same poor people were surveyed again; and (4) those who had been contacted by the campaign were compared with those who had not. This design eliminates many of the alternative explanations that can crop up in working without a control group. For instance, it could not have been the initial measurement that changed the group that had been contacted, compared with the control group, because both groups had been measured in the same way.

Nevertheless, the natural experiment still allows alternative explanations. Because the researcher does not have control over who is exposed to the independent variable, it may be that the exposed group has a different predisposition to change than the control group. In "Organizing the Poor," for instance, the campaign workers are likely to have approached those poor whom they thought they could most easily get interested in politics. Also, those among the poor who were most resistant to change might not have let the campaign workers in the door or might have been chronically absent when the campaign workers tried to contact them. Accordingly, a plausible alternative explanation in "Organizing the Poor" is that the poor who were contacted by the campaign increased their interest in politics more than those who were not contacted *simply because they were the ones who were most likely to have become more interested in politics at that time, regardless of the campaign.* This alternative must be either assumed away or controlled by using a design in which the researcher can determine who falls into the test group and who falls into the control group. A design that accomplishes this is a *true experiment*; but before going on to discuss this, let me discuss a poor cousin of the natural experiment.

The natural experiment without premeasurement. This is a design in which no measurements are made before subjects are exposed to the independent variable. This design follows the form:

1. Measure the dependent variable for subjects, some of whom have been exposed to the independent variable (the test group) and some of whom have not (the control group).
2. If the dependent variable differs between the groups, ascribe this to the effect of the independent variable.

The "Tax-Reform Mail" example is of this sort. In this design, (1) senators' votes on a tax-reform bill were noted, and (2) the votes of senators who had received favorable mail were compared with the votes of those who had not. The same kind of alternative explanation that has to be dealt with in natural experiments has to be dealt with in this design also. As in "Organizing the Poor," it may be that heavier pro-tax-reform mail went to senators who already were moving into a tax-reform position even without the mail. Such senators, about whom there might have been a great deal of speculation in the press, could have attracted more mail than did other senators.

Moreover, this design permits many additional alternative explanations beyond those that apply to a natural experiment. In the tax-reform example, it is probable that people were more likely to write letters favoring reform to senators they thought would agree with them. In other words, it might be that senators' mail did not cause their votes, but that their likely vote caused them to get certain kinds of mail. Hence, the relationship between a senator's vote on the bill and the mail she received might not be a causative relationship at all—merely a coincidence between pro-reform and pro-mail and anti-reform and anti-mail. This alternative could not apply to a natural experiment. In a natural experiment, it would have been clear from the initial measurement whether or not those who fell into the test group had initially been different from those falling into the control group. In fact, what is compared in the natural experiment is not the measured variables themselves, but how the two groups change between measurements.

To sum up, the natural experiment without premeasurement is a design in which the test group and the control group are compared with respect to a dependent variable only after they have been exposed to the independent variable. It involves the same sorts of alternative explanations as the natural experiment does, plus some others that result from the fact that the investigator does not know what the test group and the control group looked like before the whole thing started.

True Experiment

In neither of the two versions of the natural experiment just outlined did the investigator have any control over who fell into the test group and who fell into the control group. If the investigator does have such control, she can perform a *true experiment*. A true experiment includes the following steps:

1. *Assign at random* some subjects to the test group and some to the control group.
2. Measure the dependent variable for both groups.
3. Administer the independent variable to the test group.
4. Measure the dependent variable again for both groups.
5. If the test group has changed between the first and second measurements in a way that is different from the control group, ascribe this difference to the presence of the independent variable.

Because investigators can control who falls into which group, they can set up theoretically equivalent groups. (The best, and simplest, way to do this is to assign subjects randomly to one group or the other.) The advantage of making the groups equivalent is that researchers can thereby eliminate almost all of the alternative causal interpretations that had to be assumed away in the various natural experiment designs. If the groups are equivalent to start with, for example, a difference in how the groups change cannot be due to the fact that the individuals in the test group were more prone to change in certain ways than were those in the control group. Thus the problem that the investigators faced in "Organizing the Poor" is eliminated.

"Presidential Lobbying" is an example of the true experiment. Here (1) the president chose half of the House randomly to be the test group, leaving the other half as the control; (2) he took a straw vote to measure the dependent variable (vote) for both groups; (3) he lobbied the test group; (4) the bill was voted on; and (5) he compared the voting of the two groups to see whether his lobbying had made a difference. Working with this design, the president would be pretty certain that a disproportionately favorable change among those he lobbied was due to his efforts. If he had not been able to control who was lobbied, he would have been faced with plausible alternative causal interpretations.

Table 6-1 summarizes the various research designs discussed in this chapter and some of the alternative explanations applicable in each case. Each design is presented there in a symbolic shorthand that is explained in the footnote to the table. In the last column of the table, one or two of the alternative interpretations left open by each design are highlighted.

TABLE 6-1   Selected Research Designs

Type	Graphic Presentation[a]	Example from This Chapter	Selected Alternative Causal Interpretations
Observation with no control group	Test group: M * M	Agency Study, Reagan's Victory	The first measurement itself may have caused the change observed in the second measurement; or something else that happened at the same time as* may have caused the change.
Natural experiment without premeasurement	Test group:* M Control: M	Tax-Reform Mail	Those who made their way into the test group may have been more likely to change than those who made their way into the control group; or those who made their way into the test group may have been different from those in the control group even before they experienced *.

(continued)

TABLE 6-1   continued

Type	Graphic Presentation[a]	Example from This Chapter	Selected Alternative Causal Interpretations
Natural experiment	Test group: M* M Control: M M	Organizing the Poor	Those who made their way into the test group may have been more likely to change than those who made their way into the control group.
True experiment	Test group: R M* M Control: R M M	Presidential Lobbying	None of the alternatives discussed in this chapter applies. This design permits only a very few alternative explanations. Consult Cook and Campbell (1979), cited at the end of this chapter.

[a] Notation adapted from Donald T. Campbell and Julian C. Stanley, *Experimental and Quasi-Experimental Designs for Research* (Chicago: Rand McNally, 1963). In presenting the designs graphically, an asterisk (*) indicates that a group has been exposed to a stimulus or is distinguished in some other way so as to constitute a "test group"; M indicates that the dependent variable has been measured for the group; and R (used to describe the "true experiment") indicates that individuals have been assigned randomly to the groups.

DESIGNS FOR POLITICAL RESEARCH

The natural experiment without premeasurement is the single most commonly used design in political research. A few examples will indicate the broad use of the design: (1) any voting study that shows that persons of a certain type (working class, educated, male, or what have you—the test group) vote differently from those who are not of this type (the control group); (2) any of the large number of studies estimating how much better incumbent presidents do in seeking reelection when the economy has improved in the preceding year (test group) compared with those for whom the economy has not been improving (control group); (3) most "policy output" studies, such as one by Rogowski and Kayser (2002), which showed that majoritarian electoral systems (the test group; also known as single-member district, plurality systems, the kind of system used in U.S. House elections and British and Canadian elections) will tend to produce economic policies favorable to consumers, while proportional representation systems (the control group, electoral systems like those of Germany, Sweden, and the Netherlands) should strengthen the interests of producers; and (4) studies of discrimination, such as Uhlaner and Schlozman (1986), who tested whether women candidates for office were less well financed than men because of experiential attributes such as seniority, or because of direct discrimination.

In short, any research is an example of the natural experiment without premeasurement if it (1) takes two or more types of subjects and compares their values on a dependent variable; and (2) infers that the difference on the dependent variable is the result of their difference on whatever it is that distinguishes them as "types."[5] This really describes the bulk of political research.

As we saw in earlier sections, this design is far from satisfactory. It permits relatively many alternative causal interpretations, which are difficult to handle. Nevertheless, this remains the most widely used design in political science. Other designs that have the advantage of control groups are to be preferred because they require less difficult assumptions, but these designs can be used only when the researcher has more control over the test variables than most political scientists can usually achieve.

In order to use a natural experiment design, for instance, researchers must be able to anticipate the occurrence of the test factor. They also must go to the expense in time and money of making two measurements of the subjects. Even then, the attempt may misfire; for example, it may be that the test factor (especially if it is one that affects only a small part of the population) will apply to only a few of the people included in the study. That is, the investigator may be left with a control group but no test group.

Many important variables in the social sciences are not at all susceptible to study by natural experiments. Some lie in the past: people's experiences during the Depression, the colonial histories of nations, the educational backgrounds and past professions of members of Congress, and so on. Others, such as assassinations, riots, and changes in the business cycle, are unpredictable. Such variables are difficult to fit into a natural experiment design. On the other hand, some events are more easily anticipated: the introduction of a poverty program in a town, high school graduates' entrance into college, regularly scheduled political events such as elections, and so on. These lend themselves readily to a natural experimental design.

A true experiment requires even greater control over the subjects of the study than does a natural experiment. The latter requires only that the investigator be able to anticipate events, but the true experiment requires that the researcher be able to manipulate those events—she must decide who is to fall into the control group and who is to fall into the experimental group. To do this in a field situation requires power over people in their normal lives. Thus it is no accident that the example I used of a true experiment, "Presidential Lobbying," was carried out by the president. It is rare in real political situations that a researcher can exercise this kind of control over events. However, the experiment is so much more powerful than other designs—rejects alternative interpretations so decisively—that we should use it whenever possible, and probably should use it a good deal more than is now done.[6]

---

[5]It is apparent here and in the examples directly preceding this that I am taking some liberty with the notion of "control group." Where rates of participation in the middle class and working class are compared, for instance, it is not at all clear which class is the "test" group and which is the "control." The distinction is even muddier when one compares several groups simultaneously, such as voters from several age-groups. But the logic of what is done here is the same as in the strict test/control situation, where the dependent variable is compared among groups of subjects distinguished by their values on the independent variable. It is convenient and revealing to treat this sort of analysis in terms of the analogy to experiments.

[6]Kinder and Palfrey (1993, especially the Introduction) argue persuasively that we in political science have overrated the problems and barriers to true experimentation in our field.

Achen (1986, p. 6), citing Gilbert, Light, and Mosteller (1975), points out that apparently *only* randomization provides a clear-enough causal interpretation to settle issues of social-scientific research conclusively:

> Without it, even the cleverest statistical analysis meets strong resistance from other scholars, whose professional skepticism is quite natural. When the forces that determine the experimental and control groups are unknown, the imagination has full play to create alternative explanations for the data. Inventing hypotheses of this sort is enjoyable, unstrenuous labor that is rarely resisted.

It may be that in a small organization, such as a local political caucus or a portion of a campus, the investigator can carry out a true experimental design. For instance, students might conduct a political campaign among a randomly selected portion of the campus community and compare that portion over time with a randomly selected control.

It is sometimes possible to carry out true experiments on a larger scale than this, but only if the experimenter can control significant policies and manipulate them for the purposes of investigation. A good example of this sort of experiment is a study by Gerber and Green (2000), in which 30,000 registered voters in New Haven, Connecticut, were each randomly assigned one of three different approaches in a nonpartisan get-out-the-vote program. It turned out that personal visits were effective in getting people to vote, direct mail appeals helped slightly, and telephone calls made no difference at all.

An interesting example of a natural situation that produced something approximating a true experiment is the study by Howell et al. (2002) of the effects of a private education on poor children. Programs were initiated in Dayton, Ohio; Washington, D.C.; and New York City that offered children in public schools partial scholarship vouchers to attend private schools. Since there were more applicants than could be funded, children were chosen by lottery to receive the vouchers. This selection process approximated a true experiment; the scholarships were assigned randomly, and there was a control group of children who applied for scholarships but did not receive them. Thus, the two groups should have been equivalent in all respects other than the experimental treatment. The result of the study was that African American students who received the scholarships did significantly better on standardized tests two years later than African American students who did not receive the scholarships. However, the effect seemed limited to African Americans; no other ethnic group appeared to benefit in the same way. It is possible that something in the African American culture or in the situation of African American students made them especially receptive to the program.

This study comes very close to a true experiment, and therefore offers very convincing results on an important policy issue. One remaining alternative explanation is that something akin to the problem we saw in "Agency Study" was operating. The children who received scholarships knew they had won something special. Also, they knew that their parents were paying extra money beyond the partial scholarship to further their education. This may have left them more highly motivated than the students who had not won in the lottery. (In an ideal experiment, people do not know whether they are in the experimental group or in the control; the New Haven study by Gerber and Green is an example.) This worry might be lessened, however, by the fact that it was only African Americans who appeared to benefit from the vouchers; if the benefit were an artifact of children's knowing they had won in the lottery, one would think that would affect all ethnic groups in the same way.

When it is possible to construct true (or nearly true) experiments in real field situations like this, the results can be compelling. More often, true experimentation is useful for studying general aspects of small-group interactions or individual thought processes relevant to politics. For example, a group of subjects may be placed together and told to reach a decision on some question. The investigator then manipulates the way individuals in the group may communicate with each other, or what messages they see, to determine how these influence the result. In such studies, of course, true experiments are the most appropriate design, inasmuch as the investigator generally can control all the relevant variables. A good example of this sort of experiment is that of Mutz and Reeves (2005) to investigate whether rudeness and incivility in politicians' debates decreases people's trust in the political process. Students, and some other adults who were hired to take part, were randomly assigned by the investigators to watch talk show debates (staged by actors) that varied by how uncivil the debaters were to each other. Those who watched the uncivil versions showed a reduced trust of politicians and the political process, compared with the others. This true experiment was crucial to establishing the relationship between incivility and trust, since outside of a randomized experiment people who distrust politicians already would probably be more likely to choose shows in which commentators and guests are uncivil to each other. Without the experiment, one could not tell for sure which causes which.

Special Design Problem for Policy Analysis: Regression to the Mean

I have introduced you above to some simple sources of alternative causal interpretations and some simple designs to control for them. A slightly more complex problem, while it has many applications in general explanation, is especially important in evaluating the impact of policy initiatives. This is a problem most public officials and journalists do not appear to understand at all, but it is well within your range of understanding at this point.

The problem is called *regression to the mean*. If we assume that essentially everything we observe has some element of randomness to it—that is, in addition to its true core value it varies somewhat from time to time—regression to the mean will always be present. Consider a student in a course, for example. When she is tested, her measured level of knowledge is generally about right, but if she has had a bad day (isn't feeling good, has bad luck in the instructor's choice of questions, etc.), she will score somewhat below her usual level; on a good day, she will score somewhat higher. Note that this sort of random variation in a measure is closely related to what we referred to as unreliability in Chapter 4.

For our purposes here, the important thing about this is that if we observe cases at two points in time, we can expect high initial values to drop somewhat from one time to the next, and low initial values to rise somewhat. Not all of them will do this; some of the high scores no doubt are genuinely high and may even rise by the next time they are observed. But a disproportionate number of the high cases are probably cases for whom things had lined up unusually well the first time; that is, the random part of their measure is likely to have been positive. We should expect that it is unlikely they would be so lucky twice in a row, so on the average they are likely to go down the next time they are observed. Similarly, the lowest scores probably include a disproportionate number of cases that were unusually low because of a negative random factor; on the average, we should see them rise.

We should therefore be a little suspicious of a statement like: "Team learning strategies are good in that the weakest students improve, but they are bad in that the strongest students appear to be dragged down by working with the weaker ones." This might be true. But an alternative explanation could be that this is simply regression to the mean. It might be that the stronger students' scores declined because when they were measured at the beginning of the experiment with team learning, a number of them had done unusually well and then just drifted back to their normal level of performance over time. Similarly, some of the poorer students might have drifted up to their normal levels. In other words, the scores of the weaker students might have improved, and the scores of the stronger students might have declined, even if the students had never been involved in team learning. The two alternative causal interpretations can only be sorted out by using an appropriate research design. (One is given on p. 90).

One variant of this problem shows up time and again in assessing the impact of new governmental policies. How often have you seen a statement of the sort: "After foot patrols were introduced in the entertainment district, our city's murder rate declined by a full 18 percent"? What is often missed in such statements is that this effect might also be due to regression to the mean. When do cities typically institute new policies? When the problem they are concerned about has flared up! But cities' problems, like students taking tests as in the example discussed earlier, probably have some element of randomness to their measures. If the murder rate has shot up in one year, it is more likely to go down the next year than to go still higher, whether or not the city institutes foot patrols in the entertainment district. In other words, governments are likely to pick a time when a problem is at a high point (which may or may not include some random element) to initiate a policy to solve the problem. Thus, in the case of the murder rates, on the basis of the information in the statement, we cannot tell whether or not foot patrols really curbed the murders, because regression to the mean provides a plausible alternative explanation.

Does this mean that we cannot assess the impact of changes in policies? Of course not. But it does mean that we must find a research design that allows us to distinguish between the two alternative explanations. The design in the statement about foot patrols and murder rates is our old friend:

M * M

Our problem is that we suspect that the first M may have been unusually high, making it likely that the second measurement would show a decrease whether or not the intervention between the two measures has had any impact.

A design that allows us to sort this out is an *interrupted time series*, that is, a series of measurements over time that is interrupted by the policy intervention:

MMMMM * MMMMM

If the measurement that came just before the intervention was unusually high, the measurements preceding it should tend to be lower than it is. The test for whether the intervention has had an effect in this design is whether the *average* of the several measurements preceding the intervention differs from the *average* of the measurements following the intervention.[7]

The interrupted time series is graphically illustrated in Figure 6-1, with the intervention indicated by an asterisk and a dashed vertical line. Graph A illustrates an interrupted time series in which the intervention appears to have caused a change. Graph B illustrates one in which it did not. Note that in graph B, if we had looked only at the adjacent "intervention and after" measures, regression to the mean would have led us to think the intervention had had an impact.

USE OF VARIED DESIGNS AND MEASURES

I suppose that the easiest conclusion to draw from our discussion thus far is that any kind of research in political science is difficult and that the results of political research are, in the last analysis, unreliable. But this would be far too sour. I did not discuss these selected research designs to convince you not to do political research but to show you some of the problems you must deal with.

Even if you are forced to rely solely on one of the weaker designs (operating without a control group, or using a control group with no premeasurement), you are better off if you set out your design formally and measure those variables that can be measured, acknowledge alternative causal interpretations, and try to assess just how likely it is that each alternative is true. The choice is between doing this or giving up and relying on your intuition and impressions.

But there is a more hopeful side to this chapter. The various weaknesses of different designs should suggest a solution: *Wherever possible, try to work simultaneously with a variety of designs, which can at least in part cancel out each other's weaknesses.* For example, in working solely with a randomized experiment in an isolated situation, we may wonder whether the result we have obtained might be a result of something about the way the experiment was set up, rather than a "true"

---

[7]An even better design, where possible, would add a control to rule out the possibility that it was something else that happened at the same time as the intervention that caused the change:

MMMMM * MMMMM
MMMMM   MMMMM

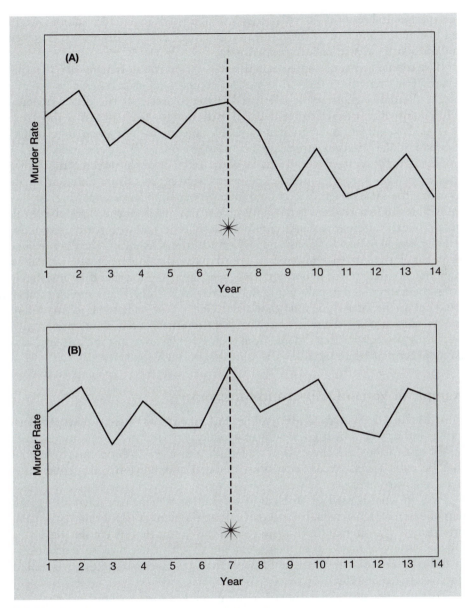

FIGURE 6-1   Examples of Interrupted Time Series

result. Relying totally on a natural experiment, we might wonder whether our results simply reflect a test group comprised of unusual people, rather than a "true" result. But if we could use both of these designs, employing either the same or closely related measures, each result would bolster the other. We could be more confident of the experimental result if we had gotten a similar result in a field situation. And we could be more confident of the result of the natural experiment if we had gotten a similar result in an artificial true experiment.

If we can mix research strategies in this way, the end result is more than the sum of its parts. The strengths of the various designs complement each other. The likelihood that the alternative explanations associated with each design are true decreases because of the confirmation from the other design. It will seem less likely to us that the result of the natural experiment is due to unusual people entering the test group, for example, if we obtain similar results in a true experiment, whose test group we controlled.

Note that the effect would not be the same if a single research design were repeated twice—if, say, a natural experiment were repeated in a different locality. Repeating the same design twice would increase our confidence somewhat, by showing us that the first result was not an accident or a result of the particular locality chosen. But the alternative causal interpretations associated with natural experimental design would in no way be suspended. Consider the "Organizing the Poor" example once again. If the campaign in one city tended to reach mainly those who were already becoming more interested in politics, thus creating the illusion that the campaign had gotten them interested in politics, there is no reason to think that a similar campaign would not do the same thing in a second city. Getting the same result in two different cities would not make it any less likely that the alternative causal interpretation was true. Using two designs that differed from each other, even in just the one city, would add more certainty than repeating the same design in a second city.

Example of Varied Designs and Measures

In his *Making Democracy Work*, Robert Putnam (1993) uses the varied-design strategy rather well. His study sought to explain variation in the quality of governmental institutions; his theory was that traditions of civic cooperation, based on what he calls *social capital* (networks of social cooperation), are what lead to effective government.

First, in what is really a problem of valid measurement (see Chapter 4) rather than one of research design, he approached the problem of measuring "government performance" by using multiple measures. To the extent that he got the same results across a variety of methods of measurement, all with their own varied sources of invalidity, he could be more confident that he had measured governmental effectiveness accurately.

To this end, he first gathered a number of statistics about governmental performance in the 20 regions that he was studying, such as the promptness with which the regional governments developed their budget documents. He then checked and supplemented the official statistics by having research assistants call government agencies in each region with fictitious requests for help on such things as completing a claim for sickness benefits or applying for admission to vocational school. (Governments' response quality varied from responses in under a week after a single letter, to responses that required numerous letters, numerous phone calls, and a personal visit over several weeks.) Finally, these objective measures of performance were supplemented by several opinion surveys in which people were asked how well they thought the regional government performed.

Once he had decided how to measure governmental performance, Putnam was faced with the question of research design. His basic design was the natural experiment with no premeasurement. The 20 regions were compared as to their level of civic engagement and the quality of their governments' performance, and those with high engagement proved to be those with a high quality of governmental performance.

To test the relationship more richly, he also added tests of *linking* relationships using the same design. For instance, he showed that the higher civic engagement was in communities, the less political leaders feared compromise. This makes sense as a component of the relationship between civic engagement and governmental effectiveness, since willingness to compromise should in turn lead to effective government. The fact that such linking relationships proved to be true under testing makes us more confident that the overall relationship was not a design fluke.

This design still suffered, though, from the possibility that the relationship was a matter of other contemporary things associated with civic engagement, such that those regions high in civic engagement were for some other reasons primed for governmental effectiveness. Putnam countered this, in part, by adding analyses over time of the form "observation with no control group." In these, he traced the development of civic involvement in regions over the past century and showed that high civic involvement in the latter part of the nineteenth century led to civic involvement and governmental effectiveness a century later. By combining the complementary strengths of varied measures and varied designs, Putnam was thus able to generate conclusions of which the reader is more confident than if they were based on a single measure or on a single design.

CONCLUSION

To pick up once again the refrain of this book, creativity and originality lie at the heart of elegant research. Anybody, or almost anybody, can take a research problem, carry out a fairly obvious test on it using one or two obvious measures, and either ignore or assume away the ever-present alternative causal interpretations. A creative researcher will not be satisfied with this but will try very hard to account for all plausible alternative interpretations. Such a student will muster logical arguments, will cite evidence from related studies, and may even vary the designs and measures in his own study. All of these techniques will help the investigator limit the number of alternative interpretations of his findings.

The suggestion made in the preceding section—to vary measures and designs—is, I think, a useful one, but it should not be thought of as the only answer. Varying designs is generally useful, but there are other ways to eliminate alternative interpretations, such as by logical argument or by indirect evidence of various sorts. No interpretation of a research result is cut and dried; interpreting a result and handling alternative interpretations of the result are difficult and challenging constituents of research.

HOLDING A VARIABLE CONSTANT

I have talked about holding a variable constant more than once in this chapter. If we want to know whether a relationship between two variables can be accounted for by a third variable that is related to both of them, we can hold the third variable constant to see whether the relationship between the first two continues to exist when the third variable is not free to vary. *Holding a variable constant* is often also called *controlling for the variable*.

The simplest way to do this is to divide the subjects into separate groups, each having a distinct value on the variable to be held constant, and then observe whether within each of these groups there is a relationship between the first two variables. If there is, it cannot be due to variation in the third variable, for within each of these groups the third variable literally is constant.

A good example of holding a variable constant is provided by the Przeworski et al. (2000) study of whether people live better in democracies than in dictatorships. They found that the life expectancy of people living in democracies was 69.3 years, while that of people living in dictatorships was just 53.3 years. Those in democracies could expect to live 16 years longer, on the average, than those in dictatorships—a big difference.

However, an obvious alternative explanation offered itself. Dictatorships were much more likely than democracies to be poor, and poor countries in general have worse health and lower life expectancies than countries that are better off. Do the longer life expectancies in democracies indicate anything about what democracy does for people, or is it just that democracies are richer countries, and that is why people in democracies live longer?

As indicated in Table 6-2, if we divide countries into groups with approximately the same per capita incomes, there still remains an advantage for democracies,

TABLE 6-2   Life Expectancy Under Dictatorships and Democracies

Per Capita Income, $	Life Expectancy, Democracies		Life Expectancy, Dictatorships		Difference
0–1,000	47.2	(11)	46.4	(215)	0.8
1,001–2,000	56.3	(39)	52.2	(144)	4.1
2,001–3,000	63.6	(34)	59.2	(59)	4.4
3,001–4,000	67.3	(30)	64.2	(44)	3.1
4,001–5,000	70.2	(19)	65.0	(25)	5.2
5,001–6,000	71.3	(23)	68.6	(18)	2.7
6,001–	73.2	(239)	67.6	(18)	5.6
Total	69.3	(395)	53.3	(521)	16.0

although it is nothing like 16 years.[8] For countries with per capita incomes less than $1,001, life expectancy in both democracies and dictatorships is low, but the democracies have an advantage of eight-tenths of a year. At all levels of prosperity, democracies have some advantage, reaching as high as an increase of 5.2 years of life expectancy for countries with per capita income of $4,001–$5,000, and an increase of 5.6 years for countries with per capita income greater than $6,000.

The number of countries falling into each type appears in parentheses, and from these we can see why the difference was so great before we controlled for the countries' per capita incomes.[9] The poorest group has 215 dictatorships, compared with only 11 democracies (countries such as India). At the other end are only 18 dictatorships with per capita income over $6,000, but 239 democracies (mostly from North America and western Europe).

The conclusion we draw from holding per capita income constant is that although most of the difference in life expectancies was due to the difference in how well off democracies and dictatorships are, a substantial difference still exists between democracies and dictatorships even when per capita income is taken into account.

The technique demonstrated here of holding a variable constant—literally separating the subjects into new little groups and doing the same analysis within each of these groups—is the simplest technique one can use to eliminate a third variable. Statistical techniques such as multiple regression, which we will look at in Chapter 9, *artificially* hold variables constant, and their effect is approximately the same as the direct technique I used here. The advantage of such statistical techniques is that they can conveniently hold several variables constant simultaneously. Doing this with the direct technique would not be easy. First, it would result in a horrendous number of tiny tables. More seriously, many of these would be based on rather small numbers of cases, and their meaning would thus be uncertain.

■ Further Discussion

I have presented here only a few examples of the more commonly used research designs, and my analysis of them has included only a sample of the possible alternative explanations for each design. A more complete treatment of research design, excellent and readable, is provided in Thomas D. Cook and Donald T. Campbell's *Quasi-Experimentation: Design and Analysis Issues for Field Setting* (1979); or more recent and even more complete (but not quite as readable), William R. Shadish, Thomas D. Cook, and Donald T. Campbell *Experimental and Quasi-Experimental Designs for Generalized Causal Inference* (2002). I have relied heavily on their approach in this chapter. Christopher H. Achen's *The Statistical Analysis of Quasi-Experiments* (1986) explores these issues with great wisdom; Chapters 1 and 2 are easily accessible to readers with limited technical preparation. A good treatment of the concept of "cause" in relation to research design is found in Blalock (1964, Chapters 1 and 2). Tingsten (1937) provides an example of unusually

---

[8]Based on Przeworski et al. (2000), p. 229.
[9]The reason the number of countries is so high is that the authors counted each country at several different points in its history; some countries appear in the data set four or more times.

careful and creative interpretations, developed in the face of quite limited research designs. Several interesting examples of improvised research designs in field research on animal behavior can be found in Eisner (2005).

The literature on the use of true experiments in political science is burgeoning. Good examples are Kinder and Palfrey (1993); a special issue of the journal *Political Analysis* (volume 10, no. 4, Autumn 2002); and a special issue, edited by Donald Green and Alan Gerber, of *American Behavioral Scientist* (volume 48, no. 1, January 2004).

One question that you might consider in connection with this chapter is: Why should theory-oriented, empirical political research be based almost exclusively on causal relationships rather than on relationships in general?

Selection of Observations for Study

So far in this book, we have looked at how you can develop a research question, measure the variables involved, and look for relationships among them to provide answers to the research question. A further important factor underlies this whole process, however. To do all these things, you must select a set of observations to look at, and your selection of cases can sharply affect or even distort what you will find. Further, it is often the case that the "selection" occurs by subtle processes other than your own choice. In this chapter, I want to alert you to the importance of case selection (whether it is done by you or by nature), and to show you some basic principles that will help you to select cases in ways that will allow you a clean examination of your research question.

A central theme in this book, which you saw especially in the two chapters on measurement and which you will see again in later chapters, is that we need to construct our research operations so that the relationships we observe among the variables we have measured mirror faithfully the theoretical relationships we are interested in. (This was the point of Figure 4-1, for instance.) It will not surprise you, then, that case selection is judged by how well it produces observed relationships that faithfully mirror the theoretical relationships we are trying to test.

Consider the following examples:

- I described earlier the strange case of the *Literary Digest*, which in 1936 predicted that Franklin Roosevelt would lose the election by a landslide on the basis of questionnaires sent to subscribers to their magazine, car owners, and those having telephone service (not a representative group of American voters in those days) (see pp. 50–51). The cases the magazine had chosen to look at (subscribers, etc.) did not faithfully mirror the American electorate.

- College students taking psychology courses are routinely used for experiments to measure psychological processes. For instance, an experiment using college students might study the effect of drinking coffee on one's ability to memorize long strings of numbers. Researchers justify doing this by arguing that the processes they are studying are universal, so even though their test subjects are not at all representative of the human population, that does not matter. The relationship they are looking for would be expected to be the same in any kind of group of people, so their students are as good as any other for the test.

• Most graduate departments admit students to their programs based in part on each student's scores on the Graduate Record Examination (GRE). From time to time, a department will consider dropping the exam because when one looks at the performance of graduate students in the department, how they did on the GRE has little to do with how well they have done in the graduate program. Therefore, it is argued, the test is a nearly irrelevant predictor of success in the graduate program and should be dropped as a tool for assessment.

However, this argument relies on data from those admitted to the program to generalize to the population of all students who might apply to the program. Clearly, the students admitted into the program are an atypical sample from the population, since they all did well enough on the GRE to get into the program. But would students who did badly on the GRE do well in the program? We cannot know, because no such students are in the group we are able to observe. Since all of the students we *are* able to observe have similarly high scores on the GRE, any variations in their performance almost surely are due to other things and cannot tell us anything about the effect of GRE scores on performance.

In this case, selection of a potentially biased sample did not result from a decision the researcher made, but inheres in the situation. Nature did it.

• John Zaller (1998), studying whether incumbent members of Congress had extra advantages in garnering votes, had to work with another selection problem dealt by nature. His theory predicted that incumbent members' safety from electoral defeat, as measured by their share of the vote, would increase with every term they served, but at a decreasing rate. So he examined the vote margins of incumbents running for reelection, at varying levels of seniority. A number of seats were uncontested, however, because the incumbent was so safe that no one wanted to take her on. So the available set of congressional races consisted only of those districts in which someone felt it made sense to challenge the incumbent.

Zaller stated his problem:

> To set [these races] aside, as is sometimes done, would be to set aside those cases in which incumbents have been most successful in generating electoral security, thereby understating the amount of electoral security that develops. On the other hand, to regard victory in an uncontested race as evidence that the MC [member of congress] has captured 100 percent of the vote would probably exaggerate MCs' actual level of support. (p. 136)

In other words, if he ignored the selection problem, he would understate the amount of safety that long-time incumbents accrue. But if instead he treated the unchallenged incumbents as having gotten 100 percent of the vote, he would be overstating their safety. (His approximated solution was to estimate from other factors the vote that the unchallenged incumbents would have gotten if they *had been* challenged, and then to insert those simulated estimates as the observations for the unchallenged incumbents—not a perfect solution, but the one that made the best approximation.)

- The general understanding when new democracies emerged in Eastern Europe after the fall of the Soviet Union was that unless they were culturally homogeneous like Poland, they were "ethnic powder kegs" that had been held in check only by Soviet repression and were now prone to explode in ethnic violence. As Mihaela Mihaelescu (2007) pointed out, however, this general impression had come about because almost all scholars who looked at ethnic conflict in new Eastern European democracies were drawn to the dramatic outbreaks of violence in the former Yugoslavia. In fact, of fourteen new states in Eastern Europe with significant ethnic minorities, only four experienced violent ethnic conflict, and three of these were various parts of former Yugoslavia.

In this case, scholars' attraction to the dramatic cases led to a strangely "selected" body of scholarship, in which the full range of possibilities did not get examined.

SAMPLING FROM A POPULATION OF POTENTIAL OBSERVATIONS

The *Literary Digest* example, the discussion of using college students to generalize to all adults in psychological tests, and scholars' choice of Eastern European countries to study, are all examples of the problem of "sampling." We usually cannot study all possible observations to which our theory applies. We cannot, for example, ask every American adult how he or she expects to vote in an election. And, though it would be (barely) possible to do detailed analysis and fieldwork in each country of the world (or of Eastern Europe), limitations of time and resources usually bar us from doing so. As a result, we usually work with a sample we draw from the universe of all possible observations to which a theory applies. As noted earlier, the guiding rule in choosing observations for study is that the relationships we are looking for in the full universe of possible cases should be mirrored faithfully among the observations we are using.

Random Sampling

When we are able to draw a fairly large number of observations, the "Cadillac" method is to draw a random sample from the full population of possible cases. In random sampling, it is purely a matter of chance which cases from the full population end up in the sample for observation; that is, each member of the population has an equal chance of being drawn for the sample. It is as if we had flipped coins for each possible case and, say, admitted into the sample any case that got heads ten times in a row. (In reality, scholars use computer-generated random numbers to identify which members of the full population should join the sample for observation.)

If a sample has been drawn randomly, we are assured that any relationship in which we are interested should be mirrored faithfully in the sample, at least in the sense that, across repeated samplings of this sort, *on the average* the relationships we would see would be the same as the relationship in the full population. Even random samples will diverge by accident from the full population. For instance, although there is a "gender gap" in American voting, with men favoring the Republican party more than women do, it would not be unusual for a sample of ten Americans to include a group of women who were more Republican than the men in the sample. Since in fact men are more likely to be Republicans than women are, most samples of ten Americans would show men to be the more Republican, but it would still happen fairly often, by chance, that the ten people you drew for a sample would show the reverse of that. If you took a large number of such samples, however, and averaged them, the average expression of the gender gap would almost surely mirror faithfully the gender gap in the full population.

The principle here is the same as that in randomized experiments, which we looked at in Chapter 6. In randomized experiments, two groups are randomly chosen, so they cannot be expected to differ in any significant way that could interfere with a causal interpretation from the experiment. In other words, randomization ensures that any two groups chosen are essentially alike. But if that is true in experiments, it must also be true when trying to generalize to a population from a sample. If any group chosen randomly from the population can be expected to be essentially the same as any other, then they must all be essentially the same as the full population.

How much variation there is from one random sample to another is hugely influenced by the size of the sample. The larger the sample, the less variation there will be from one time to another when we draw samples and look at a relationship. If you drew samples of a thousand Americans, for instance, it would happen only rarely that you could have come up with a group among whom the women were more Republican than the men. (Review the discussion of the law of large numbers, p. 61. We saw there that variation in anything we are observing diminishes as we use larger and larger samples to examine it.)

One nice thing about random samples is that there is a very precisely worked out mathematical system to ascertain, for a sample of any given size, exactly how likely it is that the sample result is any given distance from what you would have seen in the population. It is this mathematical system that allows pollsters to say of a national poll, for example, that it shows support of 56 percent for Barack Obama, within an error of plus or minus 3 percentage points.

It always seems surprising that samples do not really need to be all that large to give an accurate rendition of a population. Typically, surveys of American citizens are considered to have sufficient cases for accurately mirroring the population of 309,000,000 if they have questioned a sample of two or three thousand people. It is kind of amazing that just a few thousand out of hundreds of millions would be sufficient to estimate the population to within a couple of percentage points.

Now, while the true random sample is the Cadillac of sampling, it is rarely used for large populations. For relatively small populations, such as the population of a city, true random sampling is often feasible, and is then, of course, the method of choice. But you can imagine what it would cost to sample the U.S. population in a truly random way—sending an interviewer to interview a single person in Menominee, Wisconsin, another to interview a person in San Diego, and so on.

HOW TO DRAW A RANDOM SAMPLE

If you want to draw a random sample of a population, you need (1) a list of everyone in the population you want to sample and (2) a list of random numbers. Many such lists are published, often appearing as appendices to textbooks on statistics. You can also generate your own list, using random number generators at sites such as http://www.random.org/integers/.

A typical set of random numbers might look like these that I generated from random.org:

3451	1644	3129	6059	5927
9472	0732	4184	8373	0789
2691	7836	0854	7743	4202
3233	7486	1759	1169	2086

This is only a small part of the list of 10,000 random numbers I generated, but you can see what such a list looks like.

To draw a random sample, you would now establish a rule by which any random number would correspond to one member of the population. For instance, if there were 40,000,000 people in the population, and you had a list of all of them, you could start from the upper left corner of the list and combine pairs of numbers to make eight-digit numbers. The rule could then be that each eight-digit number you read would cause the corresponding member in the list of the population to be in your sample. For instance, the first number would be 34511644, and this would cause the 34,511,644th entry in the population list to be drawn for your sample. Next would come the 31,296,059th entry in the population list, and so on. When you reached 59279472, you would skip that random number because there are not that many people on the population list. But the next entry, 07324184, would yield the 7,324,184th entry from the population list.

You can see how difficult this can be for a large population, and why alternative, quasi-random sampling methods are generally used in these cases. For smaller populations, however, random sampling can work easily enough. For instance, if you wanted to do a survey of students at your institution, you could start with the student directory, as a population list. Your rule for sampling could then be that the first two digits of each four-digit random number would direct you to a page of the directory, and the next two digits would indicate how far down you should go on the page to draw the member of the sample. For instance, in the example above, starting from the upper left-hand corner, you would first go to the 34th page and call the 51st name on the page; you would then go to the 16th page and call the 44th name; and so on.

Quasi-Random Sampling

When a large population is involved, various methods exist to draw "quasi-random" approximations to a random sample. The National Election Study at the University of Michigan uses what is called a "cluster sample": About 100 localities are first selected, and then, within each of these, a certain number of individuals are randomly chosen for the sample. This allows the survey to use approximately 100 interviewers, one based in each of the localities chosen. Then, instead of having interviewers fly or drive hundreds of miles for a single interview, each interviewer can readily reach the 20 or 30 subjects randomly selected from her cluster. The end result approximates a random sample closely. And statistical adjustments can be made to take into account the clustered structure of the sample, so that it operates almost exactly like a random sample.

An alternative system is to draw a truly random sample of telephones by having a computer dial telephones randomly ("random digit dialing," or RDD sampling). This allows access to a random sample without the difficulty or expense of getting an interviewer to the person's door, but it is increasingly difficult to draw a sample in this way that represents the broad population accurately. In 1932, at the time of the *Literary Digest* poll described earlier, the problem with telephone lists was that only the middle class had telephones. Today, almost everyone has a telephone, so in principle RDD sampling could work well. But in practice, people's use of their phones varies so much that the group that can actually be reached by phone at a given time is problematic as a sample. Some people are at work all day, so their telephones will ring at any daytime hour but not be answered unless by a machine. Others are always gone in the evenings. Some telephones have devices to block unsolicited calls. Some families have two phone lines and therefore would be twice as likely to end up in the sample. RDD samples are rather problematic as approximations of a random sample of the population.

Looking back now at the first two examples stated, we can see from our consideration of random sampling how they might (or might not) be questionable as samples. The *Literary Digest* poll was drawn before sampling was well understood. Its sample of telephone owners, subscribers to the magazine, and those appearing on state lists of registered automobiles was simply a terrible sample, very much skewed toward the middle class and would have produced an erroneous prediction any time the middle class voted differently than the population as a whole. The sample of college students, on the other hand, might provide a reasonable basis for drawing psychological conclusions about people in general, even though they are clearly not a random sample of the full population *if* we are confident that their psychological processes are the same as psychological processes among the full population. In this case, even though the sample is not random, it is much cheaper than trying to draw a random sample of all people, and can serve as a satisfactory quasi-random sample if processes are indeed the same as for the full population.

Purposive Sampling

Sometimes we deliberately want to sample in a nonrandom way, not just for reasons of efficiency or cost, but because a deliberately constructed, nonrandom sample serves a purpose for our research. If we wanted to compare the political choices of African Americans and whites, for instance, a purely random sample (or good approximation, such as a national cluster sample) would probably not yield enough

African American citizens for a good comparison. If it faithfully mirrored the population, about one-eighth of the sample should be African American, too small a group for reliable comparisons in a sample of the usual size. One solution would be to draw a monstrously large sample, but that would, of course, be very expensive. Another solution, if the purpose of the study is to look at the politics of race, is to draw what is called a "purposive" sample.

A purposive sample does not attempt to replicate the full population. Rather, it draws subjects to maximize variation in the independent variable of interest, so that the relationships we are looking for will be very clear.[1] In the preceding example, we could sample African Americans randomly and sample whites randomly, combining them to construct a sample that is half white and half African American. Like all purposive samples, this would not work as a general reflection of the full population. If African Americans were more likely to vote Democratic than whites, for instance, the sample would give an unreasonably high estimate of the Democratic vote. But the one thing for which the sample is going to be used, estimating a relationship or set of relationships based on race, is fine. Since both African Americans and whites have been randomly (or quasi-randomly) selected, a comparison of, say, the news-watching habits of the two races should reflect accurately the relationship in the full population.

One reason that most sampling is random or quasi-random, rather than purposive, is that usually when we draw a sample, it is intended to serve multiple purposes. And we should probably also anticipate that as we proceed with analysis, we might want to look at things in the data other than what we had anticipated when we were first drawing up the sample. A purposive sample works only for the particular independent variable or variables on which we have based the sample. So it is usually safer and more useful to draw up a more general sample, random or quasi-random, rather than one focused just on the single task we start with.

Selection of Cases for Case Studies

Another kind of purposive sampling comes into play when we are dealing with such small numbers of cases that random sampling would not be very helpful in any case. A case study is an intensive study of one or a few cases. It might be a study of a particular president's administrative style, an intensive study of the attitudes and ideologies of a few people, or, as it is most frequently seen, a study of some aspect of politics in one or a few countries. In principle, even if we are looking at only two or three cases, random selection of the case or cases would reflect the full population in the long run. But in practice, the law of large numbers is working so weakly when we study only a few cases that the divergence of any case from the full population, though it will be "only random," will still be huge.[2] Under these circumstances, there

---

[1]We will see (pp. 107–109) why we do not draw the sample to maximize variation in the *dependent* variable.

[2]This is a situation that seems to fit Keynes' well-known comment that in the long run we shall all be dead. In principle and in the long run, a randomly selected sample of even just a couple of cases will mirror the full population. But any given couple of cases—for instance, the ones you plan to study—are likely to diverge sharply from the full population.

is much more to be gained by intelligently choosing the case(s) to pick up the relationship of interest, rather than by randomly drawing the case(s). If we want to study the effect of authoritarian government on economic growth, for instance, it makes sense to seek a couple of authoritarian states and a couple of nonauthoritarian ones for comparison, rather than just taking four randomly chosen states.

CENSORED DATA

The last three of the five examples in the introduction to this chapter were examples of "censored data," instances in which part of the range of cases to which a theory applies are cut off and unavailable to the researcher, either by the researcher's choice or by circumstances. In the case of GRE scores, any generalization about the importance of test scores is obviously meant to apply to all students who could apply for admission, but the researcher can see the performance only of students who were admitted to the program. John Zaller's theory of congressional elections was obviously meant to apply to all members of Congress, but he could observe election outcomes only for those members who were challenged by an opponent. In the case of ethnic violence in Eastern Europe, the theory that ancient hatreds would flare up after Soviet repression was lifted from the region obviously was meant to apply to all Eastern European democracies with large ethnic minorities, but scholars had chosen to look only at the dramatic cases in which conflict had actually occurred.

The problem of censored data is always severe, because it requires researchers and their readers to make strong assumptions about what "might have been" in the range of data that are not available. Sometimes there are reasonable ways to fill in the spaces. Zaller, for instance, estimated on the basis of other variables what vote unchallenged members might have been expected to receive had they been challenged, and inserted those estimates into his study as imputed data. And sometimes the answer is easy: If investigators have ignored some of the range but can study it, that just makes a neat and interesting study for another investigator to conduct, filling in for their short-sightedness. Mihaelescu was able to do a useful and rewarding study, just picking up on what others had not noticed: that most Eastern European states with ethnic minorities had not exploded when the Soviets left.

When Scholars Pick the Cases They're Interested In

Often, as in this example of ethnic conflict in Eastern Europe, investigators doing case studies gravitate to the outcomes in which they are interested, and pick cases for which the outcome was strong or dramatic. They then look at those cases to see what caused the thing in which they are interested. Scholars of revolution are prone to look at the Soviet Union or Cuba. Scholars of economic growth are prone to look at countries such as Korea, Taiwan, or Brazil, which have grown rapidly. Scholars of the presidency are likely to look at the administrations of dramatic presidents who had a large impact, such as Franklin Roosevelt or Ronald Reagan, rather than less showy presidents such as Calvin Coolidge.

I will argue later that choosing cases to maximize variation in the dependent variable distorts relationships, and that one should instead select to maximize variation in the independent variable or variables. But another result of choosing cases that exhibit most strongly the thing we are interested in is that it often also results in a censored data set. Barbara Geddes (2003) gives a nice example of this. She points out that a strong argument arose in the 1980s, based on case studies of rapidly developing countries, that it was important for developing countries' governments to repress organized labor to let industry develop rapidly. Most case studies of economic growth at the time focused on Mexico, Brazil, and the "Asian Tigers": Singapore, South Korea, and Taiwan. As Geddes points out, the focus on these several cases of rapid development led to a very wrong-headed conclusion.

Geddes developed a measure for how much labor organization was repressed by governments, and then placed the five frequently studied countries on a graph of labor repression, related to growth in per capita GDP from 1970 to 1981. As you can see in her graph, reproduced in Figure 7-1, all four cases fall in the upper right-hand part of the graph (b: high labor repression, rapid economic growth); and the lowest growth (Mexico's) also happens to coincide with a lower repression of labor.

As Geddes showed in work adapted here in Figure 7-2, however, if we had all of the developing countries of the 1970s before us, we would see that there was little or no advantage for the countries that repressed labor. Looking at the full range of labor repression and the full range of economic outcomes, we find about as many low-growth countries with low levels of labor repression as with high labor repression. There is very little pattern in the figure, indicating little relationship between the two variables. There may be a slight relationship; the upper left-hand part of the

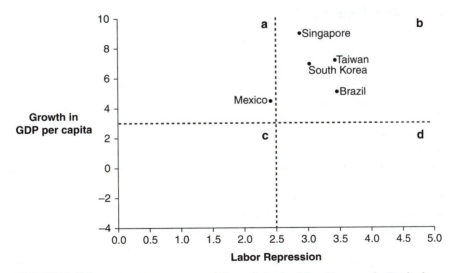

FIGURE 7-1 Labor Repression and Growth in the Most Frequently Studied Cases, 1970–1981. (GDP per Capita from Penn World Tables.)
Source: Geddes (2003), p. 101

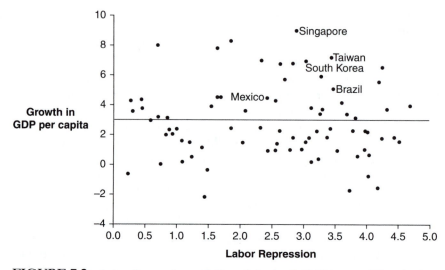

FIGURE 7-2   Labor Repression and Growth in the Full Universe of Developing Countries, 1970–1981. (GDP per Capita from Penn World Tables.)
Adapted from Geddes (2003), p. 103

figure is a little less thickly filled with cases, indicating that there were somewhat fewer low-repression countries with high growth. But overall, there is nothing like the kind of relationship that appeared from the censored data in Figure 7-1.

When Nature Censors Data

What can one do about censored data? If the data have been censored because of decisions of researchers, the problem is easy to solve, and can in fact offer a nice chance to another researcher to make a significant contribution. This is what Mihaelescu or Geddes did, for example. All one has to do in this case is to seek out a broader range of information, and bring it into the analysis.

But if the data have been censored by nature, as in the example of GRE scores, or Zaller's work on congressional elections, there are no easy solutions. The missing cases are gone and are not going to reappear. One cannot under ordinary circumstances admit to graduate school a group of students who have done badly on the GRE test to see how they perform. And one cannot decree that all congressional incumbents will be challenged for reelection.

In such cases, we are forced to draw conclusions of what might have been had the data not been censored. This means we must make some assumptions, and justify them, for drawing "what if?" conclusions. We might, for example, seek out those graduate departments that for whatever reasons do not use the GRE as a criterion, find the GRE scores of students who attended there, and see how they did. This would not be a perfect solution; it would require the assumption that departments that did not require the GRE were like other departments in every other way, which is, of course, unlikely. And it would ignore the fact that the low-GRE students admitted to those departments would be atypical as well; since they would have been rejected by other departments but ended up being accepted into the non-GRE departments, they are probably unusually high achievers in other ways. Nonetheless, despite the fact that assumptions are required, this would be better than ignoring the initial problem of censored data.

Similarly, Zaller had to make a number of assumptions to predict what vote unchallenged members would have gotten had they been challenged.

A good deal of artfulness is required to analyze data that have been censored by nature, but a creative imagination will be rewarded by substantially improved estimation. And it's a nice challenge.

SELECTION ALONG THE DEPENDENT VARIABLE: DON'T DO IT!

When we looked at selection of samples, we noted that you might usefully draw a purposive sample to get sufficient variation in the variables of interest. A very important rule, however, is that this can work well when you select cases to maximize variation on the independent variable, but that you should never select to maximize variation on the dependent variable. If you maximize variation in the independent variable, the relationship you observe will mirror nicely the true relationship, at least if you have enough cases so that the law of large numbers can work for you. But if you maximize variation in the dependent variable, you will distort the true relationship. And it does not matter in this case whether you have a large or a small sample.

Let us illustrate this with a hypothetical city with significant racial polarization. In Figure 7-3, we see the breakdown of support for the mayor, by race. These are the true population figures. Taking percentages, we find that 80 percent of whites support the mayor, but only 45 percent of nonwhites support the mayor.

In Figure 7-4, I have drawn two samples of 400 from this population, one a purposive sample to maximize variation in race and the other a purposive sample to

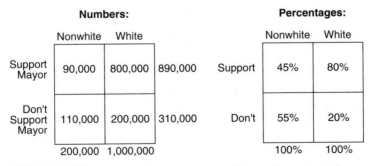

FIGURE 7-3   Race and Support for the Mayor: Hypothetical Polarized City

(A) Selection Along Independent Variable

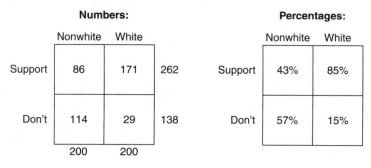

(B) Selection Along Dependent Variable

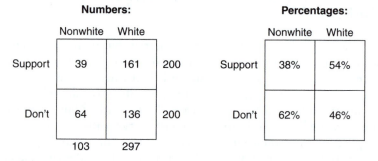

FIGURE 7-4   Selection Along Independent, Dependent Variables

maximize variation in support or opposition to the mayor. Figure 7-4 (A) shows the results of drawing 200 nonwhites randomly from the pool of nonwhites shown in Figure 7-3 and similarly drawing 200 whites from the pool of whites. While this sample is on the small side, it draws enough nonwhites to make fairly reliable comparisons with whites; and since it is drawn along the independent variable, it replicates faithfully the relationship in the full population. In the sample, 43 percent of nonwhites support the mayor (compared with 45 percent in the full population), as do 85 percent of whites (compared with 80 percent in the full population). The numbers diverge by about the amount we would normally expect in drawing a random sample of 400 cases, but the relationship is recognizably the same.[3] In fact, it is more accurate than what we would have gotten from a purely random sample of the population, since that would have produced only a small number of nonwhites, with a widely variable estimate of nonwhites' support for the mayor.

Figure 7-4 (B) shows the results of a purposive sample of the same size that maximizes variation in the dependent variable, support for the mayor. As we see,

[3]This sample, by the way, offers a good tangible example of about how much variability one gets with random sampling of this size.

drawing this sort of sample does not produce a faithful reflection of the relationship in the full population. In the full population, 80 percent of whites support the mayor, compared with 45 percent of nonwhites, a relationship of sharp polarization. But the sample maximizing variation in support appears to indicate a considerably weaker relationship, with 54 percent of whites supporting the mayor, compared with 38 percent of nonwhites. This does not present the same picture of sharp polarization.

Why is it that sampling along the independent variable produces accurate estimates of the relationship, but sampling along the dependent variable does not? It makes sense, because the purpose of the analysis is to compare nonwhites' and whites' support for the mayor. Drawing groups from the two and comparing them fits this very well. But drawing groups of supporters and opponents of the mayor and then comparing whites' and nonwhites' support does not parallel the research question in the same way. And most importantly, changing the relative numbers of supporters and opponents from what one sees in the full population changes the percent of supporters in both racial groups, in ways that distort the percentages in both groups. (Note that sampling on the independent variable distorts the proportions of whites and nonwhites in the population, but that this is actually helpful; it increases the number of nonwhites available for analysis. It leaves unaffected the percentages in which we are interested.)

SELECTION OF CASES FOR CASE STUDIES (AGAIN)

The preceding example clarifies why one should not sample on the dependent variable, but it may puzzle the reader a bit. It looks a little artificial—why would anyone do this in the first place? Actually, this does not come up often with regard to large-scale sampling. It does, however, come up time and again with regard to intensive studies of one or a few cases (so-called case studies), and the logic there is just the same as the logic of the preceding example. I chose to introduce the idea through a large-scale survey example because the problem is easier to see there, but the real importance of the argument is with regard to case studies.

It is so easy when studying a political outcome to choose a case in which the outcome occurred, and see whether the things you expected to have been the causes were present. Or, if you properly wanted to avoid the problem of censored data, you might choose two cases, one in which the outcome had occurred and another in which it had not, and see whether the things you expected to have been the causes were present. In fact, doing something like this is the most obvious and intuitive thing to do; see where the thing you're trying to explain has occurred, and try to account for it.

It is intuitive, but it is wrong, for the same reason we saw in the earlier example—namely, that it distorts the likelihood that the outcome occurs or does not occur. Choosing instead cases that represent varying instances of your explanatory variable allows you to examine the full range over which your explanation is meant to apply, but it does not fiddle at all with the likelihood that the outcome occurs, and so allows you to examine straightforwardly where the chips fall under varying circumstances.

ANOTHER STRATEGY, HOWEVER: SINGLE-CASE STUDIES SELECTED FOR THE RELATIONSHIP BETWEEN THE INDEPENDENT AND DEPENDENT VARIABLES

So far in this chapter, I have dealt with issues having to do with the following: the selection of cases; the question of sampling from a larger population; the problem of censored data; and the question of whether to select cases on the basis of what you are trying to explain or on the basis of your independent variable. This has all been aimed at research in which we are comparing cases (anywhere from two cases to thousands) to look at the pattern of the relationship between independent and dependent variables. For such research, the selection of cases affects profoundly what results you see. Case-selection forms the foundation for all of your examination of evidence, and it will work well as long as your procedures fulfill the basic principle enunciated so far in this chapter: The relationship to be observed among the cases you have selected must mirror faithfully the true relationship among all potential cases.

There is another kind of case study, however, in which you do not look at a relationship between variables across cases, but instead look at a *single* case to help clarify or illuminate a theory. For instance, Gerhard Loewenberg (1968) was struck by the fact that Germany by the late 1960s looked just the opposite of what we would have expected from theories of electoral systems. It had a proportional representation electoral system, and according to theory, this should lead to a multiparty system if the country had multiple divisions in society (see the discussion of Duverger's theory, pp. 2–3); and, Germany had demonstrated in the 1920s and 1930s that it did indeed have a richly divided society. (At its highest, the number of parties represented in the prewar German Reichstag had been 32!) But by the late 1960s, Germany had almost a two-party system.[4] How could this be? Loewenberg studied the German case in depth to see what had produced this exception to the theory, in order to refine the theory and illuminate how it worked.

Note that Loewenberg did not pick this case just in terms of the dependent variable. He did not simply pick a case with a dramatic or interesting outcome. Rather, he picked it because of the *combination* of the electoral system and historic divisions in society (independent variables) and the party system (dependent variable). When a case study is being used in this way—not to test a theory by trying it out to see how well it works, but rather to develop the theory by looking in detail at a case in which the theory is working in particular ways—we should not ignore the dependent variable in selecting our case. But we should also not select the case just in terms of the dependent variable. Rather, we should pick the case because of how the theory appears to be working, as indicated by the combination of dependent and

---

[4]Since then, the system has moved back somewhat toward multipartism. Three parties were represented in the parliament in the 1960s, with the two largest (the Social Democrats and the Christian Democrats) holding about 90 percent of the seats. Currently there are five parties represented, and the "big two" have 73 percent of the seats.

independent variables. And, we should then be clear that we are not providing a test of the theory. Rather, this is a strategy for further refinement of the theory.[5]

■■ Further Discussion

John Gerring (2007) provides a comprehensive and intelligent review of case selection. Geddes (2003) has a very nice chapter, "How the Cases You Choose Affect the Answers You Get." A good, though fairly technical, treatment of censored data is presented in Przeworski et al. (2000) in an appendix, "Selection Models." Another good treatment of case selection is King, Keohane, and Verba (1994), Chapter 4.

[5]This argument is developed in Shively (2006).

Introduction to Statistics

Measuring Relationships for Interval Data

In Chapter 6, we were concerned generally with "relationships" between independent and dependent variables. That is, we wanted to see whether the presence or absence of a test factor affected the value of the dependent variable. This was too simple, for two reasons.

First, as noted in footnote 5 in that chapter, the test factor in field research is frequently not something that is simply present or absent; rather, it takes on a variety of values. Our task then is not just to see whether the *presence or absence* of a test factor affects the value of the dependent variable, but instead, to see whether and how the *value* of the independent variable affects the value of the dependent variable. For example, in relating education to income, we do not treat people simply as "educated" or "not educated." They have varying amounts of education, and our task is to see whether the amount of education a person has affects his or her income.

Second, "relationship" cannot be dichotomized, although I treated it as a dichotomy in Chapter 6, to ease the presentation there. Two variables are not simply related or not related. Relationships vary in two ways: first, in how *strongly* the independent variable affects the dependent variable. For instance, education might have only a minor effect on income. The average income of college graduates might be $33,000 and the average income of high school dropouts might be $30,000. Or, it might have a major effect. College graduates might average $50,000, while high school dropouts average $15,000.

Relationships also vary in how *completely* the independent variable determines scores on the dependent variable. College graduates might average $50,000 income and high school dropouts $15,000, for instance, yet there might still be much variation in incomes that could not be attributed to variation in people's education. Some college graduates might make only $10,000 a year and some high school dropouts might make $80,000 or $90,000 a year, even though the *average* income of the college graduates was higher than the *average* income of the dropouts. This would indicate that although education affected incomes sharply, it was relatively incomplete as an explanation of people's incomes. Because income still varied a good deal within each level of the independent variable, there must be other things affecting income in important ways, and we often would guess incorrectly if we tried to predict a person's income solely on the basis of education. This is what it means to say that education is not a very "complete" explanation of income.

Thus variables are not simply "related" or "not related." Their relationship may be such that the independent variable has a *greater or lesser effect* on the dependent variable; and it may be such that the independent variable determines the dependent variable *more or less completely*. Generally speaking, political research is not so much concerned with whether or not two variables are related but with whether or not they have a "strong" relationship (in one or both of the senses used earlier). This can be seen in our examples of research design in Chapter 6. Although for the sake of simplicity these were presented as if we were interested only in whether or not a relationship existed, it is clear that what was of interest to the investigators in each case was finding out how *strong* a relationship existed. In "Presidential Lobbying," for instance, the president was not simply concerned with whether or not he was able to influence voting for the bill, but with how *many* votes he could swing.

Our task in evaluating the results of research, then, is to measure how strong a relationship exists between the independent variable(s) and the dependent variable. The tools we need to accomplish this task are found in the field of statistics.

STATISTICS

Although modern political scientists have begun to use statistics extensively only in the past several decades, it was actually political scientists of a sort who first developed the field, for statistics originally grew out of the need to keep records for the state. The name *statistics* derives from the Latin *statisticus*, "of state affairs."

Statistics includes two main activities: statistical inference and statistical measurement (including the measurement of relationships, with which we are concerned in this chapter). Statistical inference consists of estimating how likely it is that a particular result could be due to chance; it tells us how reliable the results of our research are. I discuss inference in Chapter 10. In this chapter and in Chapter 9, I introduce some statistical techniques for measuring the strength of relationships.

IMPORTANCE OF LEVELS OF MEASUREMENT

In Chapter 5, we saw that we have more information about a relationship between variables if we work at a higher level of measurement than if we work at a lower level of measurement. It should not be too surprising that methods of measuring relationships between variables are different depending on the level at which the variables are measured. If we know more about a relationship, we should be able to measure a greater variety of things about it. Just as higher levels of measurement yield relatively richer information about a variable, so techniques for measuring relationships at high levels of measurement give relatively richer information about those relationships.

Basically, there are two major types of techniques: those appropriate for data measured at the interval level and those suited for lower-level measurements. Recall that we mentioned two ways to measure the "strength" of a relationship between two variables: (1) by how great a difference the independent variable makes in the dependent variable, that is, how greatly values of the dependent variable differ, given varying scores on the independent variable; or (2) by how completely the independent variable determines the dependent variable, that is, how *complete* an explanation of the dependent variable is provided by the independent variable. I shall call the first way of measuring a relationship *effect-descriptive* and the second *correlational*. The critical difference between working with interval-measured data and working with data measured at a lower level is that effect-descriptive measurement can apply only to interval-scale data. Correlational measurement of one sort or another can apply to data measured at any level.

Ordinal and nominal measurement techniques cannot tell us how great a difference in the dependent variable is produced by a given difference in the independent variable, although this is precisely what is required to measure the relationship in an effect-descriptive way. The whole point of nominal and ordinal measurement is that in neither do we have available a unit by which to measure the difference between two values of a variable. This means that we cannot measure how great a difference is induced in the dependent variable by a change in the independent variable. If we are using an ordinal-scale variable, we know whether one value is higher than another, but we do not know how much higher it is. If we are using a nominal-scale variable, of course, all we know is whether the two values are distinct.

This becomes a particularly important distinction in political research, because under most circumstances, effect-descriptive ways of measuring the strength of a relationship are more useful than correlational ways. I demonstrate this in the next few sections.

WORKING WITH INTERVAL DATA

Regression Analysis

A convenient way to summarize data on two interval-scale variables so that we can easily see what is going on in the relationship between them is to plot all the observations on a *scattergram*, as in Figure 8-1. Each dot in the scattergram represents one observation (a person, state, or country, for example), placed on the graph according to its scores on the two variables. For instance, dot A represents an observation that combines scores of 3.5 on the independent variable and 5 on the dependent variable. Dot B represents an observation with scores of 12 on the independent variable and 17 on the dependent variable.

By looking at the pattern formed by the dots, we can tell a good deal about the relationship between the two variables. For instance, in Figure 8-1, we note that there are few dots in the lower-right and upper-left corners of the graph. This means

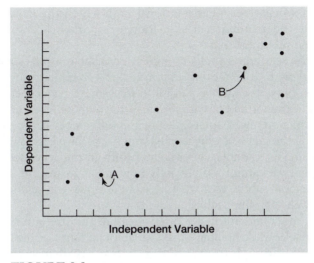

FIGURE 8-1   Scattergram

that high scores on the dependent variable tend to coincide with high scores on the independent variable, and low scores on the dependent variable tend to coincide with low scores on the independent variable. Thus we know that the two variables are positively related. Furthermore, this relationship appears to be approximately linear (see the discussion of "linear relationships" in the box on p. 71).

We have done two things so far. We have observed which way the dependent variable moves with changes in the independent variable, and we have observed that it moves at a steady rate at all values of the independent variable (a linear relationship) rather than at changing rates (a nonlinear relationship). These are both part of an effect-descriptive measurement of the relationship.

The scattergrams in Figure 8-2 illustrate various other patterns we might have observed. Graph A shows a nonlinear relationship (the dependent variable increases faster with increases in the independent variable if the independent variable has a high value). Graph B shows a linear relationship in which the dependent variable increases more gradually than in the graph in Figure 8-1.

FIGURE 8-2   Assorted Scattergrams

Graph C shows a negative linear relationship in which the dependent variable decreases as the independent variable increases. Graph D shows a pattern in which there is no relationship.

Although the scattergram tells us a great deal about a relationship, it can be unwieldy to work with. It is not uncommon in a research report to discuss 30 or 40 separate relationships. It would be painful to read such a paper if each relationship were presented in the form of a scattergram. What is more, comparing two scattergrams gives us only an approximate idea of the differences between two relationships. Comparing the graphs in Figures 8-1 and 8-2(B), we can say that in the first graph the independent variable causes greater shifts in the dependent variable than in the second, but we cannot say precisely how much greater the shifts are. If the differences were more subtle, or if we were comparing several relationships, the job would become well-nigh impossible.

Finally and most important, we often measure the strength of a relationship between two variables while holding a third variable constant (see the discussion of this topic on pp. 94–95). To do this using scattergrams may be extremely cumbersome.

For all of these reasons, it is useful to devise a precise numerical measure to summarize the relevant characteristics of a relationship shown in a scattergram. The measure commonly used to summarize the effect-descriptive characteristics of a scattergram is the *regression coefficient*.

The linear regression coefficient is derived in the following way. First, the pattern in the dots of a scattergram is summed up by the single line that best approximates it. For a linear relationship, the mathematically best procedure is to choose the unique line that minimizes the squared differences between observed values of the dependent variable and its idealized values as given by the simplifying line. This is illustrated in Figure 8-3, where a simplifying line has been drawn

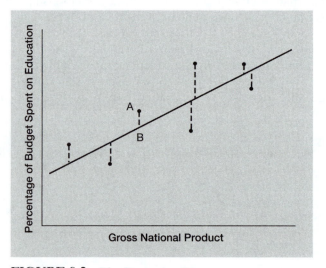

FIGURE 8-3   The Regression Line

through a scattergram with observations on seven hypothetical countries to summarize the pattern across the countries. It has been drawn to minimize the squared differences between each of the observed points, such as A and the point B at which a country having A's score on the independent variable would be expected to fall on the idealized simplifying line.

The simplifying line may be thought of as a rule for predicting scores on the dependent variable from scores on the independent variables. Its usefulness as a predictor depends on keeping the average squared value of "deviant" scores on the dependent variable as low as possible. A single summarizing line can be described more easily than a pattern of dots. In particular, a straight line such as this can be fully described by the equation

$$y = a + bx$$

where y is the predicted value of the dependent variable, x is the value of the independent variable, and a and b are numbers relating y to x. The number a, the expected value of y when x equals zero, is called the *intercept* of the regression equation; it is the value of y where the regression line crosses the y axis, that is, where x equals zero (see Figure 8-4). The number b, or the *slope* of the regression equation, shows by how many units y increases as x increases one unit. (If b is negative, y decreases as x increases; there is a negative relationship between the variables.) In other words, to find the predicted value of the dependent variable for any specified value of the independent variable, you must add a (the predicted value of y when x equals zero) to b times the number of units by which x exceeds zero.

The slope, often simply called the *regression coefficient*, is the most valuable part of this equation for most purposes in the social sciences. By telling how great a shift we can expect in the dependent variable if the independent variable shifts by one unit, the slope provides a single, precise summary measure of how great an impact

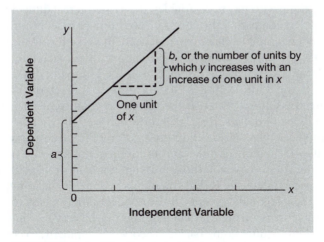

FIGURE 8-4   The Regression Equation

the independent variable has on the dependent variable. Let's assume, for instance, that the relationship between income and electoral participation is linear and can be summarized by the regression equation

$$\text{percent voting} = 50.5 + \frac{1}{2} \left(\text{income in thousands of dollars}\right)$$

This means that with every additional thousand dollars of income, $\frac{1}{2}$ percent more potential voters vote. For example, if income is \$20,000, the predicted percent voting equals $50.5 + (1/2 \times 20)$, or 60.5. If income is \$30,000, the predicted percent voting equals $50.5 + (1/2 \times 30)$, or 65.5.

Remember, however, that even though we work with neat, impersonal numbers, we do not escape the scholar's obligation to think. If we have guessed the direction of causation between x and y incorrectly, plugging in our data and getting numbers out will not make the results valid. If y causes x rather than vice versa, the formulas will still give us an a and a b, but the shift of one unit in x in the real world will *not* be followed by a shift of b units in y. Thus the arguments made in Chapter 6 apply even when we work with simple numbers like these.

The problem of comparing units. It may be seen from an examination of the concept *slope* (the number of units by which y changes with a change of one unit in x) that the slope has meaning only with regard to the units in which x and y are measured. For example, if there is a regression coefficient of -10.5 for nations' diplomatic involvement with the United States (measured by the number or magnitude of exchanges per year) predicted from their distance from the United States measured in thousands of miles, there would be a regression coefficient of -0.0105 for the same dependent variable if distance were measured in miles. That is, if diplomatic involvement could be expected to decrease by 10.5 with every 1,000 miles of distance from the United States, it would be expected to decrease by 0.0105 with every mile of distance.

If we are working with just two variables, this poses no real difficulty. But often we may be interested in comparing the effects of two or more independent variables on a particular dependent variable. If the two independent variables are measured in different sorts of units, this can be difficult. Continuing with our example, we might want to know which variable—nations' distance from the United States or the volume of their trade with the United States—has a greater impact on their diplomatic interaction with the United States. If the regression coefficient for volume of trade, measured in millions of dollars, is $+0.024$, how can we tell whether it has a greater impact on diplomatic interaction than does geographic distance, with its slope of -10? The units—thousands of miles and millions of dollars—are not comparable; therefore, the coefficients based on those units are not comparable either.

The real answer, of course, is that the numbers do have meaning, but only with relationship to their original concepts. If the concepts are not easy to compare, then regression coefficients referring to them will also not be easy to compare. The solution to the problem requires going back to theory development, to consider on what grounds your concepts can be related to each other. Apples and oranges actually can be compared, contrary to the old saying about "comparing apples and oranges," but to do so we must first specify along what dimensions our theory calls for them to be compared. We can compare them in a nutritional theory, for instance, by measuring how much vitamin C each fruit contains. Or, we could compare them in a theory of gravity by comparing their mass. To compare the effects of diplomatic interaction and geographic distance in the example above, we would have to develop in our theory dimensions along which they could be meaningfully compared.

Checking for linearity. We must be careful to make certain in using linear regression analysis that the data do fit a more or less linear pattern. Otherwise, the regression equation will distort the pattern in the data, rather than summarize it. Figure 8-5 shows a linear regression equation passed through the scattergram of a nonlinear relationship. This regression line fits the data very badly and is not a useful summary of the relationship. You should always check your data before using linear regression analysis. The best way to do this is simply to draw a scattergram (or rather, let the computer do it for you) and see whether it looks linear.

Many relationships in political science do turn out to be linear. But if the relationship you are investigating turns out to be nonlinear, that is no reason to give up analyzing it. It merely means that the relationship is more complex than you anticipated—and probably more interesting. A nonlinear regression equation may be found to fit the pattern fairly well.

In Figure 8-6, a nonlinear regression equation $y = a + b_1x - b_2x^2$ has been passed through the scattergram from Figure 8-5. It summarizes the pattern in the data more accurately. In this case, two coefficients, b_1 and b_2, are required to express the impact that a change in x will have on y, since that change is not the same at all values of x. We can see that y increases with x but decreases with the square of x. The regression equation provides a handy summary description of the effect, now a bit more complicated, that x has on y.

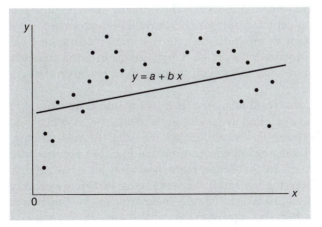

FIGURE 8-5   Linear Regression on a Nonlinear Relationship

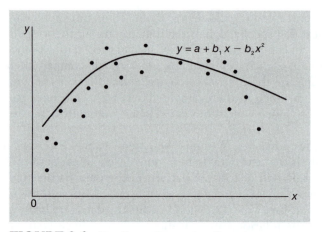

FIGURE 8-6   Nonlinear Regression Equation

Formulas are available to calculate equations for regression lines satisfying the least-squares criteria. This is particularly true for linear regression; the formulas for *a* and *b* are found in every standard statistics text, including the ones cited at the end of this chapter. But there are no set "formulas" for nonlinear regression equations, for there is an infinite variety of nonlinear equations that you might fit to any set of data. It usually is necessary to play around with alternative nonlinear equations for a while. But these, too, can be worked out readily enough.

To the extent that your research is based on a well-thought-out theory, the theory can help you to design an appropriate nonlinear equation. For instance, if your theory predicts that the dependent variable will always increase with increases in the independent variable, but at a constantly diminishing rate (a "diminishing marginal returns" model), the equation depicted in Figure 8-6 would be inappropriate because it must inevitably reverse direction at some point. An equation such as $y = a + b \log x$, as depicted in Figure 8-7, would be appropriate.

One important warning: Remember that the presentation I have made here is only a broad, introductory overview. Competence in using measures like those presented here requires more thorough training than is within the scope of this book.

Examining the residuals. Any regression line is actually a reflection of the stage that we have reached in developing a theory. Because our theory anticipates a relationship between two variables, we measure the relationship between them by calculating the regression equation for the line that best summarizes the pattern of the relationship. In this sense, regression analysis is an expression of what we already think about the subject. It may surprise us—where we expected a relationship there may be none, or it may be nonlinear, and so on. But it is an expression of what we already have been thinking about the subject.

However, the regression line can serve a further important function; by pointing out important independent variables that had not yet occurred to us, it can help refine

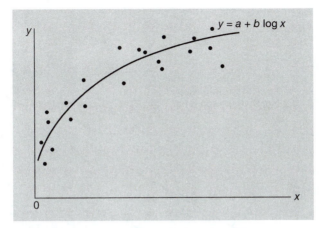

FIGURE 8-7   Model of Diminishing Marginal Returns

our theory. Looking back at Figure 8-3, note that the regression line does not provide perfect prediction of the values on the dependent variable for the cases in the scattergram. This means that there is still unexplained variation in the values of the dependent variable. Some of the observations are higher on the dependent variable than we would expect from their value on the independent variable, and some are lower. *Something else, beyond the independent variable, is also affecting the dependent variable.*

This difference between the observed value and the predicted value is called the *residual*. Examining these residuals points out to us those cases in which the "something else" has the effect of raising (or, conversely, lowering) the dependent variable. In Figure 8-3, for instance, a case such as A is one in which the effect of the "something else" is to raise the value of the dependent variable; the actual value for case A is higher than the value for B, which is the prediction from the regression line.

Now, once the cases have been sorted out in this way, we may notice that cases with similar residuals have some additional characteristic in common; this may then suggest an additional variable that may be brought into our theory. Consider Figure 8-3. On examining the residuals in that figure, you might notice that all of the countries for which educational spending was higher than predicted were democracies, and all of the countries for which it was unexpectedly low were not democracies. In this way, you might have discovered the identity of the "something else," beyond GNP, that acts as an independent variable. Notice also that it would have been difficult to identify the presence of another factor if you had not first regressed educational spending on GNP. The richest nondemocracies in Figure 8-3 show a higher rate of educational spending than do the poorest democracies, so that without the regression analysis it might not have been at all obvious that "democracy" was a variable you should use to explain levels of educational spending.

The technique of examining residuals is illustrated in Figure 8-8, adapted from V. O. Key, Jr.'s *Southern Politics* (1950, p. 48). Key wanted to measure the impact of factions in Alabama primaries, so he related counties' votes for Folsom, a progressive

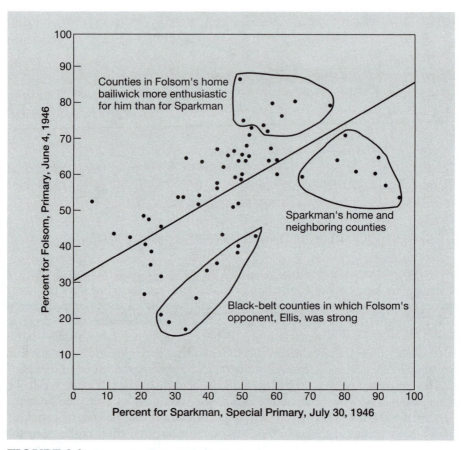

FIGURE 8-8   Example of Residual Analysis
Source: V. O. Key, Jr., *Southern Politics* (New York: Alfred A. Knopf, 1950), p. 48.

candidate in the 1946 gubernatorial primary, to their votes for Sparkman, a progressive candidate in the 1946 senatorial primary. He found a moderately strong relationship between the two. Because this meant that counties tended to lean the same way in both elections, it indicated the presence of conservative and progressive factions structuring the vote, as Key had expected. Had such factions not existed, there would have been no particular reason to expect a county to vote in much the same way in the two primaries. But the relationship was not very tight. Many counties, such as the one that gave 90 percent of its vote to Folsom but only 45 percent to Sparkman, voted far differently from what one would have expected simply on the basis of conservative and progressive factions. This indicated the presence of other variables, which were causing additional variations in the vote.

By examining the residuals around the regression line, Key got some idea of what those variables might be. In this case, it turned out that the residuals could be explained in part by the effect of "friends and neighbors." Counties in Folsom's home part of the state voted for him more enthusiastically than would have been expected on the basis of their vote for Sparkman. Counties in Sparkman's home part of the state voted less enthusiastically for Folsom than would have been expected from their vote for Sparkman (which presumably was high because he was a local boy). Similarly, the "home" counties of Folsom's opponent went less heavily for Folsom than would have been expected on the basis of their vote for Sparkman. This pointed out to Key the importance of local solidarity, one of the major forces retarding the development of stable statewide factions in Alabama politics at that time. Much of the looseness in the relationship between the votes for two candidates of the same faction was shown to be a result of people's tendency to vote for a candidate on the basis of where he came from in the state rather than the faction with which he was identified.

Users of regression analysis in political science far too rarely go on to the creative and exploratory labor of examining the residuals to see what additional variables affect the dependent variable. Usually, the spread of dots around the regression line is treated as an act of God, or as a measure of the basic uncertainty of human affairs. On the contrary, it is a trove in which new variables lie waiting to be discovered. I suspect the reason most of us do not go on to examine this trove is that we have developed a proprietorial sense toward our theories before we ever get to the point of testing them. There is a certain completeness about one's own theory, and it does not occur to us to use our theory as a "mere" starting point in the search for explanations.

Correlation Analysis

At the beginning of this chapter, I pointed out that there are two ways to measure the strength of a relationship: by measuring how much difference the independent variable makes in the dependent variable and by measuring how completely the independent variable determines the dependent variable. For interval-scale data, the regression coefficient accomplishes the first of these; the correlation coefficient accomplishes the second.

Consider the graphs in Figure 8-9. Both relationships can be summarized by the same regression line, but the value of the dependent variable in graph B is less

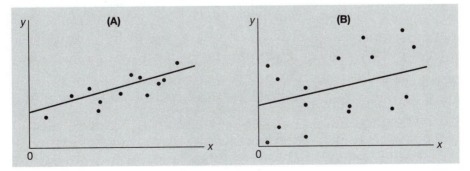

FIGURE 8-9   Two Correlations

closely determined by the independent variable than in graph A. A change in the independent variable tends to produce the same change in the dependent variable, on the average, in both graphs. But this tendency is weaker and more likely to be disturbed by "other factors," in graph B; in other words, the residuals tend to be larger in graph B than in graph A. In one sense, then, the relationship in graph B is weaker than that in graph A. The dependent variable is less a result of the independent variable, compared to "other factors" (the unknown things that cause the residuals to exist), in B than in A.

The *correlation coefficient*, r, measures how widely such a body of data spreads around a regression line. This coefficient compares a set of data with ideal models of a perfect relationship and a perfect lack of relationship, and assigns to the relationship a score ranging in absolute value from 0 to 1, depending on how closely the data approximate a perfect relationship. The two extreme models are illustrated in Figure 8-10.

In graph A of Figure 8-10, the data fall on a straight line through the scattergram. A regression line passed through them would leave no residual variation at all in the dependent variable. Thus the independent variable determines the dependent variable completely. The correlation coefficient for this type has an absolute value of 1.

In graph B, on the other hand, values of the dependent variable are combined randomly with values of the independent variable, so that any given value of the dependent variable is as likely to coincide with a low value on the independent variable as with a high one. Thus there is no pattern to the relationship. This indicates that the independent variable has no effect on the dependent variable. The correlation coefficient for this type has an absolute value of 0.

Most relationships, of course, fall somewhere between these two extremes; the closer a relationship approaches the situation in graph A, the higher its correlation coefficient will be in absolute value. Thus, the correlation coefficient provides a measure by which the strengths of various relationships can be compared, in the *correlational* sense of "strength of relationship."

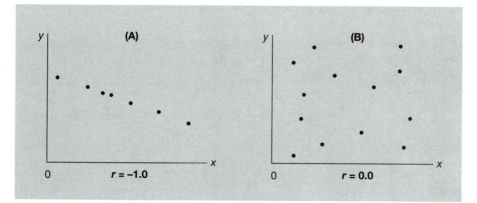

FIGURE 8-10   Extreme Models of Correlation

I have referred here only to the absolute value of the correlation coefficient. In addition to showing how closely a relationship approaches the situation in graph A, the correlation coefficient indicates by its sign whether the relationship is positive or negative. The coefficient ranges from −1.0 (a perfect negative relationship, such as the one in graph A of Figure 8-10) through 0.0 (graph B) to +1.0 (a perfect positive relationship, similar to the one in graph A but tilted up). In a positive relationship, increases in the dependent variable produce increases in the independent variable; in a negative relationship, increases in the independent variable produce decreases in the dependent variable.

Interpreting the correlation coefficient. Although it is clear enough what correlation coefficients of −1, 0, or +1 mean, there is no direct way of interpreting what coefficients between these values mean. It is true that the higher the absolute value of the coefficient, the closer it approaches the model in graph A of Figure 8-10, so that if we wish to compare two different relationships, we can say which is stronger. But it is not easy to see what the difference between them means. It is *not* true, for instance, that the difference between $r = 0.8$ and $r = 0.6$ is the same as the difference between $r = 0.4$ and $r = 0.2$. And it is also not true that $r = −0.6$ is twice as strong as $r = −0.3$. This is reminiscent of the difference between ordinal and interval measurement: We know that the higher the absolute value of r, the stronger the relationship; but we do not know *how much* stronger one relationship is than another.

Fortunately, the square of the correlation coefficient (sometimes called the *coefficient of determination*, but more often just r^2) does have a usable interpretation at all values of r. Before we can consider this, however, I must first introduce the concept of *variance*.

Variance. The variance of a variable is the average squared deviation of values of that variable from their own mean.[1] For instance, if there are just three cases, with scores of −1, 4, and 5 for a variable, their mean is $(−1 + 4 + 5)/3 = 8/3$, and their variance is

$$\frac{\left(-1 - {}^8/_3\right)^2 + \left(4 - {}^8/_3\right)^2 + \left(5 - {}^8/_3\right)^2}{3}$$

$$= \frac{\left(-{}^{11}/_3\right)^2 + \left({}^4/_3\right)^2 + \left({}^7/_3\right)^2}{3}$$

$$= \frac{{}^{121}/_9 + {}^{16}/_9 + {}^{49}/_9}{3} = 6.89$$

---

[1]The mean of any variable is its arithmetic mean, or average: the sum of all the values divided by the number of cases.

The formula for the variance of any variable x is

$$\text{variance}_x = \frac{\Sigma(x - \bar{x})^2}{N}$$

where $\bar{x}$ is the mean of x and N is the number of observations we wish to average. The Σ sign simply means that for all the observations, we are to calculate $(x - \bar{x})^2$ and then add these results together. The expression $\Sigma(x - \bar{x})^2$ is equivalent to writing $(x_1 - \bar{x})^2 + (x_2 - \bar{x})^2 + \ldots + (x_N - \bar{x})^2$, where x_1 is the observation for the first case, x_2 the observation for the second case, and so on.

The variance is a measure of how widely the observed values of a variable vary among themselves. If they do not vary at all but each has the same value, the variance will be zero. This is true because each value will equal the mean, and thus the sum of the squared deviations from the mean will equal zero. The more the values vary among themselves, the further each will be from the mean of them all, and consequently, the greater the sum of squared deviations from the mean. Thus, the more that values vary among themselves, the higher their variance will be.

The variance of the dependent variable y can be depicted in a scattergram by drawing a horizontal line at $y = \bar{y}$, and drawing in the residuals from this line, as in Figure 8-11. The average squared value of the residuals, because it is the average squared deviation of the values of y from their own mean, is the variance of y.

One way to view our goal in theoretical social science research is to note that our task is usually to account for the variance in a dependent variable. It is the variance in something that puzzles us and challenges us to produce an explanation. Why is it that some people make more money than other people? That some nations are frequently involved in wars and others are not? That some members of Congress vote for a bill and others oppose it? That some people are more politically engaged

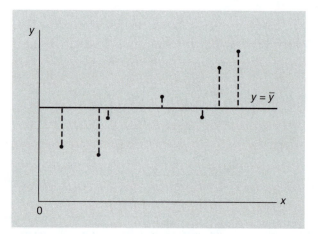

FIGURE 8-11   The Variance of y

than others? All of these questions simply ask: To what can the variance in this variable be attributed—*why does this variable vary?*

Comparing Figures 8-3 and 8-11, we should see at least a superficial similarity between the residuals around the least-squares line and the variance of the dependent variable. The least-squares line is a line passed through the scattergram in any direction such that the squared deviations of values of the dependent variable from that line are minimized. The line $y = \bar{y}$ is a *horizontal* line passed through the data in the scattergram, and inspection will suggest what is, in fact, mathematically true: This line is the one *horizontal* line that minimizes the squared deviations of values of the dependent variable from itself (see Blalock, 1979, p. 58). That is, any other horizontal line passed through the data would yield a greater sum of squared deviations in the dependent variable.

This similarity suggests that the squared deviations around the regression line may be treated as the variance of the dependent variable around the values predicted for it by the regression equation. As already noted, this is the variance in the dependent variable that is still left unaccounted for after the effect of the independent variable has been estimated.

Thus we have two variances for the dependent variable: its variance around its own mean (the "total variance") and its variance around the regression line ("variance left unexplained by the independent variable"). To the extent that the dependent variable is determined by the independent variable, this unexplained variance will be small compared to the total variance. If the dependent variable can be predicted perfectly from the independent variable, as in Figure 8-10 (A), the unexplained variance will be zero. If the dependent variable is unrelated to the independent variable, as in Figure 8-10 (B), the regression line will be horizontal, indicating that the same value of the dependent variable is predicted at all values of the independent variable; inasmuch as the line $y = \bar{y}$ is the horizontal line that minimizes squared deviations around itself, the regression line will equal the line $y = \bar{y}$ in this case. Thus the unexplained variance will equal the total variance.

Dividing the unexplained variance by the total variance tells us what proportion of the total variance is left after we have allowed the independent variable to explain as much as it can explain. As it happens, r^2 equals 1 minus this proportion, or

$$r^2 = 1 - \frac{\text{unexplained variance}}{\text{total variance}}$$

that is, the proportion of the total variance in the dependent variable that can be ascribed to the independent variable.[2] The explained variance, therefore, gives us a useful interpretation of r at all values. If you read that an author has found a correlation

---

[2]For a good presentation of this interpretation, including the proof that

$$r^2 = 1 - \frac{\text{unexplained variance}}{\text{total variance}}$$

see Blalock (1979, pp. 405–409).

of −0.30 between two variables, you should mentally square the correlation and interpret that statement: "The two variables are negatively related, and 9 percent of the variance in one is due to the other."

Another helpful way to look at this interpretation is to think in terms of prediction. Operating without any knowledge of the independent variable, our best strategy in trying to predict values of the dependent variable for particular cases would be to guess that the value in any given case is the mean. We would be less wrong more of the time than with any other guess we could make.[3] If we now add knowledge of the independent variable, our best guess becomes the value predicted from the regression equation. The magnitude of the mistakes in each case is now represented by squared deviations around the predictions. The value r^2 measures the proportion by which we have reduced our mistakes in predicting the dependent variable by introducing knowledge of the independent variable.

Correlation and Regression Compared

Our discussion so far leaves us with the question, "Is correlation or regression analysis the better way to measure the strength of a relationship?" Obviously, the answer must be, "Sometimes one is, sometimes the other." The key to deciding when to use each measure lies in the fact that the correlation coefficient reflects the variability of the independent variable directly, whereas the regression coefficient does not.

Consider the two scattergrams in Figure 8-12. The scattergram from graph A has been reproduced in graph B, except that all observations for which the independent variable is less than 2 or greater than 4 have been eliminated. The effect is to reduce the variability of the independent variable while leaving the basic relationship between the independent and dependent variables unchanged. *Under these*

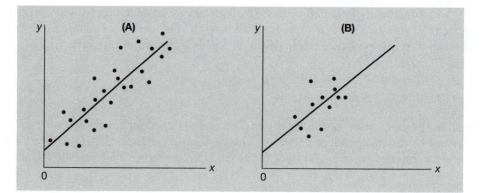

FIGURE 8-12   Regression and Correlation, with the Independent Variable Attenuated

[3]At least this is true if we think of "mistakes" as squared deviations from the true value.

circumstances, the regression coefficient in B *will be approximately the same as that in* A, *but the correlation coefficient will be sharply lowered in* B.

Let us see why this should be so. The regression line that minimized squared deviations in the full set of data in graph A should continue to minimize squared deviations in the partial set of data in graph B. Therefore, we would expect the regression coefficient to be about the same in both graphs. On the other hand, because the variability of the independent variable has been reduced in graph B, the extent of its possible effects on the dependent variable are reduced. Relative to other causes of the dependent variable, which are just as free to operate as they were in graph A, the importance of the independent variable as a cause of the dependent variable must decline. But this is simply to say that the proportion of the total variance that is attributable to the independent variable declines. In other words, r^2 is reduced.

This becomes a matter of considerable importance in field research, because generally the variability of independent variables is beyond the investigator's control. For instance, a researcher might be interested in knowing whether gender or race had more to do with whether a person voted. The researcher might use census tract data on a large city, correlating percent black with percent voting and percent male with percent voting. But the distribution of people in most cities is such that the percent black would vary greatly while the percent male would not. (Blacks are concentrated highly in some tracts and almost absent in others; men are spread more or less evenly across all the tracts.)

The fact that percent male scarcely varies from one census tract to another guarantees that this researcher would find practically no correlation between percent male and percent voting. As indicated in the hypothetical scattergram in Figure 8-13, there is near zero variance in percent male; hence very little of the variance in percent voting can be due to it. On the other hand, if residential patterns were such that percent male could vary as much as percent black does, it might be that gender would show up as a major determinant of voter turnout.[4] There is limited usefulness to a measure that would have us conclude from this that race is a more important cause of participation than sex gender.[5]

The problem with using correlation coefficients in both of these cases is that while the coefficient is affected by the particular variance of the independent variable in the data at hand, the investigator clearly intends to extrapolate from these particular data to a more general case. In the census tract study, the researcher wants to make a statement about the impact of race or gender on voting, regardless of how people are located in the city. In the GRE study, the researcher wants to make a judgment about how to treat new applicants (among whom the variability of GRE scores would be higher) on the basis of the relationship between GRE scores and grades among the students currently in the department.

---

[4]This example also incorporates a major statistical problem in some correlation and regression analyses, the *ecological fallacy*. This can occur when data on aggregate units (such as percent black, median income, and so on, for census tracts, countries, or states) are used to infer how variables are related among individuals living in those aggregate units. See Robinson (1950), Stokes (1969), and Achen and Shively (1995).

[5]Problems such as this are a result of censored data (see above, pp. 104–107)

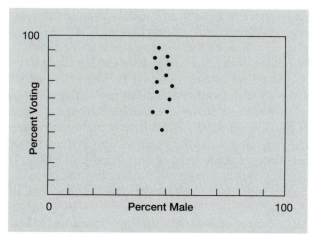

FIGURE 8-13   Predicting Percent Voting from Percent Male

A good rule is that in any situation in which you wish to extrapolate from a particular set of data to a more general case, you should use regression coefficients. Because theoretical research almost always is interested in generalizing, regression analysis usually will be superior to correlation analysis. (This advice holds despite the fact, which I mentioned earlier, that in regression analysis there is always some difficulty in handling varying units.)

There are circumstances, however, in which you may not intend to generalize, but only to describe a particular situation. For instance, someone might want to describe how a particular Congress, say the 80th or the 92nd, operated. It would then be appropriate to note that in that particular Congress, there was a negligible correlation between members' race and their votes on various bills. This would help establish what were the important factors influencing outcomes *in that Congress*. However, this would not deny the possibility of a relationship between race and voting record in any other Congress, or for Congresses in general.

Problem of Measurement Error

Our understanding of relationships between variables is intimately bound up with the extent to which we have been able to measure the variables validly. To the extent that there is *nonrandom error* in our variables, we are simply unable to state accurately what the relationship between those variables is. This should be clear from our earlier discussion of measurement error in Chapter 4.

Random measurement error also distorts the relationship between variables. Refer back to Table 4-1 (p. 53). The relationship between the two variables is increasingly attenuated from left to right, as it might appear under conditions of increasing levels of random measurement error. The scattergrams for the three sets

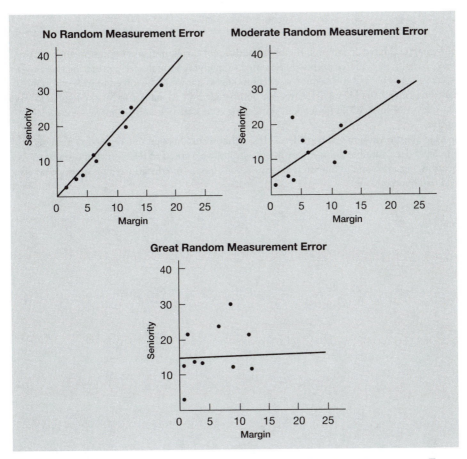

FIGURE 8-14   Relationship Under Varying Degrees of Random Measurement Error

of data drawn from Table 4-1 are presented in Figure 8-14. As progressively greater amounts of random measurement error are present in two variables, the true form of the relationship between the variables is more and more lost to us. Not only is it lost to us, but it is systematically distorted. To the extent that there is random error in two variables, they will appear to us to be unrelated. Thus there is a real danger that the only relationships we will be able to perceive are those between variables that are easy to measure accurately, a possibility that bodes ill for social science.

   If we are willing to make some assumptions regarding the nature of the random error, it is possible to correct for it, and thus reconstruct the true relationship between two variables. A good example of this technique is seen in Bartels (1993). (Unfortunately, this article and most other discussions of correcting for measurement error are difficult for the untrained reader.)

▟ Further Discussion

In this chapter, I have drawn only the broad outlines of correlation and regression analysis for interval data. In fact, I have purposely refrained from giving formulas for calculating these measures, so that anyone wishing to put these techniques to use would be forced to seek out more detailed training. David Knoke, George W. Bohrnstedt, and Alissa Potter Mee's *Statistics for Social Data Analysis*, 4th ed. (2002) is a good, standard text in statistics—one of many—for social scientists.

One question you might consider is this: What would happen in a regression analysis if the independent variable did not vary at all—if, say, we wanted to relate voting turnout to education, but everyone in our study had the same amount of education? This question looks ahead to Chapter 10.

Introduction to Statistics

Further Topics on Measurement of Relationships

In this chapter, I build on the introduction in Chapter 8 to discuss in brief how to measure three types of relationships: (1) those among ordinal and nominal variables; (2) those that involve dichotomous variables; and (3) those that involve several variables simultaneously.[1]

MEASURES OF RELATIONSHIP FOR ORDINAL DATA

As we saw at the beginning of Chapter 8, there are two main ways in which we can measure the strength of a relationship. We can measure how much change is produced in the dependent variable by a change in the independent variable, or we can measure how strongly the dependent variable is determined by the independent variable relative to other things that also help determine it.

Only for the second of these is it possible to develop a standard measure for use with ordinal-scale data. To measure how much change is produced in the dependent variable, it is necessary to have some sort of unit by which to measure that change. But this is not available under ordinal measurement. Accordingly, the most we can hope for from ordinal variables is some form of correlational analysis.

A cross-tabulation is to the analysis of ordinal variables what a scattergram is to the analysis of interval variables. Consider Table 9-1, which relates citizens' education levels to whether or not they voted in the 2008 election.

Like a scattergram, the table shows how frequently the various combinations of the two variables occur. And just as in a scattergram that shows the relationship between two intervally measured variables, a positive relationship would mean that relatively few cases should fall in the upper-left corner of the table (relatively few

---

[1]This chapter presents advanced material that can be skipped over without any loss in comprehension of the remaining material covered in this book.

TABLE 9-1   Relationship Between Education and Voting

Voted or Not	Less than 12 Years	High School Graduate	Some College	College Graduate
	Level of Education			
Voted	126	462	500	536
Did Not Vote	123	197	110	43

Source: 2008 Presidential Election Survey, National Election Study, University of Michigan.

cases with low levels of education but voting) or the lower-right corner (relatively few cases with high levels of education, but not voting). A negative relationship would imply the opposite: relatively few cases in the lower left or upper right. And no relationship at all would, of course, imply an even spread across the table. Each number in the table gives the number of people in the study who exhibited a given combination of education and voting/not voting. These are actual numbers of cases, not percentages. The table reveals a pattern between these variables, just as a scattergram does for interval-scale data.

In general, we can say that there is a substantial relationship between education and voting, with the propensity to vote increasing with education.[2] For instance, of the 249 citizens with less than a high school education, almost half did not vote, while of the 579 who were college graduates, only a few (43) did not vote. There are two differences between a table such as this and a scattergram, however:

1. Because there is a limited number of values available for each variable (four for the independent variable and two for the dependent variable), it is not necessary to use the infinite space of a plane to locate the observations. Instead, the observations are located in one or another of the cells of a table. Because so many observations are tied on each value, their presence is indicated by counting the number of observations falling in each cell and printing the number there rather than by printing a dot for each observation. If the observations were indicated by dots, as in Figure 9-1, the similarity to a scattergram would become more obvious.

2. Because there are no units with which to measure the difference between two values of a variable, the *precise* pattern in the table is meaningless. The change in propensity to vote as we move from "some college" to "college graduate" tells us nothing specific, because we do not know how much greater the education of college graduates is than of those with "some college." We do not know how much more educated the college graduates are than the others, and so we do not know from these measures how much change a given difference in "education" produces in propensity to vote.

[2]Indeed, the relationship looks to be considerably stronger than the relationship between age and voting, which we looked at in Figure 5-4.

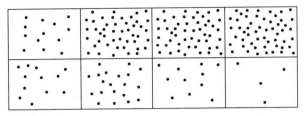

FIGURE 9-1   Scattergram Version of Table 9-1 (Each dot represents 10 cases)

Thus it is not possible to measure the strength of relationships in a way analogous to regression.[3] On the other hand, it *is* possible to develop measures analogous to the correlation coefficient. To do this, we must develop models of the perfect relationship and of perfect independence, as was done with the correlation coefficient, and also develop a measure to indicate how close the data in our table come to these two models.

One such measure for use with ordinal variables is Goodman and Kruskal's gamma.[4] Gamma is based on the idea that if there is an association between two variables, pairs of cases will tend to line up the same way on both variables. In Table 9-1, for instance, this would mean that for any pair of citizens, if one of them had more education than the other, we should expect her also to vote more regularly than the other. Note that if most pairs of citizens were like this, that would produce the pattern of a positive relationship—few cases in the upper left-hand and lower right-hand corners of a table.

All cases in the upper left-hand corner of the table, for instance, when paired up with any other case in the table, would either be tied on one or another of the variables, or would line up *differently* with it on the two variables. If paired with a case from the bottom-middle cell of the table, for example, she would have less education than that person, but would have voted while that one did not. Such a pairing would indicate a negative relationship, not a positive one, and would therefore be inconsistent with the idea of a positive relationship in the table.

Gamma's model of no relationship is a table in which half of such pairings are consistent with a positive relationship, and half are inconsistent with a positive relationship. If this is the case, then no relationship is indicated, and gamma will be

---

[3]Even though there is not a precise regression line to define residuals, however, it might still be useful to look at the "residuals" in Table 9-1—the cases that do not fit the generally positive relationship. Is there anything special, for instance, about those who have little education, but vote? Or about college graduates who do not vote?

[4]This measure was described in Goodman and Kruskal (1954). Another popular measure for use with ordinal variables is Kendall's *tau*; and, there are a number of others as well. One reason why there are varied measures is that frequently they indicate varying strengths of relationship. It is also the case that two rather different patterns will sometimes produce the same result using one of these measures. The result is useful, but also a bit ambiguous. This is simply the price we pay for the fact that ordinal measures are naturally less informative than interval measures. (See also footnote 5 on p. 139, which notes the possibility of incorporating ordinal measures as independent variables in combination with interval variables.)

zero. If all pairings are consistent with a positive relationship, however, that is the strongest possible relationship and gamma will be +1.0. If all pairings are inconsistent with a positive relationship—that is, consistent with a negative relationship—gamma will be –1.0.

To calculate gamma, we first ignore all possible pairings in which two cases are tied on one or the other variable. To make comparisons with the cases in the upper left-hand corner of Table 9-1, for instance, we would not compare with any cases with the same level of education (any in the first column), or with any that had voted (any in the first row). All possible pairings that are not tied on either variable enter into the calculation of gamma, whose formula is:

$$\text{gamma} = \frac{P - Q}{P + Q}$$

Where P is the number of pairs that are consistent with a positive relationship and Q is the number of pairs that are consistent with a negative relationship. The formula subtracts the number of pairs consistent with a negative relationship from those consistent with a positive relationship, and then divides this by the total number of pairs. If there is no relationship, P will equal half of all pairs, so will Q, and P–Q will equal zero.

P and Q are calculated as follows: each cell of the table is compared with all other cells; if it is tied with a cell on either variable, that cell is ignored. But if there are no ties, then the number of cases in the first cell is multiplied by the number in the other cell. This means that all possible pairings of cases in the two cells have been counted. (One case in the first cell is compared with all cases in the second cell; then this is repeated for each case in the first cell; the total number of comparisons will thus be the product of the number of cases in the first cell by the number of cases in the second.) If the two cells are lined up such that their pairings are consistent with a positive relationship, this product is added to P; if they are consistent with a negative relationship, the product is added to Q.

Let us illustrate this by calculating gamma for Table 9-1. Starting with the upper left-hand cell, we can make untied comparisons with three other cells—the three right-hand cells of the bottom row. All of these are consistent with a negative relationship, since cases in those cells had a higher level of education than those in the first cell, but did not vote. Therefore we add three products to Q: (126×197) + $(126 \times 110) + (126 \times 43)$. The next cell over (high school grads who voted) forms pairings that are consistent with a positive relationship with the lower left-hand cell, but pairings that are consistent with a negative relationship with the two cells below it and to the right. Thus we add to P the product (462×123) and we add to Q the product $(462 \times 110) + (462 \times 43)$.

Proceeding in this way with all cells in the table, we calculate Q to be:

$(126 \times 197) + (126 \times 110) + (126 \times 43) + (462 \times 110) + (462 \times 43) +$
$(500 \times 43) = 136{,}286$

And P to be:

$$(462 \times 123) + (500 \times 123) + (500 \times 197) + (536 \times 123) + (536 \times 197) + (536 \times 110) = 447,306$$

Thus there are 136,286 pairings of cases in Table 9-1 that are consistent with a negative relationship, and 447,306 that are consistent with a positive relationship. We now calculate:

$$gamma = \frac{447,306 - 136,286}{447,306 + 136,286} = .533$$

You can see by examining this that if there had been more pairings consistent with a positive relationship, or fewer consistent with a negative relationship, gamma would have been higher yet. And if there had been no pairings consistent with a negative relationship ($Q = 0$), gamma would have equaled 1.0.

MEASURES OF RELATIONSHIP FOR NOMINAL DATA

In relating two nominally measured variables, cross-tabulation again approximates the function of a scattergram—that is, it shows which values of one variable tend to coincide with which values of the other. However, in contrast to a table relating ordinal variables, the *position* of a cell in the table no longer tells us anything, for the order of values of a nominal variable means nothing. Consider the example in Table 9-2, in which versions A and B are equivalent. The table could not be rearranged in this way if the variables were measured ordinally.

As with ordinally measured data, all we can do in measuring the strength of a relationship between two nominally measured variables is to assess the degree to which one variable is determined by the other. Various measures have been developed to do this, just as has been done with ordinal variables. But the problem is really better dealt with by adaptations of regression analysis to nominal variable analysis. Regression adaptations for analyzing nominal variables are dealt with in the next two sections.

TABLE 9-2   Interchangeable Order in Nominal Data

Candidate Preferred	(A) Religion			Candidate Preferred	(B) Religion		
	Cath.	*Prot.*	*Other*		*Prot.*	*Cath.*	*Other*
X	20	0	0	X	0	20	0
Z	5	30	4	Y	0	0	26
Y	0	0	26	Z	30	5	4

Dichotomies and Regression Analysis

Dichotomies are classifications that involve only two categories: for example, gender (male or female), referendum vote (yes or no), or participation (voter or nonvoter). Such classifications have a useful property, which at first glance appears to be a bit mysterious: Although dichotomies are nominal scales, they can quite properly be treated as interval scales and can be analyzed using measures appropriate for such scales. This greatly expands the value and applicability of regression analysis, for obvious reasons. It means that not only intervally measured variables, but also dichotomous nominal-scale variables—and mixtures of the two—can be analyzed using regression analysis.

The trick is that because a dichotomous variable can take on only one of two values, there is by definition a common unit in which differences between values of the variable can be measured, namely the difference between the two categories. Let us call the categories A and B. Then the distance between two observations falling into category A is zero units, and the distance between two observations, one of which is in A and the other in B, is one unit. Because there usually is no natural ordering to the dichotomy, the decision of whether A is one unit greater than B, or one unit less, must be arbitrary.

An alternative way to look at this situation is to think of a dichotomy as measuring the degree to which an observation *embodies* one of its categories. The category is either present or not present for each observation. For instance, the dichotomy "gender: male or female" can also be viewed as a variable "femaleness" (or alternatively, "maleness"). Each subject is either totally "female" or totally "not female." If the difference between totally female and totally not female is taken to be one unit, women have values of +1.0 for the variable "femaleness" and men have values of 0.0. Because this is a true interval measure, it can be used together with other interval measures, such as income or age, in regression and correlation analysis.

(The same interpretation cannot be placed on nominal-scale variables with more than two categories. We would have no common unit, for example, in which to place Catholics relative to Protestants or Jews in the variable "religion." As you will see in footnote 4, however, there is yet another trick we can use in this case that will allow us to work with multiple-category variables.)

For example, we might regress income at a low-paying factory on gender, with gender equal to 0 for men and 1 for women. The best-fitting regression line might be

income = 14,000 − 2,000 gender

This would mean that the expected income of men at the factory was $14,000, since the value of "gender" for men is zero. Similarly, the expected income for women would be $14,000 − ($2,000 × 1) = $12,000. Since the independent variable can take on only two values, the scattergram for this analysis will look odd, with a set of data arrayed vertically above "gender = 0" and another set arrayed vertically above "gender = 1." A scattergram that would be consistent with these hypothetical regression results is shown in Figure 9-2.

The regression line will actually pass directly through the mean income of men at gender = 0 and the mean income of women at gender = 1. Since a regression line

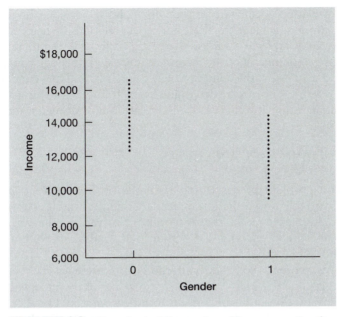

FIGURE 9-2   Hypothetical Regression of Income on Gender

serves as a convenient way of summarizing the central pattern in a set of means, there is no particular advantage to using regression analysis in cases like these, in which we are interested in the relationship between an interval-scaled variable and a *single* dichotomous variable. (Exactly the same result could be presented, more simply, by noting that the average income of men at the factory is $14,000, while the average income of women is $12,000.) Where this technique of treating dichotomous variables does become valuable is when we wish to combine a dichotomous variable with other independent variables in an analysis. This would be the case if we wished to look at the simultaneous effects of gender and education on income. There is a well-developed technique described in the section "Multivariate Analysis" on pp. 142–147 that allows us to use interval-level measures simultaneously in this way, but there is no such technique for nominal measures. The ability to include dichotomous nominal variables in such analyses is extraordinarily valuable. Such variables generally are known as *dummy variables* or *binary variables*.[5]

The value of this trick, whereby we can include nominal-scale dichotomies in the powerful technique of regression analysis, cannot be stated too strongly. However, this works only for dichotomous nominal measures used as independent variables. We cannot appropriately use them as *dependent* variables in ordinary regression. One indication that this would be problematic is that it would be impossible to construct a

[5]Techniques have also been developed for including ordinal variables in regression, but presentation of these techniques goes beyond the scope of this book. The techniques involve "ordered logit" and "ordered probit." They are variants of the logit and probit analysis presented in the next section.

meaningful correlation coefficient for such an analysis. Consider the scattergram in Figure 9-3. In any reasonable sense, there is a perfect relationship here. Above levels of $x = 10$, y is always 1; and when x is less than 10, y is always 0. But there is still "error" around the regression line. Since the regression line cannot bend, it cannot follow the jump from $y = 0$ to $y = 1$ at the point at which x equals 10 and thus cannot register the full extent to which values of y are determined by x. It is therefore incapable of serving as the "best summarizing line" to describe the relationship between x and y.

LOGIT AND PROBIT ANALYSIS

To handle the problem of describing the relationship between a continuous independent variable and a dichotomous dependent variable, statisticians have developed an alternative model that is found in two very similar variations, called *logit analysis* and *probit analysis*. I describe logit analysis here, but the general explanation holds for both.

The regression line, as you will recall, can be interpreted as the path of expected values of the dependent variable across varying values of the independent variable. From the regression line in Figure 8-4, for instance, we would predict that y would equal 9 when x equaled 1, that y would equal 18 when x equaled 4, and so on. This does not make sense for a dichotomous variable, since it can take on values of only 0 or 1. It would not make sense in Figure 9-3, for instance, to predict that the dependent variable would have a value of 0.3 when the independent variable equaled 8; this would be nonsensical.

An analogy to the expected value of a dependent variable, however, would be the probability that the dependent variable equals 1. Such a model would portray, across the variation in an independent variable, the varying probability that a

FIGURE 9-3   Dichotomous Dependent Variable

dichotomous variable equals 1. It would need to be S-shaped and bounded vertically by 0 and 1, since a probability must be positive and less than or equal to 1. Figure 9-4 provides an example. The model would predict, for example, that at $x = 5$, about 70 percent of the cases would have $y = 1$. That is, $P(y = 1)$, the probability that y equals 1, is about 0.7.

We do not have any way to work directly with such a model, but the logit model allows us to derive estimates of the sort such a model would yield. Letting $p = P(y = 1)$, the logit is the logarithm to base e, that is the natural logarithm, of $p/(1 - p)$. This is a difficult quantity to conceive! But it does embody the probability in which we are interested; and most important, the logit model allows us to use regular regression analysis to analyze a dichotomous dependent variable. It turns out that the logit can appropriately be taken as a linear function of a continuous independent variable, in the standard form

logit of $y = a + bx$

Mechanically, the way this works is that the dependent variable has values of either 0 or 1. The computer calculates from the number of 0s and 1s at given values

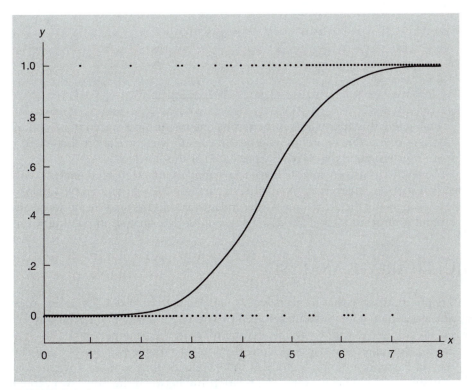

FIGURE 9-4   Path-of-Probabilities Model

of the independent variable what the expected logit of the dependent variable is across the range of the independent variable. Thus for any value of x, we know the expected logit of y, and we can proceed to analyze the relationship between x and the logit of y by regression analysis. Because the analysis is so indirect, however, the a and b in the logit equation are not intuitively interpretable. Remember, it is not y, or even the probability of y, that is predicted from x in this equation; rather, it is the natural logarithm of $p/(1-p)$. The best way to interpret logit analysis, and the way it is usually presented in studies, is to calculate by a series of transformations on the logit coefficients what the expected probability of y is at various values of x and to present those discretely. This is done by first calculating from a and b what the expected logit (the natural logarithm of $p/(1-p)$) is at each of several values of x. Then, it is straightforward to solve for p (the probability that the dependent variable is 1 rather than 0), from the natural logarithm of $p/(1-p)$. For instance, if we were interested in the effect of age on voting participation, we might perform a logit analysis and then present the results:

Age	Estimated Probability of Voting
25	0.37
35	0.58
45	0.68
55	0.70
65	0.71
75	0.71

A table like this approximates the results one might have gotten from a nonlinear regression line. There are also various analogs to the correlation coefficient for logit analyses but none that is readily presented at this level.

The ability to incorporate dichotomous variables into regression analysis, either directly if they are independent variables, or through the logit and probit variants of regression analysis if the dichotomy is a dependent variable, has made regression analysis a powerful statistical tool and the dominant tool for data analysis in political science.

MULTIVARIATE ANALYSIS

In Chapter 6, we saw that frequently it is important to hold one variable constant while measuring the relationship between two other variables. The easiest way to do this is literally to "hold the variable constant," as in the example on pp. 94–95, by separating the subjects into groups along the control variable (a group of Democrats, a group of Republicans, and a group of independents, for example, if *registration* is the variable to be held constant). The relationship between the other two variables is then measured for each group.

This technique has serious disadvantages, though. First, if we want to control for an intervally measured variable, the number of "groups" we set up might be too large. For instance, in controlling for income, we might have a group of all those with an income of $18,243, another of all those with an income of $43,402, and so on; in this case, there probably would be as many groups as there were subjects in the study. This problem can be averted by lumping subjects into a few broad categories of the independent variable, but doing so throws away a great deal of the precision in the measure—something one may not want to do.

A second and more serious problem in literally holding a variable constant is that the process quite rapidly leaves the researcher with only small numbers of subjects among whom to measure a relationship. Suppose that someone wanted to examine the relationship between occupation and voting, holding constant race and age. The investigator might divide the population into groups such as blacks aged 20–30, whites aged 20–30, blacks aged 31–40, and so on, and then look at the occupation/vote relationship for each of these groups. But the typical national survey, with about 2,000 respondents, might include no more than five or six whites aged 20–30, blacks aged 51–60, or whatever. Such small groups would give very unreliable estimates of the relationship between occupation and vote.[6]

A final disadvantage of literal controlling is that it produces a series of measures of the relationship (one measure for each group) that is unwieldy and difficult to absorb. Particularly, if we wanted to control simultaneously for more than one variable, as in our example of race and age, this might leave us with as many as 20 or 30 separate measures to consider. Especially, as noted above, any multicategory nominal variables included in the analysis will show up as a set of several dichotomous variables.

Fortunately, there is an easier way to control for a variable—at least if we are using interval-scale variables (including dichotomies that are taken as independent variables). The technique of multivariate regression allows us to look at the pattern in several variables among all of our observations (without breaking these down into separate subgroups) and to estimate what the relationship between the dependent variable and any particular independent variable would be if none of the other variables varied—that is, if each of the other variables were "held constant."

To sketch the technique in a general way, I will use as an example the case of two independent variables (w and x) and a dependent variable (y). You will recall that the relationship between two variables can be plotted in a flat space of two dimensions (represented by a scattergram). Similarly, the relationship among three variables can be plotted in a three-dimensional space, as seen in Figure 9-5. The vertical dimension is the dependent variable, and each of the horizontal dimensions is one of the independent variables. Each observation is a dot floating in three-dimensional space, located according to its values on each of the three variables. Dot A has had coordinates drawn to show how it is located in the three-dimensional space by its values on w, x, and y, where these values are p, q, and r, respectively.

Just as a one-dimensional line through the two-dimensional scattergram could summarize the pattern in a two-variable relationship, so a two-dimensional

<hr>

[6]Refer again to the box "Law of Large Numbers" on p. 61.

FIGURE 9-5   Three-Dimensional Scattergram

plane through the three-dimensional scattergram can summarize the pattern in its three-variable relationship. The plane is picked on the basis of the same criterion by which the regression line was chosen. It must be the plane that minimizes the sum of squared deviations of actual y values from the y values predicted from the plane.

This regression plane would look like a flat piece of cardboard set at some tilt in the middle of the three-dimensional space over a grid containing all possible combinations of values of w and x. By counting out a certain distance along x and then a certain distance along w, we can locate a particular combination of w and x on this grid. The height of the cardboard plane above the grid at this point is the value of y predicted from the given values of w and x by the regression plane. The regression equation associated with the plane is of the form

$$y = a + b_1 w + b_2 x$$

As in the two-variable case, a is the intercept—the predicted value of y when both x and w equal zero. Similarly, b_1 tells by how many units y can be expected to increase if w increases by one unit *and x does not change*; and b_2 tells by how many units y can be expected to increase if x increases by one unit *and w does not change*. Here b_1 and b_2 are the regression coefficients of the equation.

To calculate from the multivariate regression the y value, you would expect from a particular combination of w and x:

1. Start with a, the expected value of y when both x and w equal zero.
2. Add to this b_1 times w, or the amount by which y could be expected to change if the value of w shifted from zero to the particular value you are using. At this point, you have the expected value of y when x equals zero and w equals the particular value.

3. To this sum, add b_2 times x, the amount by which y could be expected to change if x shifted from zero to the particular value you are using and w remained unchanged. You now have the expected value of y, given these particular values of w and x.

Notice in this that b_1 describes the relationship between w and y if x does not vary, and that b_2 describes the relationship between x and y if w does not vary. In this way, without requiring us to break our observations into separate small and awkward groups, multivariate regression allows us to examine relationships with certain other variables controlled.

For example, if we had data for U.S. counties giving the percentages of African American students attending all-black schools, the median income of each county, and the percentage of African Americans in each county's population, we might find the following situation:

Let S be the percentage of African American students attending all-black schools.
Let M be the county's median income (in thousands of dollars).
Let A be the percentage of African Americans in the county's population.

On examining just the relationship between S and M, we might find that the regression equation was

$$S = 68.2 - 2.1\,M$$

This would indicate that school integration is more widespread in richer counties. The percentage of African Americans attending all-black schools decreases by 2.1 percent as the median income of the county increases by 1,000 dollars.

Obviously, however, we need to control for percent African American in assessing this relationship. It might be that the apparent integration of the well-heeled counties is simply a result of the fact that in the richer counties there are so few African Americans that there are not likely to be any all-black schools. We could test for this by adding the variable "percent African American" as an additional independent variable. The regression equation

$$S = 49.5 - 0.1M + 0.6A$$

would indicate that this is true. With the control for "percent African American" added, the relationship between median income and percentage of African American students attending all-black schools largely disappears. In the multiple regression equation, a decrease of only 0.1 percent can be expected from an increase of 1,000 dollars in median income.[7]

---

[7]This little analysis is wholly fictitious. For a multiple regression analysis of black voting registration, using county data for southern states in the 1950s, see Matthews and Prothro (1963).

This freedom from the need to "hold variables constant" physically is an important advantage of multivariate regression analysis. This is especially true when working with several variables simultaneously.[8] Because there is no satisfactory analog to this technique for use with ordinal data, we can add this to our list of arguments for trying to measure variables intervally as often as possible. Nominal variables may be included in multiple regression equations by treating them as dichotomies (refer to p. 138–140).

As in simple linear regression, it is important in multiple linear regression that the data actually fit a model in which all the relationships between the dependent variable and the independent variables are linear. Otherwise, the regression plane described by the equation we come up with will be an inaccurate representation of the relationships.

There is also an additional requirement in *multiple* linear regression. It is important that the data best fit a model in which the relationship between the dependent variable and each independent variable is the same no matter what value the other independent variable(s) takes on. In our three-variable example of w, x, and y, we had to assume that an increase of one unit in x produced the same change in y, no matter what the value of w was. Otherwise, we could not have calculated the expected value of y simply by adding a plus b_1 times w plus b_2 times x. We would have had to pick a value for b_1 that was appropriate for whatever value of x we were using, and a value of b_2 that was appropriate for whatever value of w we were using. It is obvious that this would be a complicated procedure. In fact, it is often impossible to operate under these conditions.

When this happens—when the relationship between variables A and B differs, depending on the value of a variable C—there is said to be "interaction" among the variables. A concrete example may make more clear what interaction is and how it might arise. Consider the relationship between party affiliation and how members of Congress vote on a bill. This relationship could be strong (all Democrats vote one way, all Republicans the other), or weak (less clear-cut party differences). But, the strength of the relationship itself might be related to a member's seniority. New members, who are rather dependent on party leadership for favors, might vote obediently along straight party lines. Those with more seniority, who had built up respect among fellow members, might vote more independently.

Thus, there would be interaction among the variables. The relationship between party and vote would change as the third variable, seniority, changed. Under these circumstances, a regression equation of the form

$$\text{vote} = a + b_1 \text{ party} + b_2 \text{ seniority}$$

[8]Although I have used the case of three variables in this section because that case can be represented by perspective drawings, the general multivariate regression technique applies to any number of variables. The same logic would apply to a four-variable case, with the equation $y = a + b_1w + b_2x + b_3z$, although we cannot draw a scattergram in four dimensions to illustrate it.

INTERACTION IN RESEARCH AND THEORY

Although interaction among variables is a nuisance from the standpoint of multivariate regression analysis, in itself it is an interesting phenomenon. It is exciting to think that a relationship itself may depend on a further variable. Because such interaction occurs frequently in the social sciences, it is important that you be alert to it in your research. Because "common sense" rarely gets so complicated as to suggest this sort of thing, interaction is almost always unexpected, and discovering it is fun and dramatic. As one example, Philip Converse was able to argue very neatly for the importance of a measure of ideological sophistication by showing that the relationship between social class and voting was strongly affected by it (1964, esp. pp. 231–234).[9] Among those who scored lowest in ideological sophistication, there was no relationship between social class and voting. As the score on ideological sophistication increased, however, a relationship appeared, reaching its apex among those with the highest sophistication score.

would not be appropriate. It would not be true that "vote" always increased by the same amount with a given change in "party." How much "vote" changed with a given change in "party" would depend on the value of "seniority."[10]

Like ordinary regression analysis, logit and probit analyses may readily incorporate a number of independent variables. The coefficients for the variables are difficult to interpret, since they are predicting not directly to the variable or its probability but (in the case of the logit) to the natural logarithm of $p/(1-p)$ where p is the probability that $y = 1$. As in logit analysis with a single independent variable, the results are usually made understandable by calculating from transformations of the coefficients what the probability of y is estimated to be, given varying combinations of the independent variables. For instance, if we were predicting voting for the Democratic party from age and gender, we might present the results as in Table 9-3.

CONCLUSION

You might expect me to conclude, "Go out and use these measures." However, I am more interested in cautioning you against using them unwisely. All of these techniques simplify what is going on in a set of data by screening out certain aspects of relationships. This is their great virtue, and it *is* a virtue. Still, it is your responsibility to delve a bit deeper and see just what is being screened out. For instance, each of the scattergrams in Figure 9-6 would give approximately the same regression equation,

[9]This example is a particularly interesting one because Converse demonstrated yet a second level of interaction (the interaction itself varies with gender) that I have chosen to ignore here.

[10]It is possible to add "interaction terms" to the regression equation to take into account certain types of interaction, but that goes beyond the scope of this presentation. See, for example, Blalock (1969, Appendix A, "Theory Building and the Statistical Concept of Interaction").

TABLE 9-3   Example of Results from a
Multivariate Logit Analysis

	Gender	
Age	Male	Female
25	0.52*	0.62
35	0.48	0.58
45	0.46	0.55
55	0.45	0.53
65	0.44	0.51
75	0.44	0.50

*Estimated probability of voting Democratic, for various
combinations of age and gender.

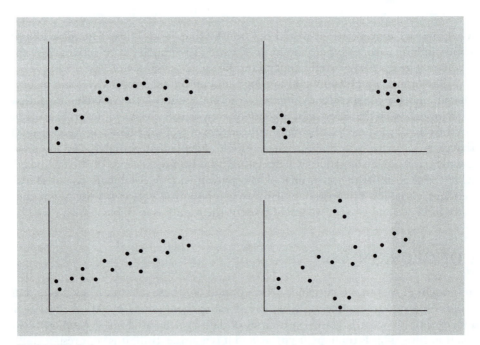

FIGURE 9-6   Four Alternative Scattergrams with the Same Regression Equations

but the relationships depicted mean quite different things. It is critical that you
examine as carefully as possible each scattergram on which you base a regression
equation, checking for nonlinearity, noting which observations are mavericks in the
relationship, and so on.

A computer can chug out hundreds of regression equations in a few seconds. It is tempting simply to call for a mound of results, especially given the uncertainty involved in working with most social science theories. Usually, however, you will be better served if you first think carefully about what you want to do, pick a limited number of relationships of interest to you, and examine each of these relationships in detail. Your measures will then be useful summarizing tools, not substitutes for a full look at what is going on.

The important thing is that you stay in charge. Use your measures and computer analyses as tools rather than ends in themselves, and keep your eye on the question you want to answer. Data will talk to you, but you must let them speak softly.

Introduction to Statistics
Inference, or How to Gamble on Your Research

As I pointed out in Chapter 8, there are two main areas of statistics: (1) measuring things, especially measuring relationships between variables; and (2) estimating how likely it is that the measure you have gotten could have occurred by chance. In Chapters 8 and 9, we looked at the first of these aspects, and now we examine the second. (I must note parenthetically that, as in preceding chapters, I do not intend to teach you *how to use* statistical tests. Instead, I present the general logic of such tests to help you understand what they mean when you see them. This approach might also serve as a useful supplement to a statistics course, which sometimes teaches students how to use the tests without putting the tests in a broader perspective.)

It is quite possible to get a particular result by chance, even though the result is not true in general. If you chose ten U.S. senators at random, for instance, it would be possible to come up with a group consisting largely of conservative Democrats and liberal Republicans. From that you might conclude—erroneously—that there was a relationship between party and ideology in the Senate, with Republicans the more liberal group.

However, if you repeatedly drew groups of ten senators, selecting the ten at random from the whole Senate, *most* of the time you would find that the Democrats in your group were more liberal than the Republicans, simply because Democratic senators do tend to be more liberal than Republican senators. But some of the time you would find that the Republicans in your sample were more liberal than the Democrats, or that the two parties did not differ at all. The problem in drawing a single group and describing the Senate from it is that you cannot know whether your group is of the first type (the relationship between the variables is the same in your subset as in the Senate as a whole) or of the second (the relationship between the variables is different in the subset from that in the Senate as a whole). If it is of the first type, your conclusion will be true; if it is of the second (a distorted sample), your conclusion will be false. This is a common problem that must be dealt with whenever anyone tries to describe a whole population of cases by looking only at a sample drawn out of the population. It comes up in conducting social science research, opinion polling, assigning television ratings, conducting market analyses, administering quality control in manufacturing, and in performing numerous other activities.

Fortunately, there are ways to determine just how likely it is that a particular result could have occurred by chance even if its opposite were generally true. By means of these techniques, we can calculate how much stock to put in our findings. It is a very close analogy to say that we can gamble intelligently on the results of our study by calculating the odds that the results are false. When we do this, we are said to measure (or "test") the *statistical significance* of our results.

In looking at how to measure relationships in Chapter 9, we found that there were qualitatively different ways to go about it, depending on the level at which the variables were measured. In measuring the statistical significance of a relationship, one broad procedure holds for all levels of data, although there are differences in specific techniques.

LOGIC OF MEASURING SIGNIFICANCE

The general procedure by which we calculate the probability that a given result could have occurred by chance, even though the true state of affairs was something other than what is indicated by the result, is the same procedure that we use in calculating the odds of any event happening.

As usual when talking about probability, let us start with a deck of cards. Given an honest deck of cards, thoroughly shuffled, you are instructed to draw a card. You know that the probability that you will draw the king of hearts is 1/52, for there are 52 cards and only one of them is the king of hearts. Next, you are instructed to do this two times, replacing the card and reshuffling after the first draw. You know that the probability of drawing a king of hearts *both times* is $1/52 \times 1/52 = 1/2704$, or 0.00037, and so on.[1]

You were able to calculate these probabilities because, given a sufficient set of assumptions, the probability that any particular result would occur could be determined. These assumptions had to account for all of the factors that could influence the outcome of the drawing. With such a set of assumptions, it was possible to calculate exactly how likely any particular result was. The set of assumptions in this case was as follows:

1. The deck has 52 cards, of which only one is the king of hearts.
2. The deck is thoroughly and honestly shuffled before each drawing.
3. The drawing is blind, so that each card is equally likely to be drawn (you don't peek, none of the cards stick together, etc.).

---

[1]The logic of this is as follows: In order to draw two kings of hearts in two draws, you must accomplish two things. First, you must draw the king of hearts on the first round. This can be expected to happen only one fifty-second of the time. Now, assuming that you have succeeded in the first round, you still can expect success in the second round only one fifty-second of the time. In other words, in the full two-draw process, you can expect to proceed to final success only one fifty-second of one fifty-second of the time.

If any of these assumptions were not true, your calculation of probabilities would be incorrect. For instance, if there were two kings of hearts (i.e., assumption 1 above was wrong), the probability of drawing one in a single draw would have been 2/52, not 1/52. Or if the deck had been stacked so as to make drawing the king of hearts likely (i.e., assumption 2 above was false), the probability of drawing one would have been greater than 1/52.

This is the way in which we normally use odds and probability. We have a set of assumptions of which we are confident. Those assumptions determine the probability that any particular event will happen. From this we know with how much confidence we can predict that the event will occur, that is, at what odds we should bet that it will occur.

Statistical inference uses this same logical structure, but turns it on its head. An example may be the best way to demonstrate this.

EXAMPLE OF STATISTICAL INFERENCE

Let us return to our previous example, taking a sample of ten senators to see whether there is a difference in how liberal the two senatorial parties are. Let us say that you have drawn such a sample and that your results are shown in Table 10-1. Of the ten senators in the sample, 75 percent of the Democrats, but only 33 percent of the Republicans, are liberal. How safe would you be to conclude from this limited sample that senatorial Democrats are on the whole more liberal?

To find out, you must proceed just as you did in our card-drawing example, by setting a list of assumptions that would be sufficient to let you calculate the probability of drawing ten senators that look like those you have, if in fact Democratic and Republican senators do *not* differ in the degree to which they are liberal. These assumptions would be:

1. The ten senators have been drawn at random.
2. There is *no relationship* between party and ideology in the "full" Senate from which these have been drawn.

Just from these two assumptions, using probability theory, it is possible for you to calculate how likely it is that you would have gotten any particular result in your sample. In this particular case, using a "chi-square" test (which I introduce later in the chapter), you can calculate that the probability of having

TABLE 10-1　Sample Result

	Democrats	Republicans
Liberal	3	2
Conservative	1	4

gotten at least as great a difference as you found between the parties, given the assumptions, is 0.264.[2] Thus there is a good chance that you could have gotten a relationship as strong as this in a sample of ten even if the assumptions that you set up were true—that is, even if there were no difference between Democrats and Republicans.

How you would then treat your research results depends on whether you are a long-shot gambler at heart, what kind of risks ride on your decision, and so on. Approximately three times out of four you would not have gotten as strong a relationship as you did if the assumptions you wish to test were true. Will you reject that set of assumptions on the basis of your sample result, accepting the one chance in four that you are wrong in doing so? If you are willing to reject the assumptions, notice that the truth is questionable with regard to only one of the assumptions in the set; you purposely have set up the test this way. You know whether or not you have drawn the ten senators at random. Therefore, in rejecting the set of assumptions, you really are rejecting only one assumption, the assumption that there is no relationship between party and ideology in the Senate. What you are saying is: "By rejecting its opposite, I am making the statement, 'There is an ideological difference between the senatorial parties.' I know that given the amount of evidence I have gathered, I am running considerable risk in making the statement. There is a probability of 0.264 that I am wrong."

HYPOTHESIS TESTING

The example we have used is a typical problem in statistical inference: We have a particular result in hand, and we wish to calculate the probability that this event could have occurred given some set of assumptions. We cannot be confident of one of these assumptions, for it involves the very thing we are trying to infer. If there is a sufficiently small probability that the event we have in mind could have occurred, given the set of assumptions, we decide to treat the set of assumptions as false. (This usually is referred to as "rejecting the hypothesis" that the assumptions are true.) And since we are confident of all but one of the assumptions (the thing we want to test), rejecting the set of assumptions really means that we are rejecting that one assumption.

We run some risk of being wrong in treating the assumptions as false. After all, the result we have observed could have occurred even if the assumptions were true. The probability we have calculated tells us precisely how likely it is that we are wrong. It tells us the probability that the result we have observed could have occurred if the assumptions we are rejecting were in fact true—that is, the probability that we are making a mistake in rejecting the assumptions. We normally will

---

[2]There is a great variety of statistical tests available to fit different circumstances of research. Statistical tests vary in the level of measurement that they require and in the particular set of assumptions that they embody. The chi-square test used here is particularly designed for testing the significance of a relationship between two nominal-scale variables. See the discussion on pp. 155–157.

reject a set of assumptions only when the probability that they could have produced the result we have observed is comfortably low.[3]

You can see now why I said that statistical inference uses the same logic as setting odds, but turns it on its head. Normally, in setting odds, we select a set of assumptions from which we can confidently predict how likely it is that certain things will happen in the future, things we have not yet observed. In statistical inference, we calculate how likely it is that an *observed* result could have occurred if some hypothetical and contrary assumption were true. If the probability is sufficiently low, we use the result to reject the assumption. Just as in everyday setting of odds, the probability shows us how likely it is that we are making a mistake.

Null Hypothesis

It is clear from our description of statistical inference that we do not test directly the statement we wish to make about a relationship. Instead, we insert its opposite—which is called the *null hypothesis*, the hypothesis we should like to reject—into the set of assumptions from which we calculate the probability. Because it is the only questionable member of the set of assumptions, if we decide to reject the set, we really are rejecting only the null hypothesis. By rejecting the null hypothesis, we in effect assert its opposite, which is the statement we wished to make in the first place.

The twisted and convoluted way one must think to understand this process is discouraging to most people when they see it for the first time. "Why," they ask, "can't we just test our hypothesis directly instead of having to turn it inside out?"

But think about how you might go about doing this. First of all, you could never test the hypothesis that your sample result was exactly the same as the true value in the population from which you had drawn the sample. Taken to a sufficient number of decimal places, it would virtually always *not* be the same as the true population value. For instance, 52.9397081 percent of voters in the United States voted for Barack Obama in 2008; no sample would have produced exactly this figure. But you would not want automatically to reject it just because your sample was not that precise a reflection of reality. Accordingly, you would pick some range of values around the true value and test whether or not the sample result was in that range. However, because you do not know what the true value is, this is a test that is impossible to set up.

In using the null hypothesis, on the other hand, a single alternative is chosen, which negates *all* possible true values that would be consistent with the statement you wish to make. For instance, in the Senate example, if you wanted to assert that your sample result was sufficiently close to the true relationship for you to accept the

---

[3]Whether the probability is "comfortably low," of course, is a difficult thing to judge. In setting odds, one usually has objective outside criteria to "help" in making the decision—an amount of money to be lost if the person is wrong, for instance. In much *engineering* research, there also will be such criteria available. In *theory-oriented* research, however, there usually are no fixed criteria, because the result is supposed to hold not just for some particular occasion, but in general. It is supposed to apply to occasions as yet unforeseen. Therefore, because objective criteria are lacking, a convention usually is followed of rejecting a set of assumptions only if the probability is less than 0.05.

TABLE 10-2   Ethnicity and Preferred Government Action Priorities

Preferred Priority	Ethnicity			
	WASP	African American	Other	Total
Employment and welfare	30	27	53	110
Foreign affairs	11	5	14	30
Environment	29	8	23	60
Total	70	40	90	200

sample result as valid, you would have to choose among an infinite variety of possible true relationships (80 percent of Democrats liberal, 75 percent of Republicans liberal; 100 percent of Democrats liberal, 51 percent of Republicans liberal; 100 percent of Democrats liberal, 1 percent of Republicans liberal; etc.). By using a null hypothesis ("there is no difference between the parties"), you can deal with a single statement that negates all possible versions of the statement you want to make. It is simply easier to disprove a specific hypothesis than to prove an open-ended hypothesis.

Example: χ^2

One popular significance test is χ^2 (chi-square), which we used in our liberal–conservative example. It is designed for use with a table relating two nominal-scale variables. Given the strength of the relationship between the variables in the table, χ^2 allows us to estimate the probability that there is no relationship between the variables in the full population from which the sample has been drawn.

In Table 10-2, a hypothetical relationship between ethnicity and policy priorities has been drawn, based on a sample of 200 respondents to a survey. We want to know whether it is safe to assert, on the evidence of this sample, that there is a relationship between the two variables.

To calculate χ^2, this table must be compared with a construct designed to show a *lack* of relationship between the variables. Such a construct is shown in Table 10-3.

TABLE 10-3   Table of Nonrelationship

Preferred Priority	Ethnicity			
	WASP	African American	Other	Total
Employment and welfare	38.5	22.0	49.5	110
Foreign affairs	10.5	6.0	13.5	30
Environment	21.0	12.0	27.0	60
Total	70	40	90	200

The entries in Table 10-3 are arrived at by calculating how many WASPs, say, would give first priority to employment and welfare if exactly the same proportion of WASPs as of African Americans and "other ethnics" favored the employment/welfare priority.[4] Thus, because there are 70 WASPs in the sample, and 110/200 of the sample favor the employment/welfare priority, we would expect to find that the sample contained 110/200 × 70 = 38.5 WASPs who chose employment/welfare. Similarly, we would expect to find that 110/200 of the 40 African Americans, or 22.0, chose employment/welfare, and so on, cell by cell, until the hypothetical table was filled. Notice that to construct a table in which the variables are completely unrelated, it was necessary to maintain the fiction that there could have been one-half of a WASP in favor of the employment/welfare priority.

Table 10-3 embodies the null hypothesis that we want to test—that there is no relationship between the variables. Each cell in the table has the characteristic (1) that its entry is the same proportion of its row frequency as its column frequency is of the total sample, and (2) that its entry is the same proportion of its column frequency as its row frequency is of the total sample. That is, the members of each row are equally likely to fall into any given column, and vice versa. This is what we should expect if the two variables were unrelated.

The question we want to ask is: Are the two tables sufficiently different that we can say, on the basis of what we found when we looked at the sample, that the full population does not look like the distribution in the hypothetical table? Chi-square is a measure of how different the two tables are. It is calculated from the formula

$$\chi^2 = \Sigma \frac{(F_0 - F_h)^2}{F_h}$$

where for each cell in the table, F_0 is the observed frequency (from Table 10-2, in this case) and F_h is the frequency predicted for the hypothetical table (10-3 in this case). Thus for each cell in the table, (1) the prediction from the hypothetical table is subtracted from the actual figure, (2) this figure is squared, and (3) the squared difference is then divided by the prediction from the hypothetical table. The results of this, from all the cells of the table, are added together (you will recall that this is what the sign "Σ" means) to give us the χ^2. The more the tables differ, the greater χ^2 will be. If the tables are exactly the same, χ^2 will equal zero, inasmuch as each cell's result will be

$$\chi^2 = \frac{(F_0 - F_h)^2}{F_h} = \frac{0^2}{F_h} = 0$$

In Table 10-4, χ^2 is calculated for the present example. Cell A is the upper-left cell of Table 10-2 or 10-3 (the cell in which WASPs choosing employment/welfare fall), cell B is the next cell to the right, cell C is the upper-right cell, cell D is the middle left cell, cell E falls at the exact center of the table, and so on.

[4]WASP is the acronym for white, Anglo-Saxon Protestant.

TABLE 10-4   Calculations for χ^2

Cell	F_h	(F_0-F_h)	$(F_0-F_h)^2$	$(F_0-F_h)^2/F_h$
A	38.5	−8.5	72.25	1.877
B	22.0	+5.0	25.00	1.136
C	49.5	+3.5	12.25	0.247
D	10.5	+0.5	0.25	0.024
E	6.0	−1.0	1.00	0.167
F	13.5	+0.5	0.25	0.019
G	21.0	+8.0	64.00	3.048
H	12.0	−4.0	16.00	1.333
I	27.0	−4.0	16.00	0.593
				$\chi^2 = $ total $= 8.444$

Sampling Distribution

Before I can show how we go from measuring the difference between the observed and null hypothesis tables to calculating the probability that the null hypothesis is true, I must first introduce the idea of a *sampling distribution*.

For any particular set of assumptions, a sampling distribution shows what proportion of the time each particular result could be expected to occur if the sampling technique chosen were repeated a very large number of times and the set of assumptions (including the null hypothesis) were true. That is, it gives the *probability* of getting a particular result if you applied the techniques you are using to a population for which the null hypothesis is true.

A sampling distribution embodies all the assumptions you make in a test, including the null hypothesis. It represents the application of probability theory to those assumptions, to calculate the probability that each possible result would occur. Some simple sampling distributions can be calculated easily. For instance, in the card-drawing example on p. 151, the sampling distribution states that the probability of drawing the ace of hearts is 1/52, the probability of drawing the king of hearts is 1/52, and so on, through all the cards of the deck. Of course, this sampling distribution depends on the set of assumptions you made in that example. The sampling distribution for a different set of assumptions would look different.

In another simple case, suppose that you had to predict the probability of getting just one head in two flips of a coin. Assume that (1) the coin is honest, (2) the flipper is honest, and (3) the coin will not stand on its edge. You can now calculate that the probability of getting a head followed by a tail is 0.25, the probability of getting a head followed by a head is 0.25, the probability of getting a tail followed by a head is 0.25, and the probability of getting a tail followed by a tail is 0.25. Because two of the possibilities involve getting just one head in the two throws, the probability of getting just one head in either of the two ways is 0.50, the probability of

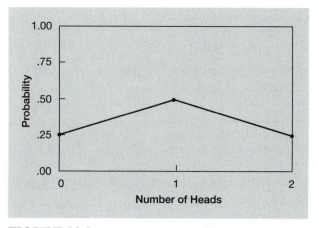

FIGURE 10-1   Sampling Distribution for Two Flips of a Coin

getting no heads is 0.25, and the probability of getting two heads is 0.25. This sampling distribution is presented graphically in Figure 10-1.

The same sampling distribution could be presented in a cumulative graph, showing the probability of getting *at least* no heads, at least one head, or at least two heads. Figure 10-2 charts the sampling distribution in this way. We always will get at least zero heads (we cannot get a negative number), so the probability of that outcome is 1.0; we could get at least one head either by getting two heads (probability of 0.25) or by getting one head (probability of 0.50), so the probability of at least one head is 0.75; we could only get at least two heads by getting exactly two heads, so the probability of at least two heads is 0.25.

These sampling distributions are simple. The sampling distributions for most statistical tests are more complex, and we must use tables developed by statisticians

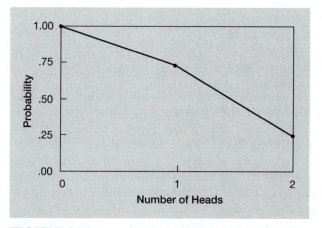

FIGURE 10-2   Cumulative Sampling Distribution for Two Flips of a Coin

FIGURE 10-3   Sampling Distribution of χ^2, for Three-by-Three Tables

to visualize them. The cumulative sampling distribution of χ^2 for a three-by-three table (a table with three categories in the rows and three categories in the columns, such as Tables 10-2 and 10-3) is presented in Figure 10-3.

Chi-square sampling distributions vary depending on the number of categories in the rows and columns of the table used. The probabilities given are the probability that a χ^2 *at least as* high as the one observed would have been obtained if the sample were drawn by random selection from a parent population in which the variables were unrelated. (Note that this is a cumulative sampling distribution, like the one depicted in Figure 10-2.) Thus, if you had found a χ^2 of 4.9, you would know that the probability of getting χ^2 as high as this was 0.3 if the variables you were working with were, in fact, not related. (The sampling distribution is based on assumptions of (1) the null hypothesis you wish to test and (2) random selection, which you know you have done.)

From this sampling distribution, we see that there is a probability of between 0.05 and 0.10 that we would have found a χ^2 as high as 8.44 from a three-by-three table if there were really no relationship between ethnicity and choice of priorities (i.e., if the null hypothesis were true). This means that we would run a risk of between 1 chance in 10 and 1 chance in 20 of being wrong in asserting on the basis of Table 10-2 that the null hypothesis is false—that there *is* a relationship between ethnicity and the choice of priorities.

To summarize these sections: A sampling distribution is a list of the probabilities that each possible event (out of a set of events) will happen. The probabilities in a sampling distribution are based on a set of assumptions. If we choose our significance test appropriately, the set of assumptions on which its sampling distribution is based will consist of (1) a null hypothesis (the assumption that what we really want to say about the data is false), and (2) a group of other assumptions that we feel certain are true. If we find from the sampling distribution that it is very unlikely, given those assumptions, that the event we have observed (in our ethnicity/choice of priorities example above, finding a χ^2 of 8.44) could have occurred, we reject the assumptions on which the sampling distribution is based. Because we are sure that all but one of those assumptions (the null hypothesis) are true, this amounts to rejecting the null hypothesis and asserting its opposite, which is what we had originally wanted to say about the data. The probability that we could have gotten the observed result if all the assumptions underlying the sampling distribution were true tells us how likely it is that we are wrong to reject the null hypothesis. Thus a significance test furnishes a useful check on our research. It tells us how likely it is that we could have gotten our results by chance alone—the probability that in fact the opposite of what we are asserting is true.

Importance of N

N, the number of cases in a sample, is always a factor in significance tests. All other things being equal, the greater the number of cases on which a statement is based, the more certain you can be that the statement is true.[5] Every significance test, accordingly, takes the number of cases into account. If each number in Tables 10-2 and 10-3 were doubled, for example, the quantity $(F_0 - F_h)^2/F_h$ would double for each cell. The χ^2 would thus be double 8.444, or 16.888. From Figure 10-3, we see that if the null hypothesis of no relationship were true, the probability of getting a χ^2 at least this high would be less than 0.01. Thus from a table showing exactly the same pattern as Table 10-2 but based on a sample of 400 cases instead of the 200 used in that table, we would run a risk of less than 1 chance in 100 of being wrong in asserting that there is a relationship between the variables.[6]

N is the most obvious factor affecting the statistical significance of findings. In many sorts of statistical tests, it is the only factor we need to worry about. But there may be others. For example, in regression analysis, the amount of confidence we can have in our estimate of what the relationship looks like is a matter not only of how many cases we have used but also of how much the independent variable varies. In the extreme case of zero variance in the independent variable, depicted in the scattergram in Figure 10-4, we are simply unable to choose any regression line. Because all the data points fall above a single value of the independent variable, an infinite number of lines (a few of which are indicated on the graph) can be passed through the data, each of which has an equal sum of squared deviations about itself. In other words, it is impossible to choose a single "best" line by least-squares criteria.

This is the extreme case. In general, the greater the variation in the independent variable, the more firmly fixed the estimate of the regression line can be and, accordingly, the more stock we can put in our findings. One way to look at this is to think of the regression line as wobbling on a fulcrum. As it happens, every regression line must pass through point $\bar{x}, \bar{y}$ in the scattergram; this is determined mathematically by the formulas for a and b. (In other words, the expected value of y when

---

[5]See the box "Law of Large Numbers" on p. 61.
[6]The following five paragraphs present advanced material that can be omitted without any loss in comprehension of other material covered in this book.

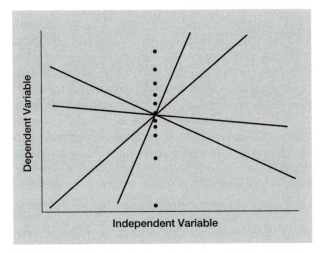

FIGURE 10-4   Regression Analysis with Zero Variance
in the Independent Variable

x equals its own mean *must* be the mean of y.) If there is relatively little variation
in the independent variable, as in Figure 10-5, the line is free to wobble a good
deal, using this point as a fulcrum. A considerable change in the angle at which the
line passes through the point $\bar{x}, \bar{y}$ will not change the size of the squared deviations
from the line by very much. This is due to the fact that for observations whose
value on x is close to $\bar{x}$, wobble in the line does not change the expected value of y
very greatly; thus the difference between the observed and expected values of y also
is not greatly changed.

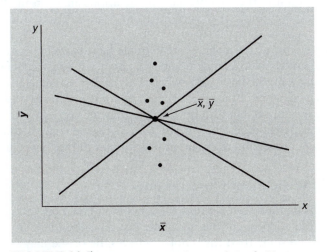

FIGURE 10-5   Regression Analysis with Little Variance
in the Independent Variable

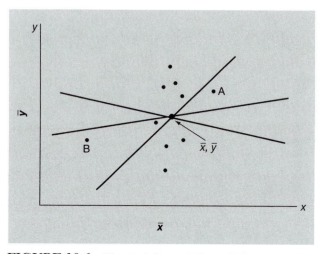

FIGURE 10-6   The Stabilizing Effect of Variance in the Independent Variable

No one of the observations is able significantly to affect the regression line in Figure 10-5. The line is simply not held firmly in place by these observations, whose values on x fall so close together. Observations with widely varying values on x, however, would hold a much firmer grip on the regression line. Two such observations have been added in Figure 10-6.

If the regression line were now to wobble through the same angles as in Figure 10-5, the size of the deviations of observations A and B (in Figure 10-6) from the line would increase dramatically. Remember, the regression line must be the line that minimizes the sum of squared deviations about itself. The regression line in Figure 10-6 cannot stray very far from points A and B without sharply increasing that sum.

Thus a few points whose x values are extreme have more impact in determining the slope of the line than do a larger number of points whose x values fall close to the mean. Accordingly, in calculating how likely it is that our estimate of a regression has been due to chance, we must take into account not only how many observations have been used in the analysis, but also how widely they are spread on the independent variable. Significance tests designed for use with regression analysis take into account *both* the number of cases and the amount of variation in the independent variable.[7]

Problem of Independent Observations

It often happens that a researcher draws a conclusion based on a set of observations that appear to be independent but are really not. Because there are in effect fewer observations in the study than the scholar believes, he or she may overestimate the

---

[7]The general extension of this problem to multivariate regression is the problem of multicollinearity. For a good expository discussion of multicollinearity, see King, Keohane, and Verba (1994, ch. 4, part 1).

strength of the evidence. The relationship in question might be due to chance, without the researcher realizing it. The difficulty here is that statistical tests will not be able to alert us to the danger, because statistical tests already assume that the data to be analyzed consist of independent observations. If the observations are not independent, all statistical tests will underestimate the probability that a relationship might be due to chance. Thus we might be inappropriately confident of our assertions.

An example may help. Consider a study that seeks to determine the extent to which "police brutality" is a function of the explicitness of guidelines issued to police patrols, with close and explicit directions presumed to be associated with low "brutality." The investigator might measure the explicitness of guidelines to patrols in the 11 towns and 63 townships of a county and relate this measure by regression analysis to the roughness with which police in each of those units handle suspects. Statistical tests might be applied to the regression results, with N stated as 74.

Unknown to the investigator, however, it might be that some of these units shared a coordinated police force. For example, all township police forces might be under the direction of the county sheriff. In this case, although the 63 townships looked like separate units, they would all be separate parts of a single police administration, with one set of guidelines and one set of expectations with regard to roughness. Thus there would in fact be only 12 independent observations (each of the 11 town forces, plus the sheriff's office), which should raise a specter of doubt about the correctness of an assertion based on these data.

The problem of nonindependent observations does not often occur in a simple form such as this, and if it does arise, it can generally be avoided by simple common sense. However, the problem occurs frequently in a more subtle (and more technical) way under the guise of *autocorrelation*. Autocorrelation occurs when observations are related to some extent but are not (as in the study of police brutality) identical to each other. For example, if we look at the relationship between trends in the economy and trends in the U.S. president's popularity, month by month, we will probably have a problem of autocorrelation. February 1943 had much in common with May 1943, for instance. Though one would not go so far as to say that gathering information from these two months is simply equivalent to having information about a single month (as we could say about any two townships in the other example), neither can we say that we have as much information here as we would have with two widely separated months.

I mention the problem at this point only to alert you to it. Partial solutions are available, but they are beyond the scope of this book. Most texts in statistics or econometrics, such as the one by Knoke, Bohrnstedt, and Mee (2002) or Kmenta (1997), discuss the problem.

SIGNIFICANCE TEST: ALWAYS NECESSARY?

Even when we do not work with a limited sample drawn from a larger group of subjects, there is a sense in which all research involves "sampling" of a sort and in which misleading results can occur by chance. For instance, we might look at all

50 states and find that the generosity of their welfare budgets is related to the degree of party competition in the states' elections. In one sense, there is no question but that this is the "true" result. Because we have included all the states in our sample, sanything we find out about them is by definition "true generally." But suppose we think of ourselves as trying to say something not just about the 50 states as they exist at this one point in time, but about "state politics." Then we must regard these 50 states as a sample drawn for us by chance and accident from a larger metaphysical population of "states"—all states as they might be in the future or as they might have been had their boundaries been drawn differently or had history proceeded differently.

The latter view seems to reflect more accurately what we try to do in developing political theories out of empirical research. There are times when we wish to describe a specific population as it exists at one point in time; this is particularly likely in "engineering" research. In such research, we frequently are interested in measuring some condition of a population so as to react to it or make adjustments in it, rather than to develop explanatory theories from it. For instance, a tax administrator may want to know how many states administer sales taxes, how great a portion of national income these states involve, and so on. What the administrator is concerned with is a description of the tax situation as it currently exists, not, by and large, with developing theories to *explain* why things are as they are.[8] In most theory-oriented research, however, we should seek a more inclusive sort of generality.

Sometimes an author claims that she need not be concerned about the possibility of chance results because her sample is synonymous with the total population of subjects (all the states, all the nations in the United Nations, all the U.S. senators, or what have you). This is a statement that should arouse suspicion. If the author is trying to draw general conclusions from the study, propositions that one would expect to be as true of states or nations or senators a decade from now as they are today, she *must* be concerned with the problem of chance results. With infrequent exceptions, then, this is a problem all of us must take seriously in our research.

POLLING AND SIGNIFICANCE TESTS

A ubiquitous activity in our society is *polling*, asking a sample of the population whom they will vote for, whether they support regulation of handguns, or whatever.[9] Typically, about 2,000 respondents are polled to describe a population such as that of the United States, and the results are reported as "accurate to within plus or minus 3 percent"—or 2 percent, or some other level of accuracy.

---

[8]Note, by the way, that to the extent that an engineer sees her task as *changing* and *reforming* patterns rather than continuing ongoing administrative procedures, explanatory theory will be relatively more important. A tax administrator who wanted to change the extent to which states relied on sales taxes to generate income would first have to try to find out why states use sales taxes.
[9]See the discussion of sampling on pp. 99–103.

This operation is a variant of statistical significance testing. Based on a given number of cases, which of course can be set as desired by the person doing the polling, and with knowledge of how the individuals have been chosen for the sample (usually some variant of random sampling), the pollster can conclude that according to the sampling distribution of percent approval that one would get using repeated samples of this sort and of this size, sample results would fall within plus or minus X percent of the true population value 95 percent of the time. Thus the pollster claims that the result is accurate to "within plus or minus X percent." Note that this does not mean that the result absolutely falls within plus or minus X percent of the true value; it means that 95 percent of the time it would fall within that range of the true value.

Note here, also, that changing N changes the width of the "plus or minus" range. If an N of about 2,000 respondents gave you plus or minus 3 percent, increasing N to 4,000 would give you a lower range, perhaps plus or minus 1 percent.

USES AND LIMITATIONS OF STATISTICAL TESTS

I have tried in this chapter to present a significance test for what it is—a useful check on research results. The real meat of research, however—the way we find out about politics—is by looking at data and seeking out relationships between variables, the sorts of things I discussed in Chapters 2 through 9.

Unfortunately, researchers often place undue emphasis on significance tests. It is a pity that looking at data requires less formal training (but more practice) than does calculating significance tests. Perhaps because they have spent so much time in courses learning to use significance tests, many researchers give the tests an undue emphasis in their research. The status of these tests should be strictly that of a secondary check on the *creative* work the researcher has done in looking at relationships.

CONCLUSION

I have tried in this chapter to give you some idea of the general logic of inference, which is the common thread running through all statistical tests. These tests vary among themselves, however, in terms of their suitability for a given level of measurement and the particular mix of assumptions (other than the null hypothesis) they require the investigator to guarantee. This is why there are so many different tests. For a description of particular tests, the reader should consult a statistics text such as the one cited at the end of Chapter 8.

■■ Further Discussion ─────────────────────────────

A particularly good discussion of the misapplication of significance tests, along the lines of the example I used, is Duggan and Dean, "Common Misinterpretations of Significance Levels in Sociological Journals" (1968). See also Winch and Campbell, "Proof? No. Evidence? Yes. The Significance of Tests of Significance" (1969).

Anyone thinking of using these tests should first take a course in statistics; barring that, however, useful presentations of the techniques are given in the text cited at the end of Chapter 8. Another very good treatment is that of Simon (1985).

For further consideration, think about the two following situations. *What is wrong in each situation?*

1. A researcher studying Congress examines the vote on 100 or so bills. For two of these votes, she finds a statistically significant relationship (at the 0.05 level) between a representative's height and the way he voted on the bill. This strikes her as a surprising finding, and she uses it as the basis for a chapter and a half of her book.

2. A large number of scholars study committee systems to see whether democracy in committee decision making leads the members to be satisfied with their work on the committee. All but one of these scholars fail to find a statistically significant relationship between these two variables. Most of those who fail to find a relationship leave that question and start to work on other things. A few of them write up their results, but these are rejected by journal editors because they are negative, not positive, findings. The one scholar who did find a statistically significant result publishes it. Net result: one published article, reporting a statistically significant relationship between committee democracy and members' satisfaction.

Where Do Theories Come From?

This has been a book about developing theories and trying them out on reality. In Chapter 2, I equated the research process with a search for elegant theories. In succeeding chapters, I have discussed various aspects of research: concept formation, measurement, data analysis. My criterion for the usefulness of any of these techniques has been the extent to which that technique aided in the creation of elegant theories. A high degree of "precision in measurement" is important, I have argued, because it allows us more flexibility in stating the *theory* we choose to work with. Measurement accuracy, whether it is a matter of reliability or validity, is important because without accurate measurement we cannot establish the connection between the data we are handling and the *theory* with which we are working. Regression analysis usually is more useful than correlation analysis, because the results of regression analysis apply generally to a *theory*, whereas the results of correlation analysis can serve only as a description of a particular situation; and so on.

In all of this, I have never dealt with the critical question: Just how does one find a theory on which to work? There is one deceptively simple answer to this question, which is to choose theories for study from the already existing body of work in political science. That is, take an existing theory and try it out on some data. I discussed some of the limitations of this procedure in Chapter 2, but the important point for my discussion here is that this answer begs the question of how the original theorist found the theory.

What makes a political scientist describe the relationship among a group of variables in a particular way? Probably it most frequently happens that the researcher observes a body of data and tries to see a pattern among them. This is the most obvious way to go about devising a theory; it follows quite naturally from the things a theory is supposed to achieve. The purpose of a theory is to provide a simplified pattern to describe a complicated jumble of observations. Would it not follow, then, that the most appropriate way to devise a theory is simply to look at the jumble of observations and pick out the most prominent pattern running through them?

Unfortunately, "observations" in political science are riddled with problems of inaccurate measurement; they are often measured imprecisely, and the nonexperimental circumstances under which we gather them make it difficult to isolate the effects of single variables. These are all problems I discussed earlier in the book. Their combined effect is to make it very difficult to look at a batch of observations and pick out the best simplifying pattern. There is so much going on in a group of observations, much of which is extraneous to what we want to do, that the pattern we ideally would hope to pick out is obscured.

This problem is not confined to the social sciences. An amusing example of the difficulty of choosing among potential explanations without the benefit of prior theory is offered by a discussion among Samuel Johnson, James Boswell, and some of their friends in 1769 about the mystery of why the residents of the Scottish island of St. Kilda caught cold whenever a ship arrived there.[1] There was at that time already speculation that illnesses were transmitted from one person to another, but Johnson regarded this as a "prejudice," and not "smart modern thought." Eventually the explanation favored by Boswell was offered in a letter from a Lady of Norfolk:

> Now for the explication of this seeming mystery, which is so very obvious as, for that reason, to have escaped the penetration of Dr. Johnson and his friend, as well as that of the author. Reading the book with my ingenious friend, the late Reverend Mr. Christian, of Docking—after ruminating a little, "The cause, (says he,) is a natural one. The situation of St. Kilda renders a North-East Wind indispensably necessary before a stranger can land. The wind, not the stranger, occasions an epidemic cold."[2]

In a similar vein, James S. Coleman described the way the theory of gravity might *not* have been devised had Galileo gone about his task in the way most data-analyzing social scientists do:

> A simple example will illustrate some of the difficulties which might arise by this kind of "brick-by-brick" approach to theory. Suppose that early mechanics had developed by the use of regression equations. Suppose, specifically, that an investigation had been carried out relating the length of time a body had fallen through the air and the velocity it attained. The relation in mechanics is that the velocity attained is equal to the acceleration due to gravity times the time the object has fallen, or
>
> $$v = gt$$
>
> where g is the acceleration due to gravity. Now if there had been numerous investigations involving different-sized bodies, different velocities, and bodies with differing densities, the investigators would have ended with numerous pairs of observations (v_i, t_i), which they would locate on a scatter diagram in order to find the line of best fit. But in every case, and especially for high velocities (i.e., objects which fell a great distance) and low-density objects (i.e., feathers), the observed velocity would fall considerably below that which the theoretical equation predicts. The resulting regression equation might have ended up including other variables,

---

[1] G. Birkbeck Hill, *Boswell's Life of Johnson*, Vol. 2 (London: Clarendon Press, 1887), pp. 51–52.
[2] Ibid., p. 52.

such as mass or density of the object; and there would have been indications that at high velocities the relation of velocity to time was not even linear. The reason, of course, would be air resistance, which has different effects as a function of the density of the object, its shape, its velocity, and other things. The regression equation would of course have been empirically correct, but it wouldn't have corresponded to the simple velocity–time relation which served as the basis for Galileo's remarkable contribution to the science of mechanics. They might even have served to confound the issue, by bringing in too soon a factor—that is, air resistance—which was irrelevant to the fundamentals of mechanics.[3]

The moral of these stories is that we almost always are better off if we have some idea of what kind of pattern we want to look for before we start to look at data. If we have in mind a particular kind of pattern, it is easy to tell, among the jumble of things we find, what is relevant to that pattern and what is extraneous. Galileo was able to ignore the effects of air resistance because he knew that they were not the thing he should use to explain the speed of falling objects.

The distinction here is between "inductive" and "deductive" theory building. To build theory inductively, the researcher scans the observations, looking for patterns. To build theory deductively, the researcher deduces (from something else, some prior expectations) what sort of a pattern to expect and then looks for it among the observations.

According to the argument I have presented so far in this chapter, deductive theory building is clearly the better of the two. The problem lies with that "something else" from which the student is supposed to deduce theories. There simply are not many well-established *premises* in the social sciences from which to deduce anything. One way of distinguishing an ongoing "science" from a "pre-science" is that the former includes a generally agreed-upon body of assumptions from which most of its theories can be deduced (Kuhn, 1962). Political science, sociology, and similar social sciences cannot be said to possess such a body of assumptions.

Lacking this base for deduction, it is hard to argue patly that theory building must be done deductively. On the other hand, it is important to bear in mind the advantages of deduction, where it is feasible. There are some tricks that may heighten your awareness of situations in which deduction is feasible. One of the best sources of deductive theory is a well-established theory from another field. Theories of epidemic growth and population dynamics, from such fields as epidemiology and ecology, may suggest theories to political scientists or sociologists. So may microeconomic theory; as noted in Chapter 1, rational choice theory drawn from microeconomic theory has been particularly fruitful for political science. A healthy awareness of major theories in fields such as these, some of which are not all that closely related to our field, can be a helpful source of theory.

The art of building a theory remains in flux in political science—partly deductive, but largely inductive. The resulting confusion can be both enjoyable and fruitful, because more than in most disciplines, it allows a place for every sort of imagination to work: literary imagination, scientific imagination, moral imagination, mathematical imagination. It is in this spirit that I have tried to stress the "craft" in the "craft of political research."

---

[3]James S. Coleman, *Introduction to Mathematical Sociology* (New York: The Free Press, 1964), pp. 100–101. Copyright 1964 by the Free Press.

Selected Bibliography

ACHEN, CHRISTOPHER H. 1975. "Attitudes and the Survey Response," *American Political Science Review*, 69 (December), 1218–1231.

————. 1986. *The Statistical Analysis of Quasi-Experiments*. Berkeley, Calif.: University of California Press.

————, and W. PHILLIPS SHIVELY. 1995. *Cross-Level Inference*. Chicago: University of Chicago Press.

ANSOLABEHERE, STEPHEN, ALAN GERBER, and JAMES M. SNYDER, JR. 2002. "Equal Votes, Equal Money: Court-Ordered Redistricting and the Distribution of Public Expenditures in the American States," *American Political Science Review*, 96, 767–777.

ASHER, HERBERT B. 1974. "Some Consequences of Measurement Error in Survey Data," *American Journal of Political Science*, 18 (May), 469–485.

BACHRACH, PETER, and MORTON BARATZ. 1962. "The Two Faces of Power," *American Political Science Review*, 56 (December), 947–953.

BARBER, JAMES D. 1972. *The Presidential Character: Predicting Performance in the White House*. Upper Saddle River, N.J.: Prentice Hall.

BARTELS, LARRY M. 1993. "Messages Received: The Political Impact of Media Exposure," *American Political Science Review*, 87 (June), 267–285.

BARTON, ALLAN H. 1955. "The Concept of Property-Space in Social Research." In Paul F. Lazarsfeld and Morris Rosenberg, eds., *The Language of Social Research*, pp. 40–53. New York: Free Press.

BATALLA, JAVIER ORTIZ. 1993. "Essays on the Early History of Latin American Central Banking," Ph.D. dissertation in economics, University of California–Los Angeles.

BERNSTEIN, RICHARD J. 1978. *Restructuring of Social and Political Theory*. Philadelphia: University of Pennsylvania Press.

BLALOCK, HUBERT M. 1964. *Causal Inferences in Nonexperimental Research*. Chapel Hill, N.C.: University of North Carolina Press.

————. 1969. *Theory Construction: From Verbal to Mathematical Formulations*. Upper Saddle River, N.J.: Prentice Hall.

————. 1979. *Social Statistics*, rev. 2nd ed. New York: McGraw-Hill.

BUENO DE MESQUITA, BRUCE, JAMES D. MORROW, RANDOLPH M. SIVERSON, and ALASTAIR SMITH. 1999. "An Institutional Explanation of the Democratic Peace," *American Political Science Review*, 93 (December), 791–808.

BUTLER, DAVID, and DONALD STOKES. 1969. *Political Change in Britain*. New York: St. Martin's Press.

CAMPBELL, ANGUS, and others. 1960. *The American Voter*. New York: John Wiley & Sons.

CAMPBELL, DONALD T., and JULIAN C. STANLEY. 1963. *Experimental and Quasi-Experimental Designs for Research*. Chicago: Rand McNally.

CARTER, LEWIS F. 1971. "Inadvertent Sociological Theory," *Social Forces*, 50, 12–25.

COLEMAN, JAMES S. 1964. *Introduction to Mathematical Sociology*. New York: Free Press.

CONVERSE, PHILIP E. 1964. "The Nature of Belief Systems in Mass Publics." In David Apter, ed., *Ideology and Discontent*, pp. 206–261. New York: Free Press.

————. 1969. "Of Time and Partisan Stability," *Comparative Political Studies*, 2, 139–171.

————, and GEORGES DUPEUX. 1962. "Politicization of the Electorate in France and the United States," *Public Opinion Quarterly*, 26 (Spring), 1–23.

————, and ROY PIERCE. 1985. "Measuring Partisanship," *Political Methodology*, 11, 143–166.

COOK, THOMAS D., and DONALD T. CAMPBELL. 1979. *Quasi-Experimentation: Design and Analysis Issues for Field Setting*. Chicago: Rand McNally.

DAHL, ROBERT. 1961. *Who Governs?* New Haven, Conn.: Yale University Press.

———. 1966. *Political Oppositions in Western Democracies.* New Haven, Conn.: Yale University Press.

———. 1984. *Modern Political Analysis,* 4th ed. Upper Saddle River, N.J.: Prentice Hall.

DALTON, RUSSELL J., and STEVEN WELDON. 2007. "Partisanship and Party System Institutionalization," *Party Politics,* 13, 179–196.

———, and HANS-DIETER KLINGEMANN. 2007. "Citizens and Political Behavior." In Russell J. Dalton and Hans-Dieter Klingemann, eds., *Oxford Handbook of Political Science.* New York: Oxford University Press.

DIEHL, PAUL F., and JEAN KINGSTON. 1987. "Messenger or Message? Military Buildups and the Initiation of Conflict," *Journal of Politics,* 49 (August), 801–813.

DIGESER, PETER. 1992. "The Fourth Face of Power," *Journal of Politics,* 54 (November), 977–1007.

DOWNS, ANTHONY. 1957. *An Economic Theory of Democracy.* New York: Harper & Row.

DUGGAN, THOMAS J., and CHARLES W. DEAN. 1968. "Common Misinterpretations of Significance Levels in Sociological Journals," *American Sociologist,* 3 (February), 45–46.

DUVERGER, MAURICE. 1963. *Political Parties.* New York: Science Editions.

ECKSTEIN, HARRY. 1960. *Pressure Group Politics.* London: George Allen & Unwin.

———. 1966. *Division and Cohesion in Democracy.* Princeton, N.J.: Princeton University Press.

EISNER, THOMAS. 2005. *For Love of Insects.* Cambridge, Mass.: Harvard University Press.

FELDMAN, STANLEY. 1983. "The Measurement and Meaning of Trust in Government," *Political Methodology,* 9, 341–354.

GEDDES, BARBARA. 2003. *Paradigms and Sand Castles: Theory Building and Research Design in Comparative Politics.* Ann Arbor: University of Michigan Press.

GERBER, ALAN S., and DONALD P. GREEN. 2000. "The Effects of Personal Canvassing, Telephone Calls, and Direct Mail on Voter Turnout: A Field Experiment," *American Political Science Review,* 94 (September), 653–664.

GERRING, JOHN. 2007. *Case Study Research: Principles and Practices.* New York: Cambridge University Press.

GILBERT, JOHN P., RICHARD J. LIGHT, and FREDERICK MOSTELLER. 1975. "Assessing Social Innovations: An Empirical Basis for Policy." In Carl A. Bennett and Arthur A. Lumsdaine, eds., *Evaluation and Experiment,* pp. 39–193. New York: Academic Press.

GOLDSMITH, ARTHUR A. 1987. "Does Political Stability Hinder Economic Development?" *Comparative Politics,* 19, 471–480.

GOODMAN, LEO A., and WILLIAM H. KRUSKAL. 1954. "Measures of Association for Cross Classifications," *Journal of the American Statistical Association,* 49 (December), 747–754.

GREEN, DONALD, and ALAN GERBER, eds. 2004. *American Behavioral Scientists,* 48, 1 (January).

GREENSTEIN, FRED I. 2000. *The Presidential Difference: Leadership and Style from FDR to Clinton.* New York: Free Press.

HAMMOND, THOMAS H., and JANE M. FRASER. 1984. "Studying Presidential Performance in Congress," *Political Methodology,* 10, 211–244.

HOWELL, WILLIAM G., PATRICK J. WOLF, DAVID E. CAMPBELL, and PAUL E. PETERSON. 2002. "School Vouchers and Academic Performance: Results from Three Randomized Field Trials" *Journal of Policy Analysis and Management,* 21(2), 191–217.

INTERNATIONAL INSTITUTE FOR STRATEGIC STUDIES. 2009. *The Military Balance, 2009.* Oxford: Oxford University Press.

JACOB, PHILIP E. 1955. "A Multi-Dimensional Classification of Atrocity Stories." In Paul F. Lazarsfeld and Morris Rosenberg, eds., *The Language of Social Research,* pp. 54–57. New York: Free Press.

KARSTEN, PETER, and others. 1971. "ROTC, Mylai and the Volunteer Army," *Foreign Policy,* 2 (Spring), 135–161.

KEMENY, J., J. SNELL, and G. THOMPSON. 1957. *Introduction to Finite Mathematics.* Englewood Cliffs, NJ: Prentice-Hall

KEY, V. O., JR. 1950. *Southern Politics.* New York: Alfred A. Knopf.

KINDER, DONALD R., and THOMAS R. PALFREY, eds. 1993. *Experimental Foundations of Political Science*. Ann Arbor, Mich.: University of Michigan Press.

KING, GARY, ROBERT O. KEOHANE, and SIDNEY VERBA. 1994. *Designing Social Inquiry: Scientific Inference in Qualitative Research*. Princeton, N.J.: Princeton University Press.

KIRK, JEROME, and MARC L. MILLER. 1985. *Reliability and Validity in Qualitative Research*. Beverly Hills, Calif.: Sage.

KMENTA, JAN. 1997. *Elements of Econometrics*, 2nd ed. Ann Arbor: University of Michigan Press.

KNOKE, DAVID, GEORGE W. BOHRNSTEDT, and ALISSA POTTER MEE. 2002. *Statistics for Social Data Analysis*, 4th ed. Belmont, Calif.: Wadsworth.

KOENIG, LOUIS W. 1968. *The Chief Executive*, rev. ed. New York: Harcourt Brace Jovanovich.

KOESTLER, ARTHUR. 1969. *The Act of Creation*. London: Hutchinson.

KROEBER, A. L., and CLYDE KLUCKHOHN. 1952. *Culture: A Critical Review of Concepts and Definitions*. Cambridge, Mass.: The Museum.

KUHN, THOMAS S. 1962. *The Structure of Scientific Revolutions*. Chicago: University of Chicago Press.

LAVE, CHARLES A., and JAMES G. MARCH. 1975. *Introduction to Models in the Social Sciences*. New York: Harper & Row.

LEITNER, CHRISTOPHER. 1997. "Of Time and Partisan Stability Revisited: Australia and New Zealand 1905–90," *American Journal of Political Science*, 41, 1104–1127.

LEVITT, STEVEN, and STEPHEN J. DUBNER. 2005. *Freakonomics*. New York: Harper Collins.

LOEWENBERG, GERHARD. 1968. "The Remaking of the German Party System: Political & Socio-Economic Factors" *Polity*, 1, 86–113.

LUKES, STEVEN. 1974. *Power: A Radical View*. London: Macmillan.

MASSEY, DOUGLAS S., and KRISTIN E. ESPINOSA. 1997. "What's Driving Mexico–U.S. Migration? A Theoretical, Empirical, and Policy Analysis," *American Journal of Sociology*, 102 (January), 939–999.

MATTHEWS, DONALD R., and JAMES W. PROTHRO. 1963. "Social and Economic Factors and Voter Registration in the South," *American Political Science Review*, 57 (March), 24ff.

MIHAELESCU, MIHAELA. 2007. *Dampening the Powderkeg: The Role of Democratic Oppositions in Fostering Ethnic Peace in Post Communist Romania and Slovakia*. Saarbrücken, Germany: VDM Verlag.

MOSTELLER, FREDERICK. 1968. "Errors," *International Encyclopedia of the Social Sciences*. New York: Macmillan.

MUTZ, DIANA C., and BYRON REEVES. 2005. "The New Videomalaise: Effects of Televised Incivility on Political Trust," *American Political Science Review*, 99 (March), 1–15.

NEUSTADT, RICHARD E. 1991. *Presidential Power and the Modern Presidents*. New York: Free Press.

NIEMI, RICHARD G., and KEITH KREHBIEL. 1984. "The Quality of Surveying Responses About Parents and the Family: A Longitudinal Analysis," *Political Methodology*, 10, 193–210.

OLSON, MANCUR. 1965. *The Logic of Collective Action*. Cambridge, Mass.: Harvard University Press.

———. 1982. *The Rise and Decline of Nations*. New Haven, Conn.: Yale University Press.

OPPENHEIM, FELIX. 1975. "The Language of Political Inquiry: Problems of Clarification." In Fred Greenstein and Nelson Polsby, eds., *Handbook of Political Science*, Vol. 1, pp. 283–336. Reading, Mass.: Addison-Wesley.

PITKIN, HANNA. 1967. *The Concept of Representation*. Berkeley, Calif.: University of California Press.

———. 1969. *Representation*. New York: Atherton.

PROTHRO, JAMES W. 1956. "The Nonsense Fight over Scientific Method: A Plea for Peace," *Journal of Politics*, 18, 565–570.

PRZEWORSKI, ADAM. 1975. "Institutionalization of Voting Patterns, or Is Mobilization the Source of Decay?" *American Political Science Review*, 69 (March), 49–67.

———, MICHAEL E. ALVAREZ, JOSÉ ANTONIO CHEIBUB, and FERNANDO LONGI. 2000. *Democracy and Development: Political Institutions and Well-Being in the World, 1950–1990*. New York: Cambridge University Press.

PUTNAM, ROBERT D. 1993. *Making Democracy Work*. Cambridge, Mass.: Harvard University Press.

ROBINSON, W. S. 1950. "Ecological Correlations and the Behavior of Individuals," *American Sociological Review*, 15 (June), 351–357.

ROETHLISBERGER, F. J., and W. J. DICKSON. 1939. *Management and the Worker*. Cambridge, Mass.: Harvard University Press.

ROGOWSKI, RONALD, and MARK ANDREAS KAYSER. 2002. "Majoritarian Electoral Systems and Consumer Power: Price-Level Evidence from the OECD Countries," *American Journal of Political Science*, 46, 526–539.

SARTORI, GIOVANNI. 1976. *Parties and Party Systems*. London: Cambridge University Press.

SCOTT, GREGORY M., and STEPHEN M. GARRISON. 2006. *The Political Student Writer's Manual*, 5th ed. New York: Longman

SHADISH, WILLIAM R., THOMAS D. COOK, and DONALD T. CAMPBELL. 2002. *Experimental and Quasi-Experimental Designs for Generalized Causal Inference*. Boston: Houghton Mifflin.

SHIVELY, W. PHILLIPS. 1972. "Party Identification, Party Choice, and Voting Stability: The Weimar Case," *American Political Science Review*, 66 (December), 1203–1225.

———. 2006. "Case Selection: Insights from *Rethinking Social Inquiry*," *Political Analysis*, 14, 344–347.

SIMON, JULIAN. 1985. *Basic Research Methods in Social Science*, 3rd ed. New York: Random House.

STOKES, DONALD E. 1969. "Cross-Level Inference as a Game Against Nature." In Joseph L. Bernd, ed., *Mathematical Applications in Political Science*, Vol. 4, pp. 62–83. Charlottesville, Va.: The University of Virginia Press.

STOUFFER, SAMUEL, and others. 1949. *The American Soldier*, Vol. 1. Princeton, N.J.: Princeton University Press.

TARROW, SIDNEY. 1996. "Making Social Science Work Across Space and Time: A Critical Reflection on Robert Putnam's *Making Democracy Work*," *American Political Science Review*, 90 (June), 389–398.

———. 1971. "The Urban–Rural Cleavage in Political Involvement: The Case of France," *American Political Science Review*, 65 (June), 341–357.

TILLEY, JAMES R. 2003. "Party Identification in Britain: Does Length of Time in the Electorate Affect Strength of Partisanship?" *British Journal of Political Science*, 33, 332–344.

TINGSTEN, HERBERT. 1937. *Political Behavior*. London: Longmans.

TUFTE, EDWARD R. 1968–1969. "Improving Data Analysis in Political Science," *World Politics*, 21, 641–654.

———. 1983. *The Visual Display of Quantitative Information*. Cheshire, Conn.: Graphics Press.

UHLANER, CAROLE JEAN, and KAY LEHMAN SCHLOZMAN. 1986. "Candidate Gender and Congressional Campaign Receipts," *Journal of Politics*, 48 (February), 30–50.

VAN DETH, JAN W. 2000. "Interesting but Irrelevant: Social Capital and the Saliency of Politics in Europe," *European Journal of Political Science*, 115–147.

WATSON, JAMES D. 1968. *The Double Helix*. New York: Atheneum.

WEBB, EUGENE J., DONALD T. CAMPBELL, RICHARD D. SCHWARTZ, and LEE SECHRIST. 1966. *Unobtrusive Measures*. Chicago: Rand McNally.

WILSON, THOMAS P. 1971. "Critique of Ordinal Variables." In Hubert M. Blalock, Jr., ed., *Causal Models in the Social Sciences*, pp. 415–431. Chicago: Aldine-Atherton.

WINCH, ROBERT F., and DONALD T. CAMPBELL. 1969. "Proof? No. Evidence? Yes. The Significance of Tests of Significance," *American Sociologist*, 4 (May), 140–143.

ZALLER, JOHN. 1998. "Politicians as Prize Fighters: Electoral Selection and Incumbency Advantage." In John Geer, ed., *Politicians and Party Politics*. Baltimore: Johns Hopkins University Press.

Index

A

abstinence-only sex education 81
Achen, Christopher H. 47, 87, 95, 129n
Acton, Lord 40
Alvarez, Michael E. 94, 111
analytic political philosophy 40
anomalies 29–30
Ansolabehere, Stephen 54–55
applied research 4
Asher, Herbert B. 46, 56
autocorrelation 163

B

Bachrach, Peter 38
Baker v. Carr 54n
Baratz, Morton 38
Barber, James David 28
Bartels, Larry M. 131
Barton, Allan H. 40
Batalla, Javier Ortiz 76
Bernstein, Richard J. 40
Blalock, Hubert M. 95, 127, 127n, 147n
Bohrnstedt, George W. 132
Boswell, James 168
Bueno de Mesquita, Bruce 26–27
Butler, David 20

C

Campbell, Angus 18
Campbell, David E. 87
Campbell, Donald T. 56, 85, 95, 165
Carter, Lewis F. 72
case studies 103–104
causal interpretations 76–77
    eliminating alternative 76–84
causation 14, 74–76
censored data 104–107
Cheibub, José Antonio 94, 111
cluster sample 101–102
coefficient of determination 125
Coleman, James S. 168–169
continuous measures 63
control group 81–83
    designs without 79–81
controlling for a variable 94–95
Converse, Philip E. 17–20, 47, 56, 147
Cook, Thomas D. 95
correlational measures of relationship 114
correlation analysis 123–128
    compared with regression analysis 128–130

correlation coefficient 124
cross-tabulation 132–134

D

Dahl, Robert 38, 40
Dalton, Russell J. 20, 29n
Dean, Charles W. 164
dependent variable 14
dichotomies 138–140
    in regression analysis 139–140
Dickson, W. J. 80n
Diehl, Paul F. 8
Digeser, Peter 38
diminishing marginal returns model 120
discrete measures 63
Downs, Anthony 5–6
Dubner, Stephen J. 31
Duggan, Thomas J. 165
Duverger, Maurice 2–3, 7n

E

Eckstein, Harry 40, 57
ecological fallacy 129n
effect-descriptive measures of relationship 114
Eisner, Thomas 31, 96
elegant research 16–17
empirical research 4
engineering research 5, 15, 23
English language 33–34
epistemic correlation 45n
Espinosa, Kristin E. 16
ethics of research 11–12
experiment, true 83–84
ex post facto argument 24

F

face validity 52
Feldman, Stanley 56
Fraser, Jane M. 56
free rider problem 7

G

Galileo 168–169
Garrison, Stephen M. 31
Geddes, Barbara 105–106
Gerber, Alan S. 54–55, 87, 96
Gerring, John 111
Gilbert, John P. 87
Goldsmith, Arthur A. 30

Goodman, Leo A. 135n
Goodman and Kruskal gamma 135–137
Green, Donald P. 87, 96
Greenstein, Fred I. 29n

H
Hammond, Thomas H. 56
Hawthorne study 80n
Hill, G. Birkbeck 168n
holding a variable constant 76, 94–95
Howell, William G. 87
hypothesis testing 153–155

I
independence of observations 162–163
independent variable 14
interaction, statistical 146–147, 147n
intercept of regression equation 117
interesting problems 10
interrupted time series 90
interval measures 62

J
Jacob, Philip E. 40
Johnson, Samuel 168

K
Karsten, Peter 68
Kayser, Mark Andreas 85
Kemeny, John 19
Keohane, Robert O. 111, 162n
Key, V. O., Jr. 121–123
Kinder, Donald R. 86n, 96
King, Gary 111, 162n
Kingston, Jean 8
Kirk, Jerome 56
Klingemann, Hans-Dieter 29n
Kluckhohn, Clyde 38
Kmenta, Jan 162
Knoke, David 132
Koenig, Louis W. 29
Koestler, Arthur 31
Krehbiel, Keith 56
Kroeber, A. L. 38
Kruskal, William H. 135n
Kuhn, Thomas S. 169

L
Lave, Charles A. 25n
law of large numbers 58, 61, 100
Leitner, Christopher 20
Levitt, Steven 31
liberal 33–34
Light, Richard J. 87
linear relationships 71, 119–120
Literary Digest 50–51

Loewenberg, Gerhard 110
logit analysis 140–142
Longi, Fernando 94, 111
Lukes, Steven 38

M
March, James G. 25n
Markov chain 19
Marx, Karl 8
Massey, Douglas S. 16
Matthews, Donald R. 145n
measurement, general problem of 42–45
measurement error 130–131
Mee, Alissa Potter 132
Mihaelescu, Mihaela 99, 104
Mill, John Stuart 5
Miller, Marc L. 56
Minneapolis Star Tribune 81
Mosteller, Frederick 56, 87
multicollinearity 161n
multidimensional concepts 32
multidimensional words 34–36
multivariate regression 142–147
Mutz, Diana C. 88

N
n (number of cases) 160–162
National Election Study 101
national integration 37
NATO 25
natural experiment 81–83
    without premeasurement 82–83
Neustadt, Richard E. 29
Niemi, Richard G. 56
nominal measures 62
nonempirical research 4
nonrandom error 49, 53–54
normative philosophy 4–5
null hypothesis 154–155

O
Olson, Mancur 6–7, 25n, 30
Oppenhem, Felix 40
ordinal measures 62

P
Palfrey, Thomas R. 86n, 96
paradox of participation 29
Peterson, Paul E. 87
Pierce, Roy 56
pilot study 51–52
Pitkin, Hanna 40
pluralism 7
political party 33
polling 164–165
positive theory 5–8

power 38–40
precision 58–67
    and describing relationships between
        variables 65–67
    enrichment of 67–71
    in measurement 62–67
    in measures 58–61
probit analysis 140–142
Prothro, James W. 20, 145n
Przeworski, Adam 20, 94, 111
Putnam, Robert D. 92–93
puzzles 24–27

Q
quantitative research 20–21

R
r 123–128
r^2 125, 127–128
random error 49, 53–54, 130–131
random sample 99–101
ratio measures 62n, 73
rational choice 6
RDD sampling 102
Reagan, Ronald 80
recreational research 4, 5–8
Reeves, Byron 88
regression analysis 114–123
    compared with orrelation 128–130
    and measurement error 130–131
regression coefficient 117
regression to the mean 88–90
relative deprivation 9
reliability of measures 45–48
    related to validity 48–49
research design 23–24, 78–85
residuals, in regression 120–123
Robinson, W. S. 129n
Roethlisberger, F. J. 80n
Rogowski, Ronald 85

S
sampling 99–103
    purposive 102–103
    quasi-random 101–102
    random 99–101
    RDD 102
sampling distribution 157–160
Sartori, Giovanni 40
scattergram 114–115
Schlozman, Kay Lehman 85
Schwartz, Richard D. 56
Scott, Gregory M. 31
Sechrist, Lee 56
selection on the dependent variable 107–109
Shadish, William R. 95

Shively, W. Phillips 20, 111n, 129n
significance, statistical 151
significance tests 163–165
Simon, Julian 166
simplicity, of a theory 15
slope of regression equation 117
Snyder, James M. 54–55
social research 2–4
social status 41–42
split-half test of reliability 47–48
Stanley, Julian C. 85
statistics 113
Stokes, Donald E. 20, 129n
Stouffer, Samuel 9
stratified sample 60

T
Tarrow, Sidney 29, 51, 52
test group 81
test-retest check for reliability 47
theory 2, 3, 14–17
theory-oriented research 4, 8, 15, 23
Tilley, James R. 20
Tingsten, Herbert 96
topics for research 21–23
trivial theory 15
true experiment 83–84
Tufte, Edward R. 31, 72

U
Uhlaner, Carole Jean 85
unidimensional concepts 32
units, comparability in regression analysis 118–119

V
validity 48–49, 130–131
    checking for 51–52
variables 14
variance 125–128
Verba, Sidney 111, 162n

W
Watson, James D. 1
Webb, Eugene J. 56
Weldon, Steven 20
Wilson, Thomas P. 72
Winch, Robert F. 165
Wolf, Patrick J. 87

X
χ^2 155–157

Z
Zaller, John 98–99
Zinsser, William Knowlton 31